Composing Digital Music For Dummies®

Cheat Sheet

The Most Used Sibelius Shortcuts

When you're using Sibelius, you soon realize that you use certain keystrokes more often than any other. Here are the shortcuts you need most often while building your tune:

- **Ctrl+Z (⌘+Z):** Undo
- **Ctrl+Y (⌘+Y):** Redo
- **Esc:** Clears the last highlighted section
- **Ctrl+[(⌘+[):** Rewinds playback to the beginning
- **Ctrl+Alt+K (Option+⌘+K):** Opens the Keypad
- **P:** Plays back from anywhere
- **I:** Adds instruments to your score
- **R:** Enters the same note repeatedly
- **Ctrl+Alt+G (Option+⌘+G):** Jumps to any measure in your score
- **Ctrl+E (⌘+E):** Enters dynamics in your score quickly
- **Ctrl+C (⌘+C):** Copies the highlighted note or section
- **Ctrl+V (⌘+V):** Pastes the copied section
- **Ctrl+1 (⌘+1):** Zooms the View to 100 percent

Magazines to Read Regularly

Keeping up on what's happening in music is important, and magazines are a great way to do it. Most of these mags also have associated Web sites, offering the latest news, reviews, and online forums.

- ***Bass Player,*** 12 issues/year, $19 for 12 issues (phone: 650-238-0300; Web: `www.bass player.com`)
- ***Computer Music,*** 13 issues/year, $117 for 13 issues (phone: 800-428-3003; Web: `www.computer music.co.uk`)
- ***Computer Music Journal,*** 4 issues/year, $245 for 4 issues online only, $272 for 4 issues print and online both (phone: 617-253-2889; Web: `http://204.151.38.11/cmj/`)
- ***Electronic Musician,*** 12 issues/year, $23.97 for 13 issues (phone: 866-860-7087 or 818-487-2020; Web: `http://emusician.com`)
- ***EQMagazine,*** 12 issues/year, $15 for 12 issues (phone: 650-238-0300; Web: `www.eqmag.com`)
- ***Guitar Player,*** 12 issues/year, $14 for 12 issues (phone: 650-238-0300 Web: `www.guitar player.com`)
- ***KeyboardMagazine,*** 12 issues/year, $12 for 12 issues (phone: 650-513-4671; Web: `www.key boardmag.com`)
- ***Mix,*** 12 issues/year, $35.97 for 13 issues (phone: 866-860-7087 or 818-487-2020; Web: `http://mixonline.com`)
- ***TapeOp,*** 6 issues/year, $30 for 6 issues (phone: 503-232-6047; Web: `www.tapeop.com`)
- ***Wired,*** 12 issues/year, $10 for 12 issues (phone: 800-769-4733; Web: `www.wired.com`)

For Dummies: Bestselling Book Series for Beginners

Composing Digital Music For Dummies®

Cheat Sheet

Web Resources to Check Out

The Internet offers all kinds of info for digital music makers. The sites listed here are just a small sample of the educational journals, independent music distributors, professional music forums, and free music legal advice you can find on the Web.

- **artistShare** (www.artistshare.com): artistShare is like CD Baby, a little. But instead of taking finished products from artists and then selling the products for them, artistShare creates a recording project, and fans of the artist invest in the music creation project.

- **CD Baby** (http://cdbaby.com): CD Baby is an online record store that sells CDs by independent musicians. It's the largest seller of independent CDs on the Web. You send them your music, they warehouse and sell it, and then pay you a share.

- **FreeAdvice** (http://law.freeadvice.com/intellectual_property/music_law/): Online for over ten years, FreeAdvice has an intellectual property and music law section, where you can find info on statutes, regulations, case law, and legal principles that affect the creation, production, distribution, or marketing of music.

- **GearSlutz** (www.gearslutz.com): GearSlutz is an online forum for professional and amateur recording engineers to share techniques and advice. Here you can find an answer to just about any question you have about recording hardware, computers, or electronic music production.

- **HipHopBeatz.com** (www.hiphopbeatz.com): HipHopBeatz.com has an impressive list of credits in producing R&B, pop, and club music. It has a huge collection of *beats* (background rhythm section tracks for producers) to sample, purchase, and download.

- **Indiana University Index of Music Journals, Magazines, Newspapers, and Periodicals** (http://library.music.indiana.edu/music_resources/journals.html): The Indiana University School of Music has put together a great compilation of music journals and magazines, newspapers, and periodicals. Here you can find links to almost every periodical or journal published about music, with such gems as *Autoharp Quarterly* and *Banjo Newsletter.*

- **Indie-Music.com** (www.indie-music.com): Another indie music connections site, Indie Music has been around as long as, or longer than, most. Here musicians can find how-to articles, underground music news, reviews, interviews, and music-biz news. Its coolest feature is a search engine that helps you locate almost any contact or company in the biz, from agents to CD replicators.

- **The Industry Resource** (www.theindustryresource.com): The Industry Resource is a place for indie artists to connect directly with music industry execs, and music industry executives to hook up with new talent. After joining, you can scroll job openings in the music biz, look at listings of industry contacts, and upload your tunes for them to check out.

- **KVR Audio** (www.kvraudio.com): This site features news and information about software audio plug-ins. It runs a searchable audio plug-in database, where you can find info on new releases, product announcements and product updates (major and minor) for VST plug-ins, DirectX plug-ins, and Audio Units plug-ins.

- **ProRec** (www.prorec.com): ProRec is an online recording business discussion forum with news and reviews. You can find lots of sites like this on the Web, but ProRec is one of the best.

For Dummies: Bestselling Book Series for Beginners

Composing Digital Music

FOR

DUMMIES®

Composing Digital Music

FOR DUMMIES®

by Russell Dean Vines

WILEY

Wiley Publishing, Inc.

Composing Digital Music For Dummies®
Published by
Wiley Publishing, Inc.
111 River St.
Hoboken, NJ 07030-5774
www.wiley.com

WILEY

About the Author

Russell Dean Vines is a music industry veteran, with more than 40 years of experience as a bandleader, sideman, composer, arranger, clinician, lecturer, and consultant.

Russ started music lessons as soon as he entered elementary school, eventually studying violin, French horn, guitar, piano, tenor saxophone, and his primary instrument, bass. He decided to become a professional musician when he was in middle school. While attending a dinner show at John Ascuaga's Nugget in Sparks, Nevada, Russ realized that the tuxedo-clad musicians in the house orchestra dressed better and probably earned more than the hard-scrabble ranchers he'd grown up among throughout the West.

At age 13, he booked his first gig, in a biker roadhouse in Reno, playing bass alongside one of the rare female baritone vocalists who could also play barrelhouse piano, and a little person on drums. Russ's featured solo consisted of blowing bubbles with a straw in a glass of water, improvising on the theme from the TV show *Flipper*. The gig paid more than his paper route and made it possible for Russ to buy cutout records on sale at the local Western Auto store. There he discovered the music of multi-instrumentalist Roland Kirk (pre-Rahsaan) and bassist Charles Mingus. The adolescent Russ found their music weird but appealing.

Down Beat magazine awarded the young bassist/composer a Hall of Fame scholarship to Berklee College of Music in Boston, where he studied with Charlie Mariano, Major (Mule) Holley, Herb Pomeroy, John LaPorta, and others. Russ learned many valuable lessons, such as:

* Don't accept a gig at a joint that has chicken-wire surrounding the bandstand.

* Playing outside has nothing to do with the weather.

* It's a mistake to leave your ax onstage between sets, because it could be in the pawnshop before you get back.

Having absorbed too much information in Boston, Russ returned to Reno, where he performed as a sideman in Reno nightspots, working with well-known entertainers including George Benson; John Denver; Sammy Davis, Jr.; and Dean Martin. For several years he played electric bass and was an orchestrator for *Hello, Hollywood, Hello,* at the MGM Grand.

Russ also worked in small towns throughout Nevada as an artist in residence for the National Endowment for the Arts. The "residence" part sometimes consisted of an elderly single-wide situated between a town's legal brothel and its liquor store.

He has composed and arranged hundreds of pieces of jazz and contemporary music that were recorded and performed by his own big band and others; founded and managed a scholastic music publishing company; and adjudicated performances at student festivals.

Always interested in digital music, Russ was able to put theory into practice when he taught himself to use a New England Digital Synclavier II, owned by Swami Kriyananda. His compositions on the Synclavier, as well as pieces written for more traditional instruments, are captured on the 1983 album *Gemini,* by Russ Vines and the Contemporary Music Ensemble. The recording was chosen as an Album of Exceptional Merit by *Billboard* magazine.

After moving to New York, Russ worked as a systems consultant for Sony BMG Music Entertainment, CBS/Fox Video, and others. He holds a gaggle of computer certifications and is now an internationally recognized authority on computer security. He is the author of ten best-selling information system security texts, including the top-selling *The CISSP Prep Guide: Mastering the Ten Domains of Computer Security* (Wiley), which reached #25 on Amazon.com and was on the site's Hot 100 list for four months.

Russ in now chief security advisor to Gotham Technology Group and writes frequently for online technical magazines, such as *The Wall Street Journal Online,* `TechTarget.com`, and `SearchSecurity.com`. He also writes on a variety of subjects, including fast cars and fun gadgets, for Jim Cramer's TheStreet.com.

Dedication

To Elzy. Forever.

Author's Acknowledgments

I would like to thank all the software, hardware, and music vendors that contributed to this book. Without their contributions, I would not have been able to provide as comprehensive a look at the current state of digital music.

I would also like to thank my associates at Wiley: acquisitions editor Mike Baker, media development associate project manager Laura Atkinson, and especially my project editor and copy editor, Elizabeth Kuball.

And a big thank-you to the musicians and friends who contributed ideas and helped me throughout the sometimes arduous writing process. A special shout-out to percussionist extraordinaire Dom Moio, guitarist and educator Tomas Cataldo, and multi-instrumentalist Howard Johnson.

Publisher's Acknowledgments

We're proud of this book; please send us your comments through our Dummies online registration form located at www.dummies.com/register/.

Some of the people who helped bring this book to market include the following:

Acquisitions, Editorial, and Media Development

Project Editor: Elizabeth Kuball

Acquisitions Editor: Mike Baker

Copy Editor: Elizabeth Kuball

Technical Editor: Ryan Williams

Media Assistant/Producer: Josh Frank

Senior Editorial Manager: Jennifer Ehrlich

Consumer Editorial Supervisor and Reprint Editor: Carmen Krikorian

Media Associate Project Manager: Laura Atkinson

Editorial Assistants: Erin Calligan Mooney, Joe Niesen, Leeann Harney, David Lutton

Cartoons: Rich Tennant (www.the5thwave.com)

Composition Services

Project Coordinator: Patrick Redmond

Layout and Graphics: Claudia Bell, Reuben W. Davis, Melissa K. Jester, Stephanie Jumper, Barbara Moore, Laura Pence, Christine Williams

Proofreader: Shannon Ramsey

Indexer: Valerie Haynes Perry

Publishing and Editorial for Consumer Dummies

Diane Graves Steele, Vice President and Publisher, Consumer Dummies

Joyce Pepple, Acquisitions Director, Consumer Dummies

Kristin A. Cocks, Product Development Director, Consumer Dummies

Michael Spring, Vice President and Publisher, Travel

Kelly Regan, Editorial Director, Travel

Publishing for Technology Dummies

Andy Cummings, Vice President and Publisher, Dummies Technology/General User

Composition Services

Gerry Fahey, Vice President of Production Services

Debbie Stailey, Director of Composition Service

Contents at a Glance

Table of Contents

Introduction

∙ ∙

*T*he world of desktop publishing has expanded to include music: Anyone with a PC or Mac at home already has the basics for a music creation studio. *Composing Digital Music For Dummies,* along with your home computer, is the fundamental toolkit you need to write music using the latest digital software.

Don't be nervous about trying your hand at writing your own digital music. If you've always loved music, but you've never thought that you could be a composer, this book is for you. If you heard about the digital music revolution, and wondered how the music you hear on the radio, the TV, the Internet, and even on your cellphone is made, this book is also for you.

About This Book

Composing Digital Music For Dummies delivers everything you need to get started making your own tunes. If you have a computer and this book, you have all the tools and information you need to build a piece of music, play it back, burn it on a CD, or print it out for others.

Composing Digital Music For Dummies simplifies the basics of composing music. In this book, I show you:

- ✔ How to use software to compose music
- ✔ The fundamentals of digital composition
- ✔ The role of MIDI and other digital tools
- ✔ How music is written and produced

I avoid advanced musical or computer techno jargon and, in a clear, friendly manner, demystify the essential steps to making your own music and making music your own.

But the big deal is: You don't have to read music or have music theory training to get started. You can begin making music *today* — and you can have fun while doing it!

The CD that comes with this book has everything you need: a demo version of Sibelius 5 (the most popular music notation software), templates to get you started, and audio files of all the examples I provide in the book.

Conventions Used in This Book

Because *Composing Digital Music For Dummies* is a reference book that you can use over and over again, I use some conventions to make things consistent and easy to understand:

- ✔ I provide keyboard shortcuts for both PC users and Mac users — music doesn't discriminate and neither do I. I list the PC shortcut first, followed by the Mac shortcut in parentheses.

- ✔ When I give you a list of steps to follow, the action part of the step is in **boldface.**

- ✔ When I define a new term, I put it in *italics,* and provide the definition nearby (often in parentheses).

- ✔ I list all Web addresses and e-mail addresses in `monofont`, so you can tell the address apart from the surrounding text. ***Note:*** When this book was printed, some Web addresses may have needed to break across two lines of text. If that happened, rest assured that I haven't put in any extra characters (such as hyphens) to indicate the break. So, when using one of these Web addresses, just type in exactly what you see in this book, pretending as though the line break doesn't exist.

One more thing: In the *For Dummies* series, acronyms are typically spelled out on their first use in a chapter, but the acronym *MIDI* is one I use so often in this book that I don't always spell it out. I talk about MIDI in depth in Chapter 4, but for now, know that it stands for *Musical Instrument Digital Interface,* and it's a way for electronic instruments made by different manufacturers to work and play together.

What You're Not to Read

I think every pearl of wisdom in *Composing Digital Music For Dummies* is cool, interesting, and useful, but I have included some stuff that you really don't need to know.

The Technical Stuff icon points out information that's fascinating for geeks like me, but that you may or may not be interested in. If you're in a hurry, you can safely skip these paragraphs without missing anything critical.

You can also skip sidebars (the text in gray boxes throughout this book). Sidebars are interesting anecdotes or historical information, but they're not essential information.

Foolish Assumptions

I don't make many assumptions about you, but I do figure that one of the following statements probably applies to you:

- ✔ You like to tinker with an instrument and make up tunes by grooving on a line or just a feeling. You may have some basic knowledge of a PC or Mac, but you're not a tech wiz or musical genius.

- ✔ You play in a band and want to arrange tunes for other players or other instruments to see what they sound like. You may have studied music in school and you may have made a few bucks on a gig or two. You know some harmony and theory, but you want to take the next step and compose digitally.

- ✔ You're a computer wizard, but you don't have any formal music training or background and you want to know how to compose music like you've heard on the latest games and Web streaming audio.

I also assume that you have a personal computer with a CD drive at your disposal — either a Mac or a PC. (If you don't have a computer, start with Chapter 4, which gives you some tips about what kind of firepower you'll need to compose digital music.) Eventually, you'll want to get more gear — and in this book I show you how to get the best bang for your buck — but I don't believe that music can only be created by those who have the most stuff, or the most expensive education.

How This Book Is Organized

Composing Digital Music For Dummies is really two books in one:

- ✔ **It's an in-depth primer on the tools that modern digital composers use to create the music you hear around you every day.** Some chapters have descriptions and links to hardware, software, and even interviews with the folks who are creating this music.

- ✔ **More important, it's a tool to help you begin to compose using these digital music tools.**

This book is modular, which means you can pick it up and read any chapter you want in any order you want.

Part I: So You Want to Compose Digital Music

If you want to compose great music using the latest and coolest digital tools, then you've come to the right place! But before you become a household name, check out Chapter 1 and get an introduction to the world of digital music, what you need to participate, and where you can go from here. In Chapter 2, you get the real scoop on who does what in the digital music industry, from video game composers to experimental electronic artists. You even get a brief rundown on how records are made. In Chapter 3, I offer up a primer on basic music notation: what the funny little dots and lines mean, and all the other marks that make up a page of music, like time signatures, key signatures, and chord symbols.

Part II: Gearing Up

In this part, you get a crash course in the hardware and software worlds of digital music composition. Chapter 4 tells you exactly what you need and don't need to start writing music like the pros. Chapter 5 is all about digital music hardware, from ready-built computer systems that play music, to futuristic gear that only a mother could love. Then in Chapter 6 I explain the ups and downs of the software side of composing; notation software, digital audio workstations and sequencers, and hip new software plug-ins that can make you sound like a guitar god.

Part III: The Basics: Building Your First Tune

Part III is where you get your hands on your first composition. In Chapter 7, you install the software from the CD and get familiar with using the templates for composing. Chapter 8 gives you the skinny on making an audio recording of your tune and how to print it out for other musicians to play. Chapter 9 shows you how to stick your toe in the water of Internet publishing, and gives you important information on the copyright and legal issues you need to know as a composer.

Part IV: Getting Fancy: Building Your Tune from Scratch

In Chapter 10, I introduce you to digital score paper, how to pick the right score paper for your band, and how to add new instruments to your score. Chapter 11 gives you the info you need to add notes using your mouse and computer keyboard; then you get fancy with your score, by adding text and bar lines. In Chapter 12, you go beyond using a mouse to enter notes, hook up a MIDI keyboard or guitar to your computer, and scan printed sheet music right into your score.

Part V: Beyond the Basics: Advanced Composing Tips and Tricks

Part V is the land of the advanced composer. If you're experienced with writing music, or you've followed this book from the beginning, these advanced composing tips and tricks will push your music to the next level.

Chapter 14 shows you how to add chord symbols for the rhythm section, add lyrics for the singers, and add color to your score. Chapter 15 lets you create a countermelody, an introduction, and an ending for your tune, all elements that make a budding composition a real piece of music. And Chapter 16 gives you some inside information on tweaking your computer's playback sound to make it more authentic, as well as some tips on mixing the sound before burning it on CD.

Part VI: The Part of Tens

A Part of Tens is the most recognizable (and some say useful) part of any Dummies book, and I think my Part of Tens is no exception. Here you find ten digital music terms that every composer should know to make the most of his music. I also have a (very biased) list of ten composers you should be aware of, as well as their contributions to the world of music. Finally, I offer up a list of the handiest Sibelius keyboard shortcuts and other assorted tips to make you the most efficient Sibelius user ever!

Part VII: Appendixes

Appendixes are usually the places in the back of a book that contain odd, arcane tidbits of information that most readers can take or leave. But I think you'll find interesting information in these two appendixes.

Appendix A gives you a little background on the concept of transposing instruments, and shows you the written musical range of most of the instruments in the orchestra. Appendix B gives you the lowdown on what I've put on the accompanying CD, such as software, Sibelius templates, Web resources, and MP3 music files. It's all stuff that's going to help you get the most out of the book and the most out of your composing.

The CD-ROM

Although I describe a lot of different types of digital music production tools in *Composing Digital Music For Dummies,* the primary software used in the book is Sibelius 5, the latest version (as of this writing) of the Sibelius family of digital music creation and notation tools. I include a demo version of Sibelius 5 on the CD, along with templates and audio MP3 files so you can hear exactly what the examples I mention in the book are supposed to sound like. Also, on the CD, I provide links to lots of other composing resources, from free software and music samples to hardware dealers and copyright advice.

Icons Used in This Book

For Dummies books are friendly, informative, and fun. One of the reasons they're so readable is because of the various graphic icons in the left-hand margins of the pages. These icons draw your attention to pointers you can use right away, warnings of impending doom, and some technical stuff you may find interesting.

Any time you see the Tip icon, you can bet you'll be getting some useful information I've gleaned from years of experience. It may be a shortcut to digital music success or expert advice for your future.

The good thing about this book is that it's a reference, which means you don't have to memorize it — you can keep it on your desk and come back to it whenever you need to look something up. But when I tell you something that you really should remember, I flag it with the Remember icon.

Composing digital music is not, by and large, a dangerous thing. You can't screw up much of anything — even the files on the CD will always be there for you to download from scratch if you don't like the changes you've made to them. But on the few occasions when you could create a serious hassle or headache for yourself, I let you know by using the Warning icon.

 The geek in me can't help but tell you about theoretical or obscure technical stuff you don't really need to know to use this book. When I do, I use the Technical Stuff icon. You can skip any paragraphs marked with this icon — but if you're as much of a geek as I am, you may want to read the Technical Stuff paragraphs first!

 When you see the On the CD icon, you can hear an audio example of the template you're working on, sounds from various music software, and other fun audio clips — all available on the CD that comes with this book.

Where to Go from Here

I've crafted *Composing Digital Music For Dummies* so you can jump in anywhere and get the info you need, without having to start from the beginning and read every page. You can skip around throughout the book, or within chapters, to find the information you need, using the table of contents and index as your guides.

If you've never written music before, or you're completely unfamiliar with how to create your own digital music, you can always start with Chapter 1 and read the book in order, downloading the templates and working through the examples as I help you create your first tune.

If you're somewhat acquainted with MIDI and digital music terms, you may want to start by checking out some of the latest software and gear in Chapters 5 and 6. You also may want to brush up on your musical notation basics in Chapter 3, or check out some legal implications of publishing your music in Chapter 9.

Whatever level of musician or computer geek you are, there's something for you in *Composing Digital Music For Dummies.* So what are you waiting for? Start composing music!

Part I

So You Want to Compose Digital Music

"I hope you're doing something online. An indie band like yours shouldn't just be playing street corners."

In this part . . .

Before you start your journey toward making a major splash in the music industry, Chapter 1 introduces you to the big world of digital music and digital music composition. Chapter 2 describes the digital music revolution and shows you how digital music is produced for CDs, podcasts, ringtones, stage, film, and TV.

In Chapter 3, you get a primer on the music notation fundamentals you need in order to get the most out of the book, such as the parts of a music score, the different notes, and what all those little dots are on a page of sheet music.

Chapter 1

Introducing Digital Music

· ·

In This Chapter

▶ Joining the revolution in digital music

▶ Gearing up: What you need and what you'll want

▶ Composing your own music

· ·

*I*n the early 1980s, a computer program was developed that caused a major shift in the music universe. The way people listen to music changed dramatically. (If you want the history behind this shift, check out the sidebar "A brief history of digital music" in this chapter.) The ways of making and selling music altered almost overnight, and the record companies are still struggling to catch up. Small, independent music composers and producers are creating new sounds and new beats. And the Web is altering forever how people acquire music.

To make the best music, you still need a good ear. Some musical education doesn't hurt, although you don't really need much — some basic knowledge of how the notes are written is all you need to get you started (check out Chapter 3 for more on that). But even *that* is changing — an ever-growing number of producers don't use scores or produce written music: They arrange beats and digital audio, and combine MIDI tracks (see "What Is Digital Music Anyway?" for more on MIDI) with vocalists into a unique sound and rhythm. You don't have to read music or have music theory training to make music today. You can make your own pro-quality sounds using the tools from any computer or music store.

In this chapter, I give you an overview of what digital music is, what kind of equipment you need to create it, and how you can get started creating your own music today.

A brief history of digital music

In 1983, the musical earth shifted, and the seismic shockwave is still being felt today. No, it wasn't the release of Madonna's first album (although that did happen in 1983). It was the creation of the Musical Instrument Digital Interface (MIDI). MIDI was released into the wild, and the musical Tower of Babel fell.

MIDI meant that different electronic music machines, which in the past could only speak their own language, could now all talk to each other and share information. MIDI meant that people could build electronic musical gear in their garage that would work with any computer.

The shift was the end result of *multiple* technological advancements that were shaking the culture, all of which combined to create digital music. These technological advancements included:

✔ The invention of the transistor, which made small, portable electronic devices possible

✔ The invention of the personal computer

✔ The development of the Internet, originally begun as ARPANET, the U.S. Department of Defense's first information-sharing network

All these elements, along with cultural shifts in the United States, made the digital music revolution almost inevitable.

What Is Digital Music Anyway?

Because digital music doesn't necessarily sound "digital" (that is, all computery and technoid), you probably don't know how much of the music you hear every day has some connection to the digital revolution. In fact, almost every piece of music you hear has been "digitized" in some way:

✔ When you buy CDs or download MP3s, you're purchasing music that was encoded digitally, whether the music is of a string quartet or a techno-pop band.

✔ If you're watching TV or a movie, you're listening to a musical score that has at least *some* digital elements and was produced using digital music software and hardware.

✔ Most recording studios use digital hardware and software to record the musicians and singers, and use digital mix-down tools and plug-ins to finish the tracks.

✔ More and more commercial pop and R&B producers are using prepackaged *beats* (collections of ready-made rhythm section tracks) and then overdubbing them with a live singer or instrumentalists.

✔ A music student who uses Sibelius or Finale to create a score and then print the parts out for their school orchestra is using digital music creation tools.

Auto-Tune

You don't even need to have a sense of pitch to sing! Auto-Tune is an audio processor created by Antares Audio Technologies (www.antarestech.com). It's used to correct pitch in vocal and instrumental performances and to disguise inaccuracies and mistakes made by the vocalist. Auto-Tune is used as a software plug-in with popular digital audio workstations, such as Pro Tools. (For more on digital audio workstations, or DAWs, check out Chapter 6.)

And the list goes on and on.

And all this digital music is possible because of the Musical Instrument Digital Interface (MIDI), an industry-standard computer program that enables electronic musical instruments (such as synthesizers, computers, and other equipment) to communicate, control, and synchronize with each other. The term *MIDI* refers to both the type of cables and plugs used to connect the computers and instruments, and to the language those computers and instruments use to talk to each other. Almost every electronic musical instrument on the market today has MIDI connectors and can, therefore, be used with other MIDI instruments and with your computer's MIDI interface.

A piece of MIDI music can be transferred back and forth between different music-composing software programs made by different vendors and still work, because it's MIDI-compliant. The MIDI language conveys information and instructions, both from the computer to the instrument and from the instrument to the computer. For example, if you tell your computer that you want your MIDI keyboard to play a note, the computer sends a MIDI message telling the keyboard which note to play. When you tell your computer that you want the keyboard to stop playing that note, the computer sends another message that stops the note from playing. MIDI files contain all the MIDI messages and timing information that are needed to play a song.

Knowing What Equipment to Get

You don't *need* much stuff to start composing digital music. But needs and wants are two very different things. In this section, I fill you in on the most basic of equipment you need to get started, and then let you know about some other cool things you'll probably want. I'll let you and your credit card work that out.

What you need

Even though you may have wanted to use me as your excuse for running out and buying a whole ton of new equipment ("But Russ says I need it, honey . . . "), I'm sorry to say I can't take the rap for that. The truth is, you don't need much to get started composing digital music. Here's the list:

- ✔ **A computer:** Any fairly new, off-the-shelf Windows PC or Mac will do the job. Your computer should have a CD-ROM drive so you can use the templates and hear the audio examples on the CD that comes with this book. (The odds of your having a computer that didn't come with a CD-ROM drive and that still works today are slimmer than the odds of all four Beatles reuniting.)

- ✔ **Headphones or speakers:** Your computer's built-in speaker is not designed to play high-quality audio, so having a set of speakers or head-phones is important if you want to hear your music played back to full effect. You can get a basic pair of headphones for $49 and a basic set of speakers for $29. Try to stay away from ear pods — they don't usually have the full-frequency response you want.

- ✔ **Music composing software:** Two types of software programs are used to input digital music into your computer and compose digitally:

    - • **Musical notation software:** Musical notation software is software that lets you enter notes into your computer, using digital score paper. Sibelius (on this book's CD) and Finale (shown in Figure 1-1) are two of the most popular programs.

    - • **Sequencing and/or digital audio workstation (DAW) software:** Originally hardware, digital audio workstation software records and manipulates audio digitally. Most current DAW software has MIDI sequencing features, and all the DAW software I use in this book has sequencing features. (For more information on sequencing, check out Chapter 6.) DAWs have a big advantage over notation programs: You don't have to know how to read music to use them. Programs such as Ableton, ACID, Cubase, Digital Performer, Logic, Pro Tools, Reason (shown in Figure 1-2), and SONAR are very popular pro-grams. And if you have a Mac, you don't have to spend a dime: GarageBand is included with every new Mac.

    I give you a full rundown of what your software choices are (and how much they'll set you back in terms of cost) in Chapter 6.

- ✔ **An Internet connection:** You can download demo or trial versions of most of the software I describe in this book on the companies' Web sites. Using free demos or trial versions is a great way to familiarize yourself with the look and feel of the software and decide whether you like it enough to buy it.

✔ **A printer:** If you're going to print out your score or parts from the notation software, a printer is a necessary piece of equipment. You don't have to buy an expensive laser printer — you can get a good inkjet printer for around $100.

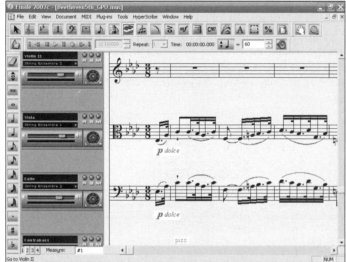

Figure 1-1:
Finale 2007 music notation software.

Figure 1-2:
The Reason 3 music sequencing rack.

What you'll want

As your musical ideas grow, you'll want a better audio system than the stock computer setup offers you. Here are just some of the things you'll find yourself adding to your wish list:

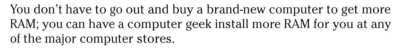

- ✔ **An external audio box:** External audio boxes attach to your computer and let you connect various MIDI devices and speaker systems, and provide a much higher quality sound. (I describe these in more detail in Chapter 4.)

- ✔ **More random access memory (RAM):** Memory is pretty cheap these days, and the more you have, the better.

    You don't have to go out and buy a brand-new computer to get more RAM; you can have a computer geek install more RAM for you at any of the major computer stores.

- ✔ **A bigger hard drive space:** Eventually, you'll need more hard drive storage to hold the rapidly increasing amount of tunes you've written. External drives, such as ones you can connect to your computer's USB port, are cheap and easy to use.

- ✔ **A MIDI controller:** The term *MIDI controller* may sound ominous, but it's really just another instrument, like a piano's keyboard. It's a way to compose your digital music in a more musician-friendly manner, by attaching a piano-like keyboard to your computer and playing the notes right into your software. (In Chapter 12, I show you how to play your notes right into the written music.)

Getting Started with a Composition

You may think that composing digital music is hard, but it's really not so difficult. Composing good music that stands the test of time will always be hard, but learning the tools to create something that's fun to listen to is easy. I provide dozens of templates and even demo software on the CD, to help you get started. After you've installed the software, you can open a template and start to build your first tune.

With digital music tools, trying out lots of different sounds and instruments is easy. You can add guitars and drums, and just copy and paste parts from one template into your digital score on the screen. You can experiment with different notes and tempos, and always go back to the way it was originally.

Digital music can be composed a bunch of ways, even if you don't read and write music. If you have a little experience with written music, notation software, like Finale or Sibelius, is a quick and simple way to write music for many different types of music groups, from small bands to orchestras.

Digital audio workstation (DAW) software, with MIDI sequencing ability, allows you to combine instruments and sounds anyway you can think of. And because it's all digital, you can just back up and undo, or erase a track and start over. You can even import samples and beats from the Web, and build your tune in new and unusual ways.

Burning your tunes

After you've created your masterpiece, you want to share it with others. You can burn it on a CD, send it to your cellphone as a ringtone, export it as an MP3 file from the Internet, or print out parts for your school band to play.

Because most music software interacts with other music software, you can create a tune using one piece of software, and then use another program to edit it into a final product, and save in different digital music formats. For example, if you used notation software (such as Finale or Sibelius) to build your piece of music, you can export it to other MIDI software, like Logic, SONAR, ACID Pro, or other programs. These programs let you change the sound of the piece dramatically (for example, by adding special effects, synthesizer sounds, and even vocal samples).

Using notation software to print out parts for other musicians to play is probably the greatest boon to composers since the invention of the eraser. Now, instead of laboriously writing out each part by hand for every instrument (called *copying* in the music biz), you can just push a button, and every part will be printed out by your desktop printer, and in the right key for each instrument!

Publishing your stuff

Besides burning CDs and emailing MP3s, you have other ways to share your original music. Internet publishing may work for you. Web sites let you share your tunes and help you reach a wide audience. And independent (indie) music distributors give the new artist a bigger financial share of his music than traditional record companies did.

If you compose music using Sibelius, you can post, sell, and share your music on the Web at its online sheet music store, SibeliusMusic (www. sibeliusmusic.com). Then anyone using Sibelius's free Web browser plug-in, Scorch, can read, play back, and print your music right from the site.

Indie music publishers offer many options for a new composer. Less rigid than the traditional record companies, they offer your fans CDs and downloads, and give the new artist on the scene greater product control.

But every creative composer needs to be aware of copyright pros and cons. You have to protect your music. Even if you're feeling generous and decide to distribute it to your fans via the Web, you still need to make sure your original work is copyrighted and you're not using someone else's copyrighted material.

The U.S. Copyright Office (www.copyright.gov) is where you register sound recordings or printed music for copyright protection. Other organizations that help protect the rights of authors, musicians, and digital artists include the Authors Guild (www.authorsguild.org) and the Electronic Frontier Foundation (www.eff.org). You should also check out Creative Commons (www.creativecommons.org); they provide tools that let you specify the terms of use for your work.

If you use *samples* (pieces of other people's compositions) in your work, you need to be sure you have permission from the composers, unless the samples you're using are from the *public domain* (music with a copyright that has expired).

Look, Ma — No Hands! Composing from Scratch

Of course, using the templates is really only one way to compose. When you get your composing sea legs, you'll want to stretch out and try your hand at composing from scratch. But you can't start building your opus immediately — you have some decisions to make.

One decision is what the score paper should look like. The term *score paper* is a throwback to the old days of composing, when orchestral compositions were written on manuscript paper. Digital music notation software still uses the term *score paper,* but now it refers to the format you use to build your tune.

What type of score paper you should use depends on what kind of musical group you're writing for: choir, pop band with a vocalist, jazz big band, school marching band. Every type of band uses a different type of score paper.

Other decisions a composer makes is what kind of instruments will play the tune, the tempo of the piece, the rhythmic feel and style, the chord progression, and probably the most obvious element, the notes.

You can enter notes into your computer in a variety of ways:

- Enter each note, one at a time, using either a MIDI controller or your mouse and keyboard.
- Connect your MIDI keyboard to your computer and record your playing right into the software as the tune plays.
- Import your music from other software programs, using different digital file formats, such as MIDI, and change it to your liking.
- Scan printed sheet music right into your computer.

If your tune is for a pop group, a rock band, or a hip-hop loop, the drum track will be very important. Your drum part can be created a lot of different ways, such as recording a live drum set or playing a MIDI controller programmed with drum sounds. You can also import prerecorded samples, loops, and beats.

Most MIDI compositions use more than one track for the drum part. This lets the composer import a sample or manipulate MIDI data for just one piece of the drum set (called the *kit*) without affecting the other piece. A digital tune commonly has separate tracks for the bass (kick) drum, the snare drum, the hi-hat, the ride cymbal, and other elements (like Latin percussion) that the composer wants to use. You can then add effects, like reverb, or adjust the volume of each part independently.

Taking Your Music to the Next Level

If you want to kick up your music and run with the big dogs, you need to know how to write chord progressions, countermelodies, intros, and outros.

The chord progression is a fundamental part of pop, jazz, country, rock, and lots of other types of music. A *chord progression* is the framework of chords that are used in your tune. *Chord symbols* are written to specify which chord should be played and when. A songwriter may create the chord progression at different stages of composing, either after he's made up the melody or, first, before he thinks of a melody to go with his lyrics.

In professional music situations, like a jazz combo performance, the chord progression is called the *changes,* and the pros are expected to know the changes to a lot of music, both popular and not so popular (like jazz standards).

Many guitarists don't read the dots and squiggles that make up music notation. This is why most music also writes the guitar part in *tablature* format, in addition to the regular note format. Tab (as it's called) lets the guitarist know exactly where to place his fingers.

Lyrics are important to have in a score, if there's going to be some vocalizing. All notation software lets you add lyrics, so when you print out the parts, the singer gets a part, too.

You also want to add finishing touches to your music, by composing countermelodies, and introductions and endings for the tunes. A countermelody is a series of notes that isn't the main melody, but may be played at the same time as the melody.

When you really get into composing and want to take your music to the next level, your first step may be to build your own basic home studio, like the one shown in Figure 1-3. In this simple studio setup, your MIDI keyboard controller goes into your computer using a USB connection, and the output audio goes to an external receiver with speakers, or directly from the speaker outputs on your computer's audio card.

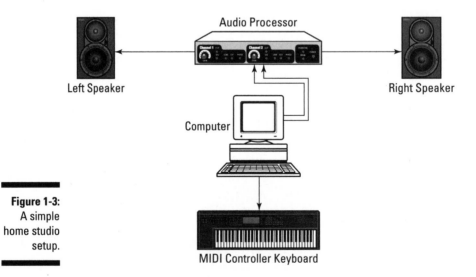

Figure 1-3:
A simple
home studio
setup.

However you follow your musical muse, digital music will be there for you to use as creatively as you'd like. As Meshell Ndegeocello told me: "I believe these advancements in technology create an environment of seekers and followers, mediocrity and genius. . . . For a moment I'm transported to when I was a teen and got my first multi-track recorder, electronic drum machine, and MIDI sequencer. I'm still the same as I was then. I just want to make some groovy sounds."

Chapter 2

The Digital Music Revolution

*W*e're in the middle of a revolution. It's as dramatic as the Russian Revolution or the French Revolution (although not as bloody). And although it's dramatic, it's hard to *notice* the revolution, because we're in the middle of it looking out, and everything looks the same as it did yesterday.

But the revolution is noticeable when you step back and look at the difference from generation to generation. It parallels the information revolution — and it's part of it. It's an outgrowth of the rock 'n' roll revolution — and it benefits from it. And it's a result of the personal electronics revolution. And because we're in the middle of it, we don't know how it will end.

In this chapter, I introduce you to the digital music revolution — the *hows*, *whos*, *whys*, and *wheres*.

Music Goes Digital

Today, anyone with a computer can have a complete digital music studio at his fingertips. Similar to how desktop publishing changed the print business and opened it up to many new players, digital music tools mark the beginning of personal composing. Technology is making it easier to compose, perform, record, and promote your own music.

With the rare exception of purely live music, such as fine art concerts or school band events, most music you hear today has some, if not all, digital elements. Most commercial music is built from digital tracks, then overlaid with live musicians or vocalists. Even purely acoustic music is probably recorded digitally and may be distributed digitally.

A composer can use this software with or without a specialized musical background. Instead of using paper and pencil to write music, the composer uses digital devices to create music and can instantly hear what he has created. And rarely before has a composer created his own instruments and invented a method of using them, before creating his compositions.

How the bits become notes

Digital music is made two ways:

- ✔ **An analog source, such as a voice or acoustic guitar, is digitally recorded using a digital audio workstation (DAW).** This recording can be made in a studio, with a lot of fancy, expensive equipment, or in your home with a microphone plugged into your laptop computer. The only real difference is that the musician is playing into a software program that stores the music as computer bits, rather than onto a roll of tape.

- ✔ **A digital source, such as a MIDI controller, sends computer data to a sequencer program.** In this example, the music is generated digitally by the controller, and then recorded, stored, and manipulated by the software digitally. So the music is never in acoustic form during the process — at least not until people listen to it.

The final digital music file is then formatted in such a way to allow you to listen to it on your computer or a portable device, like an MP3 player.

The most common digital music format, MP3, is very popular because of its small size and ease of distribution on the Internet. MP3 is an audio data compression format. After the music files are recorded, they're very large, because they contain so much data. Audio data compression reduces, or *compresses,* the size of the file so that it can easily be shared on the Web and played in small devices. This compression reduces the quality of the audio a little, however, and some audiophiles don't care for the sound of the MP3 format. But the ability to distribute your music on such a large scale generally outweighs the concerns composers have about loss of fidelity. And the MP3 compression processing can be customized, in an attempt to achieve the highest fidelity possible.

There are other audio data compression formats, such as Microsoft's Windows Media Audio (WMA) and Apple's Advanced Audio Coding (AAC). Some of these formats use digital rights management (DRM) encoding, which is a way to prevent the files from being shared illegally. But DRM is not flawless, and computer geeks are always coming up with ways to bypass the encoding. Therefore, the record companies are continually trying out new ways to control access to the music, and prevent people from sharing the files without paying for them.

A great Webzine that has tons of useful info about digital music is Create Digital Music (www.createdigitalmusic.com). It's a community site for musicians using digital music technology, and has news, reviews, tips, features, and commentary about digital music making.

It's all software all the time

The music business is going into the software world big time. The first digital studios were all hardware-based, with the software written specifically for each piece of hardware. But now the music studio has gone virtual, with many small and large software programs doing the things machines used to do.

For centuries, composers used lined manuscript paper and pencils to write out parts for each instrument. Not all instruments play the same notes at the same time, and not all instruments are in the same key, so each part had to be written by hand. Producing a score for anything from a jazz quartet to a 90-piece orchestra was a painstaking chore — expensive and time-consuming. And, of course, all those notes had to be exact and legible!

Now, parts for instruments in different keys can be transposed with a few clicks of the mouse, and pristine copies can be produced on a standard printer. This is a large shift in thinking for the music world, and moves professional arrangers, home digital music tinkerers, and music students onto a more level playing field.

Many different types of digital music software are out there. I examine each of these types in more detail in Chapter 6, but here's an overview:

 ✔ **Musical notation software:** Notation software replicates the writing of a musical score, but you use your computer rather than a pencil and paper. Notation software, like Sibelius or Finale, is constantly expanding its features. Now most notation programs have added the ability to do work like a DAW, using plug-ins and external sound sets.

- ✔ **Digital audio workstation (DAW):** Originally a hardware device, today a DAW is a software program that records, edits, and plays back digital audio. Some have MIDI sequencing features, as well as a host of other features that make the major products able to manipulate digital music in myriad ways.

- ✔ **Samples and sound sets:** A *sample* is a short digitized piece of music that can be used by your music software. It may be a short horn passage, a hot drum solo, or an other-worldly sound, for example. Collections of samples are sometimes called *sound sets,* which are libraries of samples and sounds that can be added to your programs to expand the palette of instruments available for your compositions.

  Sampling is taking a portion of an existing song, an existing recording, or both, and putting them into a new song. This is done with a *sampler,* which can either be a piece of hardware or a computer program. The term sampler can also refer to the use of sound sets in a digital composition.

- ✔ **Plug-ins:** Plug-ins are small pieces of software that can be used by different DAW programs. Plug-ins increase the functionality of your DAW program, by adding features that the original manufacturer of the DAW didn't include. Plug-ins probably constitute the fastest growing segment of the music software business, with new plug-ins doing more things than ever before. For example, you can get plug-ins that make your digital track sound like a specific type of electric organ or old-time synthesizer, or add studio effects, like reverb or noise reduction.

An excellent Web site to find free, shareware, or demo plug-ins is the plug-ins section of the Hitsquad Musician Network (`www.hitsquad.com/smm/win95/PLUG-INS/`). Here you can find plug-ins for every operating system — Windows, Mac, and Linux — and almost every possible combination of effects or virtual instruments.

The day of a digital artist

The author of the *Rock Licks Encyclopedia* (Alfred Publishing), guitarist Tomas Cataldo (`www.tomascataldo.com`) is a longtime performer, educator, and studio musician. In addition to private instruction and workshops, Cataldo teaches at the National Guitar Workshop (`www.guitarworkshop.com`).

After studying at the Berklee College of Music in Boston, Tomas was a regular fixture on the studio session scene. This changed, however, when in 2002 Cataldo got an Apple G4 and started working in his home studio with digital music files. A studio producer either uploads a music file to a file server for his access, or sends Tomas the file via instant message. He then inserts the file into his Logic software and records his solo guitar part, adding, say, a screaming guitar lick to video games such as Need for Speed, Ghost Recon, and Red Steel. He then returns the completed file to the producer, and gamers around the world can feel the excitement!

Who Does What in the Music Biz

The music business is a lot more than just getting a band together, playing, and recording. The creative artist, or even the not-so-creative artist, can make an impact in many ways.

In general, music-oriented people can get involved with the music biz in the following ways:

- ✔ **Creating:** Composer, arranger, orchestrator, jingle writer, songwriter
- ✔ **Performing:** Performing artist, session musician, orchestra member, background vocalist, conductor
- ✔ **Producing and engineering:** Producer, engineer, post-production engineer, music editor
- ✔ **Business management:** Booking agent, business manager, Artists & Repertoire (A&R) coordinator, entertainment attorney, publicist

In the following sections, I give you a closer look at these roles.

The creators

The composers, arrangers, and orchestrators work with music directly, either creating new pieces out of whole cloth, or adapting existing music for other uses.

Composer

A composer creates either instrumentals or songs. He may compose for film, television, live performance, or recording sessions. The job could be to provide the orchestral dramatic underscore to a film, or create music to be released on the soundtrack CD. The composer may not necessarily be the arranger or orchestrator, but he provides the raw material for the other two.

Arranger

An arranger provides musical arrangements of a musical composition or song for an artist, band, orchestra, or other ensemble. The arranger determines the way the piece sounds, by deciding many elements of the music, such as the harmonic structure, rhythm, tempos, voices, instruments, and many other aspects of a composition. These choices may be based on the specifications supplied by the performing artists, the music producers, or the conductors.

An arranger should have experience as a music copyist (writing parts for all the instruments), be comfortable with writing scores, and play more than one instrument. Advanced training in music theory, composition, harmony, and orchestration is a requirement. A film arranger provides the musical arrangements for a film, video, or TV segment.

Orchestrator

The orchestrator is responsible for transposing music from one instrument or voice to another in order to accommodate a particular musician or group. Similar to an arranger, the orchestrator writes scores for an orchestra, band, choral group, individual instrumentalist, or vocalist, but usually does not reorganize the piece of music to the extent that the arranger does. Sometimes the orchestrator may also be the conductor during a film scoring session.

Jingle writer

A jingle writer may be a composer, a songwriter, or a lyricist who specializes in writing music for radio and TV commercials. The jingle writer tries to represent an advertising client in a musical form. A successful jingle writer must be able to compose short, attention-grabbing segments very quickly.

Songwriter

A songwriter may be either a freelance songwriter or a staff writer with a publishing company. He usually writes both music and lyrics. Popular commercial songwriters usually produce and perform their own material.

The performers

The performing artists are what people most commonly think of when they hear the word *musician*. They play, sing, and even conduct orchestras for audiences everywhere.

Performing artist

A performing artist is simply someone who performs, plays an instrument, or vocalizes with a band. He may work as a solo act with or without backing musicians, or be packaged as part of a group by an agent. He may perform all original material or do cover versions of popular music in a nightclub.

The performing artist may be hired for a wedding, to perform on stage, or to sing the lyrics to a jingle. In the case of the performing artist, what you hear is what you get. That is, the marketability of the artist is directly related to the skill of the performer.

Session musician

The session musician could be a studio musician, a recording session player, a sideman with a house band, a freelance musician playing society dates, or a backup musician supporting a name act on the road. He may work on many different types of musical projects, such as recording dates, TV and film scores, records, jingles, and other types of gigs.

The main responsibility of the session musician is to back up the performing artist either in a recording studio or during a live performance. Session musicians are usually hired by a contractor and paid union scale, set by the American Federation of Musicians.

The session musician must be an excellent sight reader — able to play any sheet music presented to him flawlessly the first time through. He is also often called on to perform on more than one instrument, for which he is paid more (a practice called *doubling*).

Orchestra member

The orchestra member is an instrumentalist in a large ensemble, such as an orchestra. Similar to the session musician, a member of an established orchestra has a very demanding job, one that requires a vast knowledge of musical repertoire, a high level of musical skill, excellent sight reading, and doubling abilities. He must have a lot of experience playing with large groups, and needs to be prepared, by studying the material to be performed before rehearsal. Most orchestra members are represented by the American Federation of Musicians.

Background vocalist

Many famous vocal artists started out as backup singers for major and minor acts. Background vocalists sing the backup parts to support the lead singer. They also support other singers and musicians on studio sessions, in jingles and commercials, or on live gigs. Most backup vocalists work freelance, although they may be able to land long-term employment traveling with a performing artist.

One of the toughest parts of being a background vocalist is the need for flexibility. They have to be able to adapt to any musical style almost instantly, sight-read music easily, and harmonize and improvise, all without missing a beat.

Conductor

A conductor does more than just wave his arms around and smile at the audience. The conductor must prepare the orchestra and help them give the best performance they can. This also means helping plan the musical season, handling business-related issues, picking the repertoire, and managing the rehearsals.

The conductor must be an excellent musical performer, and have a deep knowledge of musical repertoire. He needs a high level of interpersonal skills, because he is the most visible representative of the orchestra and must interact with the public in a strong, confident manner.

He must also have leadership ability, because he will have to manage and interact with composers, performers, arrangers, and orchestrators, and a host of other music professionals.

The producers and engineers

This section describes those who work with music in the production, engineering, or editing side of things. This could be in a recording studio, on a film or TV production set, or in post-production just before a product is released.

Producer

The producer is the creative force behind a television, video, film, or studio recording project. He oversees all aspects of the project, including contracting the musicians and managing the budget.

Some producers work with artists, bands, and record labels to produce recordings, while others work with composers to create the sound for various multimedia projects. A producer should have a good musical training and skill, and a high level of technical and studio experience.

Recording engineer

A recording engineer is responsible for operating the sound console and other recording equipment during the music recording session. He often has to set up the studio's recording equipment before the session, sometimes even the music stands and chairs for the musicians.

An important part of the engineer's job is to try to understand what the producer or band's manager wants the finished product to sound like. It's the engineer's responsibility to create a recording that meets the producer's desires. This is a very difficult part of the job, because the engineer must be able to meet the expectations of the artist or producer, who may not be able to describe in technical terms what it is they want.

Mastering engineer or post-production engineer

The mastering engineer is sometimes called the post-production engineer. He's the last engineer to work on a project, and makes the final adjustments to polish off the project for release. He's responsible for taking the final studio mix and adding the finishing touches, such as equalization (EQ), final effects processing, and compression (such as MP3).

Film music editor

A film's music editor is responsible for synchronizing the music with the film and mixing the music for the film's soundtrack. He must have a very high level of knowledge of the technology used in synchronizing music tracks to film or video. This technological knowledge has to be coupled with a good musical intuition, an awareness of how music can make or break a dramatic scene, and he must posses an excellent ear for nuance.

The suits: Business and management roles

As in all business endeavors, the business and management types need to be involved, to make sure the studio, record label, and so on are operating profitably. The music biz has some unique business roles; some people work for the label, others work for the artist.

Booking or talent agent

Booking or talent agents may work for the artist, working to secure performance engagements, or for a club, looking for entertainment acts to place in a venue. They're usually paid a percentage of the artist's fee for an engagement, or a flat rate by the venue. Their success is often directly related to how many good contacts they have in the music business.

An agent who works for an artist is generally involved in negotiating with promoters or clubs and setting the fee. Therefore, it's considered a conflict of interest for the agent to be paid by both the artist and the club for the same engagement.

Business manager

A business manager handles the financial affairs of artists or bands. He may have a degree in business administration with a concentration in management or accounting. The business manager must have a thorough knowledge of accounting, taxes, and excellent negotiating skills. He usually interfaces with the label's attorney during contract negotiations.

Artists & Repertoire coordinator

The task of the A&R coordinator is to find and sign new talent for the recording company. In addition to listening to demo recordings, watching videotapes of acts, and visiting clubs and showcases, the A&R coordinator may also be responsible for locating new tunes for established artists to perform.

Entertainment attorney

An entertainment attorney usually specializes in one of three fields of the entertainment industry: music, sports, or film/TV. He may be on staff, on retainer with an entertainment business, or freelance.

The attorney handles any contractual matters regarding artists and the label, such as copyright laws, band agreements with managers and publishers, and any other endeavor that requires legal or contract advice.

Publicist

Publicity is the lifeblood of both a performing artist and the record company. The publicist may be a freelance publicist, who is hired directly by artists to manage their press needs, or be on staff at a record label, to direct the publicity effort for the bands signed to the label.

The publicist writes press releases, talks to the media about his clients, and arranges interviews for the artists, all in an effort to get his artist's name in front of the public as often as possible.

Your Role as a Digital Musician

The creative musician has always had to be very flexible to survive, by donning various hats: composer, arranger, performer, educator, producer, sound engineer, concert prompter, and even car parker. You can work in the music biz in many different roles, maybe in ways you hadn't even thought of.

With the decentralization of music taking hold, often the entire path of a music project — from creation to mixing to selling — can be done by a single person with fairly limited resources. This new digital music environment allows — actually, *requires* — music creators to cross-categorize. The technology doesn't pigeonhole creators into narrow categories; it lets the creative artist work in many realms.

Bands are also forsaking the embrace of the big labels and forging out into the wilderness of direct downloads to fans. One of the most visible bands doing this is Radiohead (www.radiohead.com/deadairspace), which released its recordings only through a Web site (www.radiohead.com), in digital download, vinyl, and CD formats.

In this section, I show you some of the ways a creative musician can get involved in the new digital medium.

The art of the record deal

Yes, I know, except for the rare companies that press vinyl, no one makes records anymore. But it's still called the record business, even though it's been CDs for years, and now the majors are embracing new forms of distribution, like online streaming.

I don't have enough space in this book to cover the entire record business. And because this book is focused on composing digital music, not playing and recording with your band, I'm just going to give you a high-level lowdown on what's usually involved. But fair warning: My advice is not intended to take the place of legal advice, and your results may vary.

Berklee College of Music has a great series of online courses about the music business (www.berkleemusic.com/school/courses/music_business). You can get the inside info on how to develop a strategy to break into the music industry, how to create and operate your own publishing company, and how to promote and place your songs. Other music schools have similar courses of study.

It looks simple: You make a CD, sell it at gigs, and get some radio stations to play it. With any luck, you make enough money from that CD to make another one. But major recording and distribution of your work is more complicated. That's one reason a lot of the composers I mention in this chapter have their publishing companies handle the details. It's a lot of paperwork and hassle, and you're better off spending your time composing and performing.

But if you're dying to know what happens if you sign with a major label, here are the basic steps:

1. **You sign an agreement with a major label and give the record company your recordings.**

2. **The record company creates the product — presses the record, burns the CD, or whatever.**

3. **The record company sends the product to a distributor, which wholesales it to stores or distributes it digitally.**

4. **The record company starts a marketing campaign.**

When you get your first contract offer, you'll probably be so thrilled that all you'll want to do is sign on the dotted line. But don't sign anything without making sure it's the right contract for _you_.

Whether you know someone in the biz, or a record exec hears your band at a gig and goes ape, it still will all come down to the contract. And just as you wouldn't buy a house or a car without examining all the details, or getting a lawyer to examine it for you, you shouldn't sign your artistic life away without being very careful.

The contract doesn't have to be very complicated, but you should try to anticipate as many obstacles as possible. Most label contracts have some core elements, like the details of the deal, the length of the term of the contract, the location of the record sales, and the all-important money stuff, like the advance and expenses.

Deal or no deal

You need to know what the record deal covers. It may depend upon whether you've already recorded tracks for an album, or you're negotiating for the label to release upcoming albums your band will record.

A common record deal may be

- ✔ A licensing deal for one album only, which you've already recorded
- ✔ A licensing deal for one recorded album, adding a deal for the label to release more future albums from you
- ✔ A recording agreement for you or your band to record albums that the label will release in the future
- ✔ A licensing or recording agreement that has *right of first refusal* (the record company gets to opt in or out on your album, before any other company) on your future recordings

The contract term

The *contract term* is the length of time the record company owns the album and its licensing rights. This is not as simple as it appears, and the term of the contract can be a big source of contention with established artists.

The label wants the term of the contract to be as long as possible, and can range from a couple of years to infinity. A five- to ten-year contact term is common, but the bigger labels may want a longer term. It's also common to include an option to renew the term of the contract, if agreed upon by both parties.

Location, location, location

A record label contract should state where the company has the right to sell the album. For example, if your band already has a U.K. deal, and the record company you're negotiating with is a U.S. company, the company can't sell your record in the U.K.

The contract will cover areas where the record label has distribution but where the band does not already have an existing agreement. Often a clause is inserted into the contract stating that the label can seek licensing or distribution deals in other territories.

Show me the money

An *advance* is money paid upfront to the artists, and then deducted from future earnings of the band. It's common for an unknown band to get no advance (or a very small advance), because the record company can't yet gauge how easily it'll be able to recoup that advance from the album sales. Often indie labels don't even make advances, because if money is tight, it actually works out better in the long run to have the label spend that money on promotion.

The contract must specify how and when you can expect to be paid. You won't be paid until the label makes back the money it has spent on the album, and deducted the amount of the advance. Then the contract needs to specify how the profit will be divided.

The royalty world

Besides whatever deal you strike with your record label, there are two other ways you can get paid for your tunes:

✔ **Mechanical royalties:** Mechanical royalties are a royalty paid to you whenever a copy of one of your songs is made. This means when a record label presses a CD of your song, you're due a mechanical royalty.

✔ **Performing rights royalties:** Performing rights royalties are royalties paid to you whenever one of your songs is performed, either live or broadcast. If you're a member of a performing rights collection agency, like BMI or ASCAP, the agency will keep track of performances of your music, collect payment from whatever organization is performing it, and pass the royalties on to you. (Like everything in the music biz, it's a little more complicated than that, but that's the basic story.)

The most common profit divisions are either a 50/50 split, or a percentage deal. A smaller indie label will often go for an even 50/50 split (which eases the accounting chores), but larger, major labels almost always want a percentage deal, with you getting less than 50 percent of the profit (and the record company getting more).

Because you won't make money on your album until the label makes back all the money it spent on the album, it's a good idea to get the label to agree on a spending cap in the contract. A spending cap says the record company will consult the artist or band after spending a specified amount, before it continues to spend more on album promotion or expenses.

The extra fine print

Of course, a lot of optional elements may be included on your contract. You (or your lawyer) will need to be on the lookout for several ways the label can stick you. Some of these are

✔ **Acceptance and delivery:** Sometimes major labels assert the right to refuse to release a record that is different from the record they thought they were getting. This is a sore point with a lot of artists, but new groups may not be able to eliminate it initially. Smaller, indie labels rarely use this clause.

✔ **Accounting:** Some artists require the right to have an accounting firm audit the record company's books once a year, to make sure everything is on the up and up in the royalty area.

✔ **Licensing deals:** There are other ways the label makes money from the music, such as licensing the album to a label in another territory or licensing a track to a movie, TV show, or Broadway show. How the royalties are split in such cases must be defined in the contract.

Promoting your tunes on the Web

The Internet has changed how a composer gets his music heard. Once upon a time, the record companies had that all tied up nice and neat, and you were either on the inside with them, or on the outside looking in. Now all it takes is a few mouse clicks to instantly offer your tunes to millions.

But it still takes more than just technical know-how to ensure those millions will start to *listen* to your opus. In this section, I cover a few things you should know to make the best use of your time on the Web, and maybe make a few bucks in the process.

Creating a Web site

I like MySpace (www.myspace.com) and almost everyone uses it (so should you), but your Web site should be a real, dedicated site (like www.yourname.com). It doesn't have to be complicated or fancy, with all the latest technological bells and whistles, but it needs to have basic information for your fans, and include

✔ Information about you and your music

✔ Recording news and concert dates

✔ A mailing list for your fans to keep up-to-date about you and your band's activities

The press and media will also want to use your site, so you should have good, high-quality digital photos for reproduction; an updated bio; and press releases about upcoming concerts or general news.

 Offer short audio clips of your tunes for free download, and be sure to update your site regularly. People will stop visiting if it never has any new info or music. And if you're really feeling generous, you can give away the entire file of the tune.

Selling your music on your site

After you start to drive traffic to your site and folks are downloading the sample music, you can start to think about actually charging for your music. Build a page that lets your fans buy your tracks, both in CD format (mailed to them) or in MP3 format (which they can download).

The artist should get paid first

ArtistShare (www.artistshare.com) was founded in the fall of 2000 by musician and computer consultant Brian Camelio. Its purpose is to be a place where fans fund the projects of their favorite artists in exchange for the privilege of "participating" in the creative process.

Brian created ArtistShare to be unique, because the fans donate to the creation of the product, rather than buying a piece of product or download, after it's been created. Brian explains: "So my theory was, as a form of DRM [digital rights management] copy protection, what we do is have the fans pay for the music before it's made. And then it's moot — it doesn't matter. Once it's out there, the artist has been paid. And, of course, there's going to be residual income after it's released, but a business model shouldn't be based on that. I saw the music industry becoming more of a service industry than a retail industry."

ArtistShare is also branching into other media. Brian says, "We have our first film project launched [in October 2007] — it's an independent film. We're going to use the same model because the same thing is going to happen to the film industry. Anything that can be reproduced digitally, once it's out there, it's in the ether. The limitations on the technology will be lifted in the next few years. So we're preparing for that as well. So this goes beyond jazz and beyond music, into any other art form. Any art form that the fans are interested in the creative process."

Brian still thinks the major studio model is viable, however, because "the labels still have the ability to put some muscle behind PR. And I think the labels need to go in that direction, of just basically being PR firms. And possibly bringing in new revenue streams, such as live music and merchandising, which they're already doing."

Processing payments, such as credit card numbers, is big business — and a big hassle, unless your old man owns a payment processing service provider. And big-time security issues are involved with handling credit card numbers directly, so get aligned with a service that can provide links on your site to accept payment.

One way is to get a merchant credit account from a bank and download its credit card processing software. This lets your fans process their cards right on your Web site. An established company that does this is PayPal's CyberCash service (www.paypal.com/cybercash).

Other digital music distribution Web sites, such as Napster (www.napster.com) and eMusic (www.emusic.com), offer a nonexclusive contract to distribute your tunes on their site. These can lead to a good source of revenue, if the word gets out that you're hot!

Bret Primak: Multimedia developer

One successful multimedia developer is Bret Primak (www.planetbret.com). Bret is a journalist and playwright who has recently begun documenting legendary jazz artists through video, aiding them in building their Web sites, and helping to bring them into the new digital age. Through new media he's been able to work with such creators as Walter Bishop, Jr.; Billy Taylor; David Liebman; Sonny Rollins; and Joe Lovano.

He's posting on YouTube (www.youtube.com), the video sharing site, and putting his videos on a YouTube channel called JazzVideoLand (www.youtube.com/jazzvideoland). Bret currently has around 144 videos posted, with more than a million combined views.

He feels that "creative musicians, regardless of their age or idiom, recognize the need to embrace the new media, because the way the music is sold and distributed is moving toward digital a lot faster now — it's starting to speed up. The older artists, like Sonny Rollins, because they themselves don't use the technology, are supportive but they don't necessarily understand it. Younger people are totally into it, use the technology, and totally embrace the distribution of music in this way."

Bret also feels that the traditional music labels are still having a difficult time adjusting to the new digital dynamic:

> I don't think the labels are going to last. I think the labels blew their chance to be part of this when, instead of trying to build a business model when the whole file-sharing started, taking the enthusiasm and the momentum, what they did was say they were just going to sue. They may have put the nails in their own coffin by doing that.

Radiohead is a perfect example. What the record business forgot was that people place value on the music. And they may share it, but they are going to recognize that it has value, and they are going to pay for it, and they are paying for it on iTunes. It took Apple and iTunes to make it viable. The labels could have done that four, five, six years ago, when the whole thing started.

Since video is Bret's area of expertise, he sees the trend as being toward small, home-style studios, for digital video, as well as digital music production:

> Video production is changing dramatically. People can now produce video for a very low cost and distribute it immediately over the Internet. The same thing that has happened to the music business is going to happen in the movie business as well.

> I can make a movie now, I can capture video onto my computer, edit it, and put it up on the Internet. It's not a feature film, but it allows people to create things and distribute them to a large audience. People are still going to want to go to the theaters and see the $50-million epic, but independent films, and filmmakers who just want to make short films, that's just going to get bigger and bigger and bigger.

> People want to do it themselves now. These tools that are available to create music and video are incredible. Now many more people are involved in creativity and using these tools. Not all of them are going to become successful filmmakers or artists, but just the doing of it is something that people really enjoy.

Working in the digital music business

Earlier in this chapter, I show you who does what in the music biz, but in this section, I cover a few additional new roles that specifically require *digital* music skills. These jobs didn't exist a few years ago, but business is booming.

Sequence programmer

A programmer uses music sequencing software or notation software to produce tracks for film, video, theater, television, and recording scores. Sometimes the programmer creates a track for a composer or music editor to give him an opportunity to hear the composition before it's fully scored for an orchestra. This allows the composer to identify errors in the score before the full orchestra starts to play it, when the recording costs are very high.

Music synthesist

This is a more general designation that refers to the electronic creation, modification, and control of sound. Although a music synthesist can function as a programmer, it involves a wider field of career opportunities in music education, live performance, digital composition, music production and editing, and hardware and software design.

Multimedia developer

The multimedia developer is an interactive multimedia specialist. He produces and formats audio (and sometimes video) content for an artist's CD-ROM, digital downloads, videos, and Web site. The multimedia developer combines various digital formats — such as text, images, video, animation, or sound — to create a complete interactive environment for the composer, performer, or band.

At the Barricades: Talking to Some of the People at the Forefront of the Revolution

Some composers do more than just embrace the new digital media, they exploit and thrive on it. I talked to a group of digital composers, producers, distributors, and artists who represent the wide range of digital possibilities for the creative artist, and I share their insights in this section.

Morton Subotnick

Music as performance art has been around longer than recording, of course. And notating music on paper was the first step in capturing the transient sounds of music for posterity.

Morton Subotnick personifies the digital music revolution. He has overseen the evolution from electronic music being a pure fine arts exercise, to the complete takeover of the music biz by digital music production. Never before has a single person or event encapsulated such a change in music, or any art form, for that matter.

Subotnick is one of the pioneers in the development of electronic music and an innovator in works involving instruments and other media, including inter-active computer music systems. The work that brought Subotnick celebrity was *Silver Apples of the Moon* (1966–1967), which was commissioned by Nonesuch Records, marking the first time an original large-scale composition had been created specifically for the disc medium — a conscious acknowl-edgment that the home stereo system constituted a present-day form of chamber music.

Subotnick is also pioneering works to offer musical creative tools to young children. He's the author of a series of CD-ROMs for children, a children's Web site (www.creatingmusic.com), and he's developing a program for classroom and after-school programs that will soon become available internationally.

Subotnick is amazed at how much has changed in such a short time:

> You can look at the sketches of Leonardo da Vinci, the flying machine and such, and consider how many centuries it took for that actually to come. In the '50s, I was only thinking that we were at the beginning of some-thing, just the start. Although I foresaw the move toward the individual and the home and all of that stuff, I thought electronic music was going to be fine art music. Because pop in the '50s was ballads and jazz, I didn't know the enormous pop movement that would take place.

> So now it's not this complex aesthetic experience, it's a very direct music experience, an experience you could have in any village anywhere in time. And that's pretty interesting, it's really a fascinating time.

As the world's digital information flow increases in tempo and size, and music becomes part of that programmed information flow, Subotnick's MIDI performances still retain a high-wire aspect, since they're live:

> [A]t a performance level, it's like the materials inside the computer are a surfboard, and I'm surfing. Because you can also fall apart. Because you're going in real time. And that's the difference between information management and what you're doing here. You're at peril always. You can do something you can't get out of.

James Bernard

Another creator riding the digital wave is James Bernard (www.myspace.com/jamesbernardmusic). His first album, *Atmospherics,* was released in 1994 on Rising High. He has released tracks on Isophlux Records, Analog Records, BML Records, and now on Three Sixty Records (www.threesixty records.com/jamesbernard.html).

In 1997, Bernard formed the act Expansion Union, whose song "Playing with Lightning" from the album *World Wide Funk* was featured in the hit movie *Blade* and was used on the multi-gold-selling soundtrack CD from the film.

Bernard works for Propellerhead Software as in-house artist relations and all-around Reason expert. He travels the world, performing and giving demos and training seminars on Propellerhead products.

Bernard thinks the large studio will always have a place in the creation of music "when it comes to things like recording a full band and orchestral pieces." He continues:

> The DIY [do-it-yourself] method of recording is great for most music genres, but some rely on [more than] the "sound" and tools/gear that a large studio has to offer. There is a certain "vibe" to "going to the studio" to record that is hard to capture in a garage, basement, [or] living room.

Bernard is one of the digital artists who fully embraces the digital download distribution model:

> The majority of the music I release and sell is only available digitally. I see it as the "going green" phase of the industry in a sense. Less waste product in CDs that don't sell and fuel needed to transport/ship them. I applaud bands like Radiohead who have embraced the new model and are able to thrive without the need for a major label. It's a sign of the times.

James is another artist who switched from hardware to software, and has greatly expanded the way Reason is used by all composers:

> I used to do everything on hardware. Lots of little boxes like the Roland TB-303, [Roland] TR-606, [Roland] TR-808, [Roland] SH-101, and many other analog synths. It took forever to get things all set up when I had some inspiration. And if that inspiration hit while I was away from the studio, I was out of luck.

> Now I have my studio with me and can jot down ideas anytime. If I'd had software like Reason 14 years ago, I would have written thousands of songs instead of a hundred or so. And now any sound I hear in my head I can achieve.

For me, Reason is the fastest way for me to get my musical ideas out of my head and into a finished piece of music. It's the perfect piece of software for me in that it looks and feels just like the hardware.

I think as the new digital model expands I would love to see devices like iPods and cellphones actually run Reason natively on them. Then I can just send a Reason song file to someone instead of MP3s!

You can listen to some of James Bernard's unique and original digital compositions on the CD at `Author/Chapter 02/Audio Examples/ James Bernard`.

Meshell Ndegeocello

Musicians who've been playing for decades are also seeing big changes in the music business because of the advent of digital recording and distribution techniques. Someone who has seen the rise of digital music creation and distribution, is Meshell Ndegeocello (`www.meshell.com`). An accomplished bassist and prolific songwriter, Ndegeocello was born in Germany; raised in Washington, D.C.; signed her first recording deal at 23; and has been nominated for nine Grammy Awards.

She's appeared on recordings by Basement Jaxx, Indigo Girls, the Blind Boys of Alabama, and the Rolling Stones's 1997 album *Bridges to Babylon,* playing bass on the song "Saint of Me." Her biggest hit was a cover version of Van Morrison's "Wild Night," sung with John Mellencamp, which reached no. 3 on the Billboard charts.

Ndegeocello's music has been featured in a number of film soundtracks, including *How Stella Got Her Groove Back, Batman and Robin,* and *Down in the Delta,* and she can be seen in the documentary movie *Standing in the Shadows of Motown,* singing the Miracles's "You've Really Got a Hold on Me."

Ndegeocello believes these advancements in technology create an environment both of seekers and followers, mediocrity and genius:

For the creative individual who spends many an hour learning and adapting to the latest recording software, social and music sites, or blogs, the vastness of one's universe can be infinite or very comfortable, predictable, or trite, perhaps due to the users' limited ability and sheer lack of curiosity.

She says the paradox of people-powered self-made music "allow the average unskilled musician to fulfill [her] dreams of making music, often bringing about great invention and freshness or the flipside: mediocre, well-constructed garbage. The Internet as well allows for a mask, but one of your own design. Then there is no one other than yourself to blame or reward for your success or failure."

Tom Salta

One of the world's top video game composers is Tom Salta (www.tomsalta. com). Tom is an award-winning composer of electronic and orchestral music for film, television, and video games. Recording under the artist name Atlas Plug, Salta's grooves grace many TV shows, commercials, and film promos.

Tom's home studio is the center of his composing universe. He uses Logic Studio on a Mac. Beginning with Logic's predecessor, Notator Logic on the Atari ST, he's been using Logic since the early '90s. He also has some PCs with GigaStudio for access to additional sound libraries.

In addition to an admirable list of composing credits, Salta's contemporary and traditional Japanese musical score for the video game Red Steel won IGN's 2006 Award for Best Original Score. And his orchestral score for the Xbox 360 video game Tom Clancy's Ghost Recon: Advanced Warfighter (GRAW) was nominated for Best Video Game Score at the 2006 MTV Video Music Awards (VMAs).

The movement of digital music creation from software to hardware has impacted the way Salta creates music:

> The evolution of 'working in the box' has definitely increased both the speed at which I can work, and the palette of sounds at my disposal. Now, within my DAW, all my instruments, settings, and my entire mix can be instantly saved and recalled. I can jump around between projects much faster than I could years ago. Also, I don't have to worry about hardware synths and mixers breaking down.

But Salta is the exception, rather than the rule, regarding success in the digital music world:

> Even with all the new outlets out there for the independent artist, most artists are not making a living out of selling their music. I see the key reason for this being a lack of marketing. That's still what the majors have over the indies, marketing muscle (money).

> Another issue is that since nearly anyone can create a decent sounding recording in his bedroom on any budget these days, there is a huge amount of mediocre and downright horrible music out there. This makes it even more important to market yourself so you can stand out from the crowd.

> I do think there is a lot of opportunity for new independents to connect with their audience. But at the end of the day, it takes an extreme amount of time, dedication, marketing, and persistence to get a fan base and make it grow.

Hear a couple cuts from Tom Salta's 2004 album *2DaysOrDie* on the CD at Author/Chapter 02/Audio Examples/Tom Salta.

Howard Johnson

Multi-instrumentalist Howard Johnson (www.hojozone.com) has seen lots of changes in the music industry since he first recorded in the mid-'60s. Johnson has been playing music since he was a boy in Alabama. He taught himself the baritone saxophone and the tuba after relocating to Ohio.

Johnson moved to New York City in 1963 and worked with Charles Mingus, Hank Crawford, and Archie Shepp. In 1966, he started a 20-year off-and-on association with Gil Evans. Johnson's four tuba group Substructure performed with Taj Mahal, and, in the late '70s, he formed a different tuba band called Gravity that, in 1996, finally had the opportunity to record (plus play at the Monterey Jazz Festival).

Johnson has recorded with Crawford, John Lennon, Paul Simon, The Band, Jack DeJohnette's Special Edition, Gato Barbieri, Jimmy Heath, Bob Moses, George Gruntz's Concert Jazz Band, and Paul Butterfield's Better Days, and was a member (and for a time the bandleader) of the Saturday Night Live Band between 1975 and 1980.

Johnson has seen recording technique radically evolve since the 1960s. Now the whole idea of using a big studio to record commercial music has given way to the small, portable laptop studio:

> I just did a whole series of jingles for Men's Wearhouse. The early ones were done in New York studios, but the last couple, I went up to the jingle composer's house and went into his little sugar shack where he had a microphone and a laptop. I just playing into the microphone and he used Pro Tools.
>
> He laid down the initial tracks with his guitar, bumped the bass part down an octave from his guitar, and had people come in and play keyboards, not only for keyboard parts, but also for other sounds. So his little laptop and microphone are a studio. The other musicians could come in and record at different times, whenever they could. He didn't have to book studio time, didn't have to get everyone there at the same time or any of that — he just had his own deadline, and people could come up when they could.

Howard tells an interesting story about the first time he recorded with The Band:

> When I went to their first rehearsal, I was still a little suspicious of them, of whether these guys are really even musicians or not. The arranger for the session [was] Allan Toussaint [and his] luggage had been stolen, so he had to rearrange everything overnight. He was in Robbie Robertson's house trying to arrange the tunes for the horns by listening to an old

cassette player that had dying batteries. But this meant that he arranged everything in the wrong key.

When we got to the rehearsal, we realized right away that something was terribly wrong. A tune that was supposed to be in the key of G, for example, was in the key of F♯. This meant we'd have to have the arrangements rewritten overnight for the next day's session.

But then they did something that really impressed me. The Band played these tunes in these new weird keys, so the other musicians could play the written arrangements for that day's recording session. They had to transpose and play, say, in the key of F♯, tunes that they had been playing in the key of G for many years.

Now if this had been today, those arrangements could have been transposed and printed out during a half-hour break, using notation software, a laptop, and a printer.

Chapter 3

Music Notation Basics

In This Chapter

▶ Identifying the basic elements of written music

▶ Making sense of the basic parts of a page of music

▶ Understanding the time signature

▶ Looking at chord symbols

*Y*ou may not ever need to *read* sheet music to *compose* music. Most music composition software don't require that you understand all the ins and outs of instrument ranges, notes, clefs, and bar lines to have fun creating interesting music. But if you do take the time to learn how to read music, you'll be way ahead on the composing curve. Like learning another language or computer skill, reading music opens a whole new world of ability to you, improving the quality of your compositions.

In this chapter, I fill you in on the basic elements of written music. If you already know how to read music, you may want to skip this chapter — or read it for a brush-up on the terminology.

The Four Main Elements of Musical Notation

Similar to hearing a foreign language spoken for the first time, reading what looks like fly specs on a piece of paper can seem impossible at first. But reading music isn't really that hard. People say that when you start to think in a foreign language, you know you're fluent in it. Well, when you start to think in music notation, it's a sure sign that you're starting to compose!

Musical notation has many different elements, but here are the four main pieces of information that a written note gives you:

- **Pitch:** The name of the note, and how high or low it sounds
- **Duration:** How long the note sounds; from short to long
- **Expression:** How the note is played — loud or soft, intensely or serenely, and so on
- **Articulation:** How the note is attacked, determining whether the note is short or long, hard or soft, or varying

In the following sections, I introduce you to these elements.

Pitch

The very first thing you usually notice about a note is its *pitch*. A note is composed of two elements:

- **Notehead:** The little oval symbol that's either filled in or open.
- **Stem:** The bar attached to the notehead, sometimes with a flag on the end.

Where the notehead sits on the five-line *staff* tells you what pitch to play (A, B, C, D, E, F, or G), with the notes sounding higher in pitch as the letters move up the staff. After you get to G, the next note is A (not H!).

An *accidental* is a little sign that sits in front of the note and changes its pitch either half a step up (the sharp sign [♯]), or half a step down (the flat sign [♭]). (I describe accidentals in more detail in "The key signature," later in this chapter.)

Duration

The shape of the notehead and whether it has a stem attached determine how long the note is to be played — its *duration*. The duration is relative to the beat of the music, which is determined by the score's *time signature*.

For example a whole note (o) could mean the note is held for four beats, while a half note (♩) is held for only two beats, depending upon the time signature. Each one of the following note durations is half again shorter than the one before:

- ✔ **Whole note (o):** Usually the longest note, it's a hollow oval *without* a stem.

- ✔ **Half note (♩):** Held half as long as a whole note, it's a hollow oval *with* a stem.

- ✔ **Quarter note (♩):** Held half as long as a half note, it's a solid notehead with a stem.

- ✔ **Eighth note (♪):** Held half as long as a quarter note, it's a solid notehead with a flag.

- ✔ **Sixteenth note (♬):** Held half as long as an eighth note, it's a solid notehead with a double flag.

This list could continue through thirty-second notes, sixty-fourth notes, and so on. Figure 3-1 shows a staff of music with five different note lengths.

Various Note Lengths

Figure 3-1:
Musical
notes are
played in
different
lengths, or
durations.

Expression

Expression is a term describing how loud or soft a note or passage is played. Expression instructions can come in different forms on the sheet music.

A *dynamic marking* is a letter or group of letters under the staff that tells the musician how softly or loudly he should play the musical passage. Here are some dynamic markings, from loud to soft:

- ✔ **Fortissimo (*ff*):** Very loud

- ✔ **Forte (*f*):** Loud

- ✔ **Mezzo-forte (*mf*):** Moderately loud

✔ **Mezzo-piano (*mp*):** Moderately soft

✔ **Piano (*p*):** Soft

✔ **Pianissimo (*pp*):** Very soft

A wedge-shaped symbol below the staff is either a *crescendo* (◁) or a *diminuendo* (▷), which is also known as a *decrescendo*. These tell the player to make a dynamic change over the length of the wedge, rather than all at once, like a dynamic marking. *Crescendo* (or just *cresc.*) means to increase the volume gradually, and *diminuendo* (or *dim.* or *decresc.*) means to lower the volume gradually.

Sometimes the expression is described in words above the staff, like *Softly*, or *Agitato* (agitated). Most musical phrases are Italian, because Italian music was considered the highest form of written music when the notational system was refined, during the Renaissance Era.

Expression words can also tell the player to speed up or slow down. A gradual increase in tempo is usually indicated by the term *accelerando* (or just *accel.*), written below the area where the composer wants the music to speed up. If the composer wants the piece to gradually slow down, she'll write *ritardando* (or just *rit.*) or *rallentando* under the staff where she wants the music to slow down.

Articulation

Articulation is how smoothly the note is to be played. A note can be played very smoothly (or *legato*) or detached and clipped (or *staccato*). The articulation can be indicated by marks above the notes, a line for legato or a dot for staccato. An *accent mark* above a note tells the player to make the note stand out and play it a little louder than the other notes.

A special articulation mark called a *slur* is a curved line that connects two different notes. It means that the player should move from one note to the other smoothly, without breaking the sound.

Figure 3-2 shows three articulation symbols and a slur.

Figure 3-2:
Articulations tell the musician how smoothly to play a note.

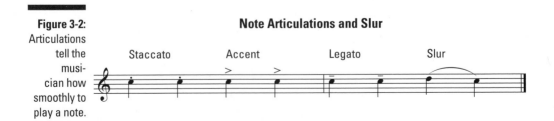

Note Articulations and Slur

Staccato   Accent   Legato   Slur

The Parts of a Music Score

A music score or piece of sheet music includes much more than just notes, expressions, and articulations. All these parts combine to create the environment the player uses to perform the piece of music as the composer intends. (And you thought all a musician had to do was just blow!)

Here are the basic parts of a page of music:

- ✔ **Staff:** Five lines that are used to place the note
- ✔ **Ledger line:** For those notes that have to be above or below the staff
- ✔ **Clef:** A symbol at the start of the music that tells the player which lines of the staff will match which notes
- ✔ **Key signature:** A series of flats or sharps at the beginning of the piece that tells the player which notes are flat or sharp throughout the piece
- ✔ **Time signature:** Two numbers, one on top of the other, that tell the musician the beat of a tune and which notes get which duration. Also called a *meter signature,* it looks like a fraction (but don't get confused and think of it as one, because it's not).
- ✔ **Bar line:** A vertical line through the staff that indicates each time signature grouping of note durations

In the following sections, I explain each of these in greater detail, along with some other elements of a music score.

The staff

Music is written on a five-line system called a *staff.* A group of these on a music score page are called *staves.* The noteheads are placed in the spaces between the lines, on the lines, or in the spaces above or below the staff.

Each alternating space and line corresponds to the letters A through G. The bottom line is called the *first line,* and the bottom space is called the *first space.*

The vertical position of the notehead on the staff indicates which note is to be played. As the notes go up the staff, their relative pitch goes up (gets higher); as the notes go down the staff, their pitch goes down (gets lower).

The notehead can be placed with the center of its notehead intersecting a line (known as *on a line*) or in between the lines, touching the lines above and below (known as *in a space*). For example, if an E is on the first line, then the next space is the letter F. The next line above the F is the letter G. The next higher note above G, on the second space, is A.

Most piano music has two staves, commonly for the right and left hands. This is sometimes called the *grand staff* or *great stave*. Notes that fall outside the range of the staff are placed on or between ledger lines added above or below the staff (see the next section for more on ledger lines).

Exactly which notes are represented by which staff positions is determined by a *clef* placed at the beginning of the staff; the clef identifies a particular line as a specific note, and all other notes are determined relative to that line. (See the "Clef" section, later in this chapter, for more on clefs.)

Ledger lines

Sometimes a note sounds lower or higher than the staff can accommodate. You can extend the staff, either above or below, by adding very short additional staff lines called *ledger lines*. The notes that rest on these lines move up and down alphabetically on the ledger lines just as they do on the normal staff lines. Ledger lines virtually extend the staff above or below to keep the space/line alternation going. Figure 3-3 shows a musical passage requiring ledger lines.

Ledger Lines

Figure 3-3:
Ledger lines
let you
extend the
staff.

A ledger line is created by drawing a short line parallel to the lines on the staff, either above or below the staff, depending on where the note should sound.

Notes that are on more than three or four ledger lines above or below the staff are usually considered too hard to read. If you have such notes in several measures, switching to a different clef is usually preferable. It's also common to write *8va* if the notes should sound an octave higher than written, or *8vb* if the notes should sound an octave lower than written.

Why is music written this way?

What we use today as musical notation evolved historically from the Western European musical tradition. The founder of what is considered the standard music stave was Guido d'Arezzo, an Italian Benedictine monk who lived from 995 to 1050. Today the five-line staff is the most commonly distributed form of notated music and is widely accepted as the standard way to distribute sheet music and study music.

Of course, there are myriad other ways to notate music, such as numbered musical notation, also known as *jianpu* in China. And new notation schemes are continually being patented and employed in contemporary music, such as guitar tablature, and graphic symbols, employed by experimental composers such as John Cage and Morton Feldman.

Music notation seems unnecessarily complicated and ungainly at times, because what people are doing is imperfectly translating an aural medium into a visual one. This means that no notation system will represent the music *exactly,* but then the various interpretations of a single piece of music by different musical artists is one of the great joys of music.

Clef

Telling the player what letter names reside on which line or space of the staff is the job of the *clef.* Located at the left edge of the page, at the beginning of the music, it works in conjunction with the staff to tell you what pitch is associated with which line and space. Although several types of clefs exist, you'll mostly use two clefs: the *treble clef* and the *bass clef.*

The treble clef

The treble clef is called a *G clef,* because the curly center of the symbol wraps around the second line of the staff, the G line. The treble clef puts the G above middle C on the second line. Figure 3-4 shows the names of all the lines and spaces on the treble clef.

All Lines and Spaces for the Treble Clef

Figure 3-4:
All the lines and spaces on the treble clef.

The bass clef

The bass clef is called the *F clef* because the colon part of the clef symbol (:) is centered on the F line of the bass staff. The bass clef puts the G below middle C on the top space. Most two-stave piano music has a treble clef on top with a bass clef on the bottom. Figure 3-5 shows the names of all the lines and spaces on the bass clef.

All Lines and Spaces on the Bass Staff

Figure 3-5: The lines and spaces of the bass clef.

The neutral clef

The *neutral clef,* also known as the *percussion clef,* is not really a clef in the same way the other clefs are. It identifies *clefless* music — music with no precise pitch — and is primarily used to notate parts for percussion instruments, with instructions written above or below the part to indicate what percussion instrument is to be played.

Percussion parts don't always have five lines in the staff. They sometimes have only one line.

Some percussion instruments are pitched, however. Mallet percussion instruments (such as the vibes and the marimba) use the treble clef, and the timpani uses the bass clef.

Figure 3-6 shows a percussion part using a neutral clef.

Neutral, or Percussion Clef

Figure 3-6: The neutral, or percussion, clef is used for music with no precise pitch.

Wood Block

Tablature

If you play guitar, or another plucked instrument like a mandolin, you've probably seen music written in tablature format, rather than traditional notes. In this case, a TAB-sign is used instead of a clef, and, instead of five lines like a normal staff, it may have six lines, to correspond with each of the six guitar strings. The number of lines varies with the number of strings of the instrument. This can vary from four to six for a bass, five or six for a banjo, or even various numbers of strings, if the stringed instrument is exotic or unusual.

Tablature is very useful for learning how a particular guitar part is played, because the TAB can show more performance details than standard notation can. When blues artists bend notes or rock guitarists use nonstandard techniques to get an unusual sound, tablature makes it much easier for a player to understand and visualize how the piece was played.

Figure 3-7 shows a simple melody in both standard notation and tablature.

Figure 3-7: "Twinkle, Twinkle, Little Star" in standard notation and guitar tablature.

Twinkle, Twinkle, Little Star

The key signature

Because of the use of flats and sharps, more than just seven notes (A through G) are possible. The *key signature* tells the player which notes will be flat or sharp throughout the entire piece of music. Key signatures are generally written immediately after the clef at the beginning of a line of musical notation.

For example, if every B in the tune should really be a B flat (B♭), then the composer will create a key signature that specifies this. If sometime during the song you want the B♭ specified in the key signature to be a regular B, a natural sign

($\natural$) is put in front of the note. A natural sign means that the key signature is overridden just this one time, and the musician should play the natural note. In this case, the natural sign would be called the *accidental*.

By now I bet you've noticed that I keep referring to the seven letters of the alphabet, A through G, that make up the notes. If you play an instrument, especially a piano, bass, or guitar, you're probably aware that there are 12 different notes in each octave. The letter notes are called natural notes. An *accidental* raises or lowers the pitch of each of these half a step, to make the full complement of 12 notes. An accidental changes the pitch of the note, either higher or lower, differently from the pitch indicated by the key signature.

Looking at a piano keyboard, like the one in Figure 3-8, you can see that the white keys represent the seven natural notes. The highlighted note is called *middle C,* and you can see that there are five different black keys.

Figure 3-8:
A piano keyboard with middle C highlighted.

Because these black keys don't have names of their own, they're referred to by their white-key names, their natural letter name, along with additional symbols called flats or sharps.

Enharmonics

On the keyboard, there are seven white keys, but only five black keys for every octave. Only five of the natural notes use sharps or flats. Two notes, E and B, do not have corresponding sharp (to the right) black keys. If you raise an E half of a step — that is, *sharp it* — it becomes a natural F. Similarly, if you sharp a B half a step, it becomes a C. *Enharmonics* are notes that can be called by different names. Thus, a C is the enharmonic of B♯, and a B is the enharmonic of C♭.

The modern system of tuning, which divides the octave into 12 notes — 7 white and 5 black — is called the *12-tone equal temperament* or just *equal temperament*. Although it evolved over several centuries, it was solidified as the primary way to pitch instruments after Johann Sebastian Bach composed *The Well-Tempered Clavier,* a collection of solo keyboard music.

The black key to the right of a white key (a half-step higher), uses the sharp (♯) symbol. Looking at the sample keyboard in Figure 3-8, the black key to the right of middle C is C sharp (C♯).

If you're going to play the black key to the *left* of a white key (a half-step lower), it's called a flat (♭). Looking at Figure 3-8 again, the black key to the left of the B just below middle C is B flat (B♭).

The time signature

The time signature (also known as the *meter*) specifies how many beats are in each measure and what note duration constitutes one beat. It looks like a fraction, but it's actually two numbers sitting one above the other.

These two numbers tell you two different things. The top number tells you how many beats will be in each measure. For example, if the top number is a 4, it means that each measure, or bar, will have four beats in it — one-two-three-four — then a bar line ends the bar and signals the start of another measure. If the top number is 3 and the bottom number is 4, which is a common time signature for a waltz (3/4), each bar will have three beats in it — one-two-three, and a quarter note makes up one beat.

The bottom number of the time signature tells you which type of note, or duration of note, is considered one full beat. If the bottom number is a 4, which is very common, a quarter note gets one beat. If the bottom number is a 2, a half-note gets one beat.

In a musical score, the time signature appears at the beginning of the piece, immediately following the clef and key signature. Some music may change the time signature during the song, for example, from 4/4 to 3/4 and back to 4/4. Figure 3-9 shows a stave of music which starts out in 4/4 time, changes into 3/4 time, and then back into 4/4 time again.

Let's Change Time Signatures

Figure 3-9:
Time
signatures
can change.

Remembering the lines and spaces

Although you'll eventually get used to which notes are on which lines and spaces of the treble clef, you can memorize the letter names of the lines by using the mnemonic "Every Good Boy Does Fine." This helps to remember the letter names of the treble clef lines from the first line to the top line, EGBDF. A mnemonic you can use to remember the treble clef spaces is "Face," which stands for FACE, the spaces from bottom to top.

Another good mnemonic, "Good Boys Deserve Fun Always," will help you remember the lines of the bass clef from the bottom to the top, GBDFA. And you can use "All Cars Eat Gas" (or "All Cows Eat Grass," if you're more rurally inclined) to remember the spaces of the bass clef, ACEG from the bottom to the top.

Bar lines

A *bar* or *measure* is a segment of time defined as a given number of beats of a given duration, as defined by the time signature. Both terms — *bar* and *measure* — are used interchangeably; they mean the same thing.

A *bar line* is a vertical line through the staff, which separates bars. How often the bar line occurs is determined by the length of the measure. For example, a time signature of 4/4 would indicate that a complete measure consists of four beats of quarter notes.

The bar line can overlap multiple staves, too. Piano music is usually noted with two staves — treble and bass clef — joined by a single bar line.

Other elements

You need to be aware of a few other important music notation elements, and I cover them in the following sections.

Repeat sign

The *repeat sign* is a symbol that indicates that a musical section should be repeated. The repeat sign has a double bar line with two dots (see Figure 3-10). The music between the two repeat signs is meant to be repeated (that is, played again).

Repeat Signs

Chord symbols

Most popular sheet music has chord symbols notated above the measures that correspond to the chord. In published sheet music, this could be a chord diagram in TAB style (see "Tablature," earlier in this chapter), which shows where to place your fingers on the guitar to make the chord, as shown in the first measure of Figure 3-11.

The fingering chosen by the music publisher is almost never the way the original guitarists played the chord, but it's a starting point. Publishers like to show a simplified version of the chord, so the sheet music reader doesn't have to have professional skills to play the tune.

Chord Symbols

Sometimes the chord symbol is just the name of the chord, as in the second measure of Figure 3-11. Especially in jazz composing, most of the rhythm section (piano, guitar, and bass) parts may consist entirely of chord symbols.

The overall pattern of chords in a tune is called the *changes* in jazz. Also in jazz, when an instrument is instructed to ad lib a solo, commonly the chord symbols, or changes, are all that's indicated on the part. The jazz musicians are expected to know all the chords and scales that the composer may want to use in the piece.

Tie

A *tie* is a short curved line that connects two notes of the same pitch. The tie tells the player to not strike or articulate the second of the two notes, but to leave the first note sustained for the combined time value of both notes. A tie is similar to a slur (see "Articulation," earlier in this chapter), but the note pitch doesn't change.

Augmentation dot

A dot directly to the right of a notehead increases that note's time value by one-half. For example, if a half note is equal to two beats in 4/4 time, a dotted half note is equal to three beats.

Rests

Obviously, music doesn't have every instrument playing all the time — it would get very boring very quickly if it did. Every piece of music has spaces in it, which makes it real music — even if the space just gives the horn player a chance to breathe!

A *rest* is an interval of silence in a piece of music, marked by a sign indicating the length of the pause. For each note value, there's a corresponding rest symbol:

- Whole-note rest (-)
- Half-note rest (-)
- Quarter-note rest (♩)
- Eighth-note rest (♪)
- Sixteenth-note rest (♪)

This list of rests continues on through thirty-second rests, sixty-fourth rests, and so on. Figure 3-12 is like Figure 3-1, except that, instead of notes, there are the corresponding rests.

Figure 3-12: Rests give a musician a short breather.

Rests

Whole Note Rest | Half Note Rest | Quarter Rests | Eighth Rests | Sixteenth Rests

When an instrument has a rest of longer than a whole note, say, several bars of rest, it's called a *multiple-measure rest*. A multiple-measure rest is usually written as a solid bar with a number above to indicate how many measures the player must rest until playing again. Figure 3-13 shows what a multiple-measure rest looks like.

Figure 3-13:
A multiple-measure rest is a rest longer than a whole note.

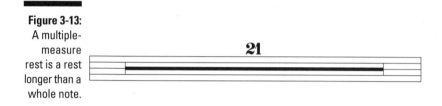

Part II
Gearing Up

The 5th Wave   By Rich Tennant

"Well, here's your problem. You only have half the ram you need."

In this part . . .

Here I give you a rundown on what you need to start
to compose music — from the latest in computers
to cool hardware and software. Chapter 4 describes the
digital composing hardware you need in order to get the
most out of this book, what computer parts you'll want
before you start composing, and how to use digital instruments with your computer.

Chapter 5 delves into some cool digital music gear you
can use to make music, like sound modules, audio breakout
boxes, preamps, and weird MIDI controllers. In Chapter 6,
you enter the software side of music composing. I show you
some of the exciting digital music software packages that
are revolutionizing the music industry, what they do, and
why you want them.

Chapter 4

Digital Composing Hardware

. . . .

In This Chapter

▶ Getting your computer ready for composing

▶ Plugging musical instruments into your computer

▶ Understanding MIDI and how it works

▶ Getting other nifty gear you know you want

. . . .

*T*he computer hardware you have at your disposal will make a big difference in your ability to compose and make your own music. But here's the good news: Bigger is not always better (at least where computers are concerned), and the microchip revolution has provided remarkably good-quality sound and features in small, inexpensive boxes.

Gone are the days when a digital synthesizer had to cost tens of thousands of dollars and take up a large part of a room, like my first New England Digital Synclavier II did in 1982. Now you can make top-quality tunes with a standard PC or Mac, and a couple hundred dollars' worth of hardware and software.

This chapter fills you in on the computer hardware you need for composing digital music, tells you what some of the terminology means, and shows you how the composer (that's you!) connects different MIDI instruments to create music.

Getting Your Computer Ready

In order to compose digital music, you need a computer — but it doesn't matter whether you have a Mac or a PC, and your computer doesn't have to be a high-end, state-of-the-art workstation. In fact, you don't really need anything else but this book and a computer. Of course, when you get bitten by the digital-music bug, you're going to want to get some of the cool gear I describe later in this chapter. But for now, it's just you, me (this book), and your computer.

What you need: The minimum setup

When you're getting into digital music, it's easy to convince yourself that you need the latest and greatest equipment to get started. But if you only have the setup I describe in this section, you'll still be able to compose music with this book as your guide.

A basic computer

Any personal computer built in the 21st century (and some from the late 1990s) is heavy-duty enough to handle the templates and basic note entry. If you're using a PC, the minimum setup you need to be able to run the demo software and load the sample templates from the CD that comes with this book are outlined in Appendix B.

If you have, or you're thinking about buying, the Windows Vista operating system, a couple of points are important:

- ✔ Most composing software is compatible with Windows Vista, but be sure to check the Web site of the software maker to see if there are any known compatibility issues.

- ✔ Installing the software can cause problems sometimes, and you may have to log in as Administrator to install or run it.

The fundamental tools you'll use to compose with this book are the mouse and keyboard. Every computer — desktop or laptop, PC or Mac — has a keyboard and a mouse. The majority of digital composing is done by clicking and dragging or cutting and pasting, so having a mouse you like is important. (If your mouse doesn't fit your hand or your wrist starts to hurt after using it for a while, look into the multitude of other mouses on the market — your local office supply or computer store is sure to have a wide selection.)

If you get some MIDI gear like the kind I describe in the "Composing with MIDI Instruments" section, you'll need to plug the gear into your computer somehow. The most common methods use your computer's USB, FireWire, or MIDI ports. If you're not sure which ports your computer has, consult your user manual or contact the computer's manufacturer.

When you get your tune finished, you may want to share it with others, like a proud parent. Be sure your computer's CD-ROM drive is a CD/R-type drive (not a read-only drive). This way you can burn audio-compliant CDs and play your tune on your sound system or in your car. And believe me — the commute to work is a lot more fun if you're listening to your own tracks instead of the radio.

Speakers and headphones

You're going to want to hear what you composed, so you'll need speakers and/or headphones.

The MIDI revolution

Musical Instrument Digital Interface (MIDI) revolutionized electronic music when it was introduced in 1983. What it meant to musicians is that, for the first time, synthesizers and other instruments from different vendors could be connected together and all be played at the same time, and a piece of MIDI music could be moved back and forth between different music-composing software programs.

The actual computer code that makes this happen may look very complicated, but it makes everything much simpler (and you don't have to understand the computer code to benefit from MIDI). The code creates a common language that all MIDI-compliant devices can understand,

regardless of the model, make, or features of the keyboard, digital workstation, computer, MIDI guitar, or whatever.

And because it's a computer program, MIDI can control other things than just musical instruments. An entire live theatrical production can be controlled by MIDI: The sound effects, sound mixing board, lighting, and curtains all can be run from a single computer! (If you don't believe me, go to the MIDI Manufacturers Association Web site at `www.midi.org/about-midi/ msc/mscchart.shtml` and check out the amazing list of the Broadway and Las Vegas shows that use MIDI sound and show-control programs.

Pretty much every computer made today has a sound card built in. If you get serious about digital music, you'll want to buy a specialized digital audio card like the ones I describe in the "Audio sound cards" section, later in the chapter. But for now you can plug speakers directly into your computer through the built-in sound system.

What you'll want

When you get further into digital music composing, you'll find yourself wanting to take things up a notch. In this section, I fill you in on the kind of setup that's a step up from the basics.

A computer system

I'm always a little suspicious of the "minimum" setup requirements described on the side of a software box. They're usually just the bare minimum you need to install and run the program, without any bells and whistles, so you won't be scared away from purchasing the software if you have a low-end system.

But if you *really* want to use the software, without having to wait forever for it to load or do something, look for the "recommended" setup on the side of the box. It's often a much more realistic description of what you're going to need to have fun! Also, if you're going to use scores with a lot of instrument sounds, you'll need more memory than the minimum setup.

Here's my recommended setup for Windows:

- ✔ Windows XP or Vista
- ✔ 2.5 GHz processor or faster
- ✔ At least 1GB of RAM
- ✔ At least 3.5GB of free hard-drive space
- ✔ DVD-ROM drive
- ✔ An ASIO-compatible sound card (not a sound chip on the motherboard — see the "Audio sound cards" section of this chapter for more information)

ASIO is short for Audio Stream Input/Output. It's a protocol for *low-latency digital audio*. ASIO lets recording studios process their audio via software on the computer instead of using thousands of dollars' worth of separate equipment.

- ✔ A separate graphics card, like an Accelerated Graphics Port (AGP) or PCI Express (PCIe) card, is a good thing to get. When you order your PC, you may have the option to upgrade to a better graphics card. If you can afford it, do it. The built-in graphics processor on a standard PC is usually not the greatest. If you have computer geek potential, you can also buy one and install it yourself.

Here's my recommended setup for Macintosh:

- ✔ A G5 or Intel processor
- ✔ At least 1GB of RAM
- ✔ 3.5GB total hard drive space
- ✔ DVD-ROM drive

With this setup (for the PC or Mac), you can load the sound banks that come with the software, and make the sound more realistic and less "computery."

Audio sound cards

One piece of audio gear that's going to make a big difference without costing a lot of money is an audio sound card, like those made by Creative (www.creative.com) or Turtle Beach (www.turtlebeach.com). No internal, factory-built PC sound system is going to be able to handle well the heavy-duty audio and MIDI sounds you'll be crankin' out.

An audio sound card can either be a piece of equipment you insert into your computer, or an external add-on box that attaches to a port on the computer (such as the USB port). High-end audio cards are sometimes called "prosumer" cards, because they're designed to bridge the gap between music hobbyists, and professional digital music creators.

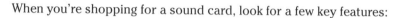

Whether you get an internal sound card or an external add-on box may depend upon how comfortable you are with taking the case off your computer and adding or subtracting parts. Some external boxes also have internal cards that come with them. So even if you want to get an external sound box because you don't want to go mucking about inside your PC, you might have to anyway. Be sure to check on how the card connects to your PC, if opening up your computer is a concern to you.

You can get any computer store to plug the card into your computer for you — for a fee, of course.

When you're shopping for a sound card, look for a few key features:

✔ **A card that can handle at least a 48 kHz sampling rate, with a 24-bit sampling size:** A good sound card has a high sampling rate, something you'll need when you start to record your own sounds.

✔ **An audio card that's ASIO-compatible:** A card with ASIO helps your computer process the sound faster and is the favorite of musicians and sound engineers.

✔ **A card that has speaker and headphone outputs:** How music devices interface with (plug into) the audio card is important. Also, separate ¼-inch microphone and audio inputs are nice, so you don't need to get an adapter to plug in your guitar or mic.

✔ **A card that has MIDI in/out connectors:** This is important if you're going to advance beyond entering notes into the software with your mouse, and you'll use a digital keyboard or guitar.

The two companies that make the most popular audio cards for home computers are Creative's Sound Blaster and Turtle Beach. Expect to pay $50 to $250.

I use a Creative Sound Blaster Audigy2 Platinum EX. It has a card that plugs into your PC and a nifty external box that has connectors for MIDI, FireWire, USB, mic, guitar, digital audio, and regular stereo RCA phono jacks. I can control all input and output by controls on the box, and it has a cool infrared remote control. (I love anything with a remote control.) Another advantage of an external sound box like the Audigy is that it has a preamp built into the mic and guitar inputs, which boosts the signal enough for the computer to recognize it. Otherwise, you'll need to get a separate preamp, which I discuss in the following section.

Sound Blaster has a new (as of this writing) version of the Audigy2, called the Sound Blaster X-Fi XtremeGamer Fatal1ty Pro Series, which has an Audio Creation Mode with every bell and whistle you can think of for recording digital audio.

Creative also makes a laptop version of the Audigy, called the PCMCIA Sound Blaster Audigy 2 ZS Notebook. It's a cute little PCMCIA card that slides into your laptop or notebook, and gives your laptop all the sound power of a desktop.

Speakers and headphones

Speaker systems for computers have gone way beyond the original tinny 3-inch beeping speaker. Depending on what type of sound card you use, you can get everything from a nice pair of desktop speakers to a full 7.1 THX Surround Sound theater sound system for your PC.

A lot of companies make good speaker systems for your computer, in a wide range of prices. Speakers come in pairs, three-piece systems (called 2.1), and advanced six-piece systems (called 5.1). Expect to pay in the $25 to $150 range for good speakers.

Don't cheap out on the speakers — your tune will only sound as good as the speakers do. If you can, avoid a simple pair of speakers and get at least a 2.1 system, which usually consists of a pair of small speakers for your desk, and a powered woofer, which sits under it. I like the feel of a booming bass.

Good speaker systems are made by Altec Lansing (www.alteclansing. com), Creative Labs (www.creative.com), Logitech (www.logitech.com), JBL (www.jbl.com), and Harman Kardon (www.harmankardon.com). I use a Cambridge Soundworks 2.1 speaker system, which has a nice pair of small left/right speakers that sit on my desk, and a larger woofer for the bass tones, which rests on the floor underneath my desk.

Headphones are useful if not everyone in your house or apartment building wants to hear you compose at all hours of the night. Frankly, I don't understand why they *wouldn't,* but having a pair of headphones is a good idea anyway.

Headphones come in a ton of sizes and prices. AKG (www.akg.com), Sony (www.sonystyle.com/headphones), and Sennheiser (www.sennheiserusa.com) offer good headphones at every level of the price spectrum, from around $30 to $125. I prefer the larger studio size "cans," which fit over the head and are comfortably cushioned. I use a pair of $99 Sennheiser HD 280 Pro headphones that really cancel outside noise (which is a big help when the neighbor's dog starts up). I also have a pair of behind-the-neck portable Sony headphones for on-the road listening.

The smaller portable phones are useful, but stay away from ear buds, as they don't usually have a full frequency response. You'll want to hear every frequency, from low to high, and your phones will need to be comfortable for long-time wearing.

Whichever type of headphones you get, be aware that you may need to get an adapter to change the plug size of the input, depending upon what your sound system requires. Smaller portable headphones commonly use the mini plug popular with portable electronics, while the larger headphones and most pro gear uses a ¼-inch jack size. You can buy adapters that change male mini to female ¼-inch and vice versa. Note what kind of headphone input your audio card has, and get the right adapter from a place like Radio Shack, if you need it. Some headphones, like the Sennheiser, include plug adapters with their products.

Printers

If you want to print out your music, from simple single-line lead sheets to full orchestral scores and parts, you'll need a printer. A laser printer is best, because inkjets tend to frequently run out of the black ink required for all the parts, and are usually slower than lasers.

You can spend a lot of dough on large-format printers that print big scores and parts full size, but unless you're going to do professional work for a music company or orchestra, a simple home laser is fine. I use a Hewlett-Packard LaserJet 1100, and it's been running fine for years. You can get a decent black-and-white laser printer for around $200.

If you're going to be printing parts for musicians to play, get printer paper with a weight rating of 32 pounds. The thickness of printer paper is based on weight — the thicker the paper, the higher the weight rating. Most regular cheap copy paper is 20 pounds, which is fine for most printing. But musicians need a thicker page to stay on a music stand, and a laser printer can handle the 32-pound weight fine. You can sometimes find card stock with a weight around 60 pounds, if your printer can handle it.

Composing with MIDI Instruments

If you had to pick the one idea that began the digital music revolution, most musicians would pick MIDI. MIDI, invented in 1983, stands for Musical Instrument Digital Interface. It's a computer communications standard that allows electronic instruments to send and receive data in real time. (For more information on MIDI, check out Chapter 17.)

After you've gotten your computer all set up, you want to start looking at some MIDI gear that will help turn your ditty into a full-fledged orchestral opus.

You don't need musical proficiency to input notes into your composing software. Even if all you can do is click and drag, you can still compose with just the mouse. But if you're willing to play a little piano or guitar, MIDI keyboard controllers and MIDI guitars will put you right in the middle of the real action — and for not a lot of money.

MIDI controllers defined

A MIDI controller can be anything that uses the MIDI language to talk to other MIDI-compliant devices. Although it's most often a piano-style keyboard, it can also be a MIDI-compliant guitar, or bass, too.

It doesn't have to be an electronic instrument, either. Breath controllers mimic saxophones and trumpets, violin players have their own string controllers, and drummers have MIDI percussion instruments.

So although you and I still think of these as instruments, as far as the computer is concerned, they're all MIDI controllers.

Playing with keyboard controllers

The modern descendant of the acoustic piano is the portable digital keyboard. Because most digital keyboards are MIDI-compliant, they're the primary way today's music is composed.

A grand piano will always be an impressive piece of furniture, and for a pianist a good acoustic piano has no digital equal. But the portable keyboard has a lot of advantages over its big grandfather:

- ✔ It doesn't need tuning, ever.

- ✔ You can put it in a closet when you're not using it.

- ✔ You can play it with headphones and not bother the neighbors.

- ✔ It will probably fit in your car (maybe even in a subcompact one).

- ✔ Best of all, you can plug it into your computer and make it sound like hundreds of different instruments or create your own other-worldly sounds.

Today's keyboards are easy to set up and play, and even the cheapest digital keyboard now has MIDI connectors to connect to your computer.

When picking out a digital keyboard like the one shown in Figure 4-1, the choices can be overwhelming, but remember these things:

- ✔ **Your budget:** It's usually the number-one consideration.

- ✔ **The level of your musicianship:** If you're a professional-level pianist, it's probably important for you to have a real weighted piano feel.

✔ **Features you need (and those you don't):** Do you need a lot of internal instrument sounds? What about an internal speaker to hear the keyboard when it's not hooked up to your sound card?

✔ **MIDI-compliance:** The keyboard has to be MIDI-enabled, with MIDI in and out ports to attach to other MIDI devices or your computer. USB ports that make it easy to attach your MIDI device to your computer are pretty standard, too.

The digital keyboard arena is dominated by Roland (www.rolandus.com) and Casio (www.casio.com), with Korg (www.korg.com) and M-Audio (www.m-audio.com) also providing popular entry-level through professional-level MIDI keyboard controllers. Here's a breakdown of your keyboard options:

✔ **Good:** At the affordable end of the spectrum, many manufacturers make good, usable, digital keyboards in the $100 to $200 range. Casio makes several styles of electronic keyboards that can be used as MIDI controllers, as well as stand-alone keyboards with built-in speakers. The street price of the new Casio CTK-810 (refer to Figure 4-1) is around $149. It has a ton of sounds, lots of rhythms, and USB connectivity. You'll want to shell out more money for the power adapter, however, because it runs through batteries pretty quickly.

✔ **Better:** A little farther up the food chain is E-MU System's Xboard 61 61-key MIDI controller, which uses USB and sells for around $250. I especially like the M-Audio Oxygen series of 49-key and 61-key MIDI keyboard controllers. I use an Oxygen 61, which has both USB and standard MIDI connections. *Note:* The Oxygen keyboards don't have any internal sounds or speakers, so they can only be used as MIDI controllers, not as stand-alone keyboards.

✔ **Best:** Even better is Casio's upscale PX-310, which goes for $800. It has an 88-key scaled hammer-action keyboard to replicate an authentic grand piano feel.

Korg has debuted a feature-packed digital keyboard controller and synthesizer called a microX, which you can find for about $650. Even though it has a small 25-key velocity sensitive keyboard, it has a huge number of preset sounds and options for editing your tunes.

Before you get any MIDI keyboard controller, be sure your sound card or computer has the proper ports. If the keyboard you want uses a USB connection, make sure your PC or sound system has a USB port. The same goes for MIDI in/out connectors and FireWire ports. Nothing is more frustrating than getting your beautiful new baby home and realizing you can't hook it up. And be sure you have all the necessary cables. If you're not sure, ask the salesperson.

Figure 4-1:
The Casio
CTK-810
digital
keyboard
synthesizer
and MIDI
controller.

If you want to get an all-in-one music machine with all the bells and whistles, check out Korg's TRITON Extreme. It's a loaded music workstation with a keyboard, synthesizer, and sampler for creating your own sounds. The TRITON Extreme has a built-in sequencer that can record, edit, and play back music. Plus, it has a cool touch screen, making menu navigation quick and easy. But get ready to put out big bucks for it — the prices for the TRITON Extreme range from $1,500 to $2,300, depending on whether you get the 61-key, 76-key, or 88-key model.

Take a pair of headphones when you go shopping for your keyboard, because most music stores are as loud as the runway at O'Hare. Also, if, like me, you're not the world's greatest pianist, you'll be less intimidated by playing in public. The headphones give you more confidence to try out all the features of several different models. And don't be shy in asking for help understanding the keyboard's various features or to ask for a demonstration. The salesperson shouldn't make a commission if he makes you feel like a jerk.

Composing with guitar

You don't need a MIDI keyboard — you can get the music into your computer in other ways. If you play a guitar, you can play right into your computer, whether you have a MIDI electric guitar or just a regular electric guitar.

Electric guitar

You can plug a regular electric guitar directly into your computer's audio card, if it has a microphone input jack. This means your setup has a preamp built in, which it needs to boost the sound volume to a level that the computer can use.

Most pros use guitar preamps to increase and improve the sound of the instrument. If your audio card doesn't have a preamp built in, or you just want to get a better sound, you'll need to get a preamp to boost the sound. Models from L. R. Baggs (www.lrbaggs.com), D-TAR (www.d-tar.com), Fishman (www.fishman.com), and PreSonus (www.presonus.com) all work great. Expect to pay from $100 up to the sky.

MIDI guitar

Preamps (see the preceding section) will boost your sound enough to be able to record directly into your computer with digital recording software, like Sound Forge, but if you want to input MIDI data using your guitar (instead of a keyboard), you'll have to convert the guitar output to MIDI format.

Often an external box, called a *MIDI interface,* does the trick. Roland's GI-20 GK-MIDI Interface (shown in Figure 4-2) detects the signal from any electric guitar or bass equipped with a 13-pin divided pickup, and converts your electric guitar sound into MIDI signals that your MIDI software can use. The GI-20 costs from $400 to $550, depending upon whether you already have the required divided pickup, like a GK-2 or GK-3.

Figure 4-2:
The Roland
GI-20
GK-MIDI
Interface.

MIDI guitar conversion has been a dicey proposition over the years, with glitches, compatibility, configuration, and latency a big problem. Early MIDI guitars had serious issues generating the sound quickly enough to use on a gig. It's much better now, and for the purposes of this book, it should work well enough to input notes into the book's templates. But be warned: MIDI guitar is still a temperamental animal.

Better than using a MIDI conversion kit for your electric guitar is a specific type of guitar that connects directly into your MIDI in connectors, called a *MIDI guitar.* In a MIDI guitar, the electronics circuitry that converts the signal into MIDI data is built right into the guitar — you don't need preamps or conversion kits. The only downside: It's more expensive.

A popular MIDI guitar is the iGuitar (www.iguitar.com) from Brian Moore Guitars (www.brianmooreguitars.com). Depending upon the body shape and features you want, it'll set you back about $1,200 to $2,000. You can get the iGuitar with either a 13-pin or USB connector.

Composing with bass

I sometimes use a bass guitar to record directly into the computer. This approach is useful when laying down a heavy bass line as the first part of a tune, and then building the rest of the instruments on top.

Like a guitar, you need a preamp for recoding. You can use the audio card's built-in preamp, but the notes may be too low for the card to hear properly, so a bass needs its own preamp. Like guitar preamps, lots of bass preamps are out there — but they're a little more expensive, running from $150 to $900, depending on how many features you want.

Bass is even harder than guitar to convert well to MIDI, because the low frequencies are difficult to detect and use by the MIDI system. The Roland GK-3B Divided Pickup for Bass (shown in Figure 4-3) costs about $180 and converts the signal for use by synthesizers, such as Roland's V-Bass and GR-20 guitar synthesizers.

Figure 4-3:
An electric
bass with
the Roland
GK-3B
Divided
Pickup for
Bass
attached.

Why is it hard to "MIDI" a guitar?

On a regular electric guitar, the vibration of the strings is detected by magnetic pickups, converted to an analog electric signal, and then amplified so that humans can hear it (especially the neighbors). MIDI needs a digital signal, not an analog one, so you need some way of converting the audio output into a MIDI-readable digital form.

A digital keyboard has this MIDI circuitry built in, and it's easy for MIDI to read each note played. However, a guitar has a much more varied input than a digital keyboard, because the same note can be played in several different places on a guitar, and bending the note presents even more choices.

Chapter 5

Getting Cool Gear

• •

In This Chapter

▶ Reconnoitering ready-built music computers

▶ Measuring music production centers

▶ Surveying stand-alone MIDI modules

▶ Eyeing all those extra bits you'll need

• •

I admit it: I love getting and using cool music gear. But I've trained myself to not run out and get the first version of a new shiny toy until I at least know what it does.

But my love for new music doodads presents a problem: The future of digital music is in the software, not the hardware. A ton of great MIDI hardware modules and workstations are out there, but unless you need these machines for a live gig, the *real* advancement in digital music is sure to happen in the software arena.

This reality doesn't mean that you won't get any neat stuff. You'll still need a computer, and you'll want to get a keyboard controller, a MIDI interface, speakers, and maybe a tone module or two.

Investing a ton of money in the latest MIDI machine doesn't make sense when you consider that:

✔ It will be cheaper next year.

✔ It will have more features, more sounds, and run faster next year.

✔ You can probably get a software VST or DXi plug-in that does the same thing for a lot less money. (See Chapter 6 for more info on VST and DXi.)

Of course, it doesn't hurt to just *look* at some of the cool digital music gear that's out there. And if you gotta have it, you gotta have it!

Using All-in-One Music Centers

I'll let you in on a secret: You're not going to need all this stuff to use this book. In fact, you don't really need anything more than the basic setup I describe in Chapter 4.

But all this cool gear shows you how versatile the digital music scene can be. Sounds that once were the sole domain of high-end, expensive studios in a few big cities can now be yours at home or onstage.

Ready-built music computers

Maybe you don't want to spend most of your precious composing time ana-lyzing the various hardware and software choices before you buy a machine to produce digital music. Installing software, contacting tech support, and managing updates and patches probably isn't the best way for you to use your time.

If you're nodding your head, then you'll want to check out companies that sell turnkey or custom computers solely for music production. Turnkey systems arrive with all the hardware and software you need preloaded and configured at the factory. You don't have to worry about hardware or soft-ware conflicts, whether the software will work with the hardware you want, and whether the computer will be powerful enough to handle your great opus.

Many companies will furnish or build a computer to fit your needs, load all the software you want, and provide customer support any time of the day or night. Often, these computers are heavy-duty music processing machines, so you'll probably pay a bit more than if you got the pieces separately and installed it all yourself. But unless you're a geek, the ease and peace of mind can be priceless.

One large company that has an excellent reputation is Carillon (www. carillondirect.com). Carillon has a long-standing reputation for quality, includes a massive amount of software with the PCs it sells, and has a huge support team, with a dedicated Web site (www.carillonsupport.com) just to resolve issues and provide after-sales support. It has a cool new rack-mountable computer called the Cubase T.I.–Total Integration system — which will set you back £999 (around US$2,000). Carillon's systems are designed to combine hardware and software in a way specifically designed to suit musi-cians moving over to computer-based music production for the first time, or those who already use computers but want an optimized, "off-the-shelf" digi-tal music production setup.

Buying used MIDI equipment

The Internet has revolutionized buying and selling almost everything, especially computer and musical equipment. Not only can you compare the features of a piece of gear you want from one manufacturer with the features from another, but you can comparison-shop to get the best price from huge online retailers.

And you can look for used gear, too. If a keyboard is MIDI-compatible, for example, it may not have all the features of today's version, but it will still work with your DAW and other MIDI devices. I purchased a Yamaha YS200 in 1989, and you can still find it online for almost nothing.

Some caveats about buying used gear over the Internet, however:

✔ **Shop at a reputable firm or auction house, like eBay (www.ebay.com), and find out as much about the seller's reputation as you can.**

✔ **Pay with PayPal (www.paypal.com) if you can.** PayPal has dispute resolution procedures.

✔ **Because you can't play it to test it, get good digital pix of it from all angles, and get the seller to guarantee that it's in working condition.**

✔ **Don't expect the device to be perfect.** It may have some scratches and some knobs may be gone, but it should still largely work as it did when it was new.

Another great company that makes custom and turnkey systems for serious composers and musicians is VisionDAW (www.visiondaw.com). VisionDAW makes rack-mount digital music workstations that include DAWs, GigaStudio, KONTAKT systems, as well as custom systems with multiple central processing units (CPUs). Its machines are more expensive than some brands, running from $2,000 to $4,000, but many composers in the music industry swear by VisionDAW and say it's the best comprehensive music production PC built.

Some other popular companies that build music computers, either turnkey off-the-shelf or to your custom specs include the following:

✔ **PCAudioLabs:** www.pcaudiolabs.com

✔ **Professional Audio Solutions:** www.proaudiosolutions.com

✔ **Rain Recording:** www.rainrecording.com

✔ **TrueSpec Systems:** www.truespec.com

Stand-alone music workstations

In the old days, all digital music development was done on hardware devices, with software integrated into the device. Then the Mac with Pro Tools made high-quality computer-based recording feasible. Today, digital music products for Windows have opened the door to music production for everyone.

But for many professional studio producers, hardware products still reign, and stand-alone music workstations have a serious and dedicated following.

Generally, you'll find three types of music workstations:

- **Keyboard workstations** combine traditional keyboard synthesizer features with built-in sequencing, sampling, and other features.

- **Sequencing workstations** are hardware devices that have sequencers, maybe with some synthesizer ability and effects, but no keyboard.

- **Sampling workstations** are similar to sequencers, but their emphasis is on sampling rather than sequencing.

Keyboard workstations

Some musicians are just more comfortable with using a keyboard-style music workstation than a computer or some space-age machine. Keyboard workstations have a fairly long pedigree in the music business — some of the first multifunction digital music machines in the '80s were keyboards. They had some synthesizer features like polyphony, were multitimbral, and had some primitive sequencing ability.

Some of the tried-and-true keyboard workstations are made by long-time manufacturers in the music business, like Korg (www.korg.com), Kurzweil (www.kurzweilmusicsystems.com), and Roland (www.roland.com). But they offer new instruments with amazing features, like the Korg M3 ($2,500), the Kurzweil K2600 ($4,600), and the Roland JUNO-G ($1,200). These keyboard workstations are the cream of the crop, with every feature you could want, including weighted keys, tons of sounds and effects, and the durability you get from a professional-grade instrument.

Open Labs (www.openlabs.com) makes two unique models of keyboard workstations — the NeKo and the MiKo:

- **NeKo:** The NeKo runs from $4,000 to $7,400 and is a complete, self-contained, computer-based keyboard workstation, with a built-in Intel Core 2 Duo processor. It's capable of hosting up to 300 plug-in sounds and effects at once, playing over 500-voice polyphony, recording over 64 audio tracks at 24/96 simultaneously, and cloning virtually any other electronic keyboard or rack-mount sound.

- **MiKo:** The MiKo (shown in Figure 5-1) is a little less expensive than the NeKo, running from $3,000 to $3,400. It's a compact unit designed for working in a project studio or performing live. It simplifies creating beats, allows live multitracking, and includes DJ/VJ capabilities.

Figure 5-1:
The Open
Labs MiKo
keyboard
workstation.

Sequencing workstations

Several of the companies that make keyboard workstations also make sequencing and sampling workstations, which makes sense because the technology is similar to each workstation — just the features and product design are different.

The Korg Electribe EMX-1 ($500) is a sequencing workstation that offers synthesis, sequencing, drum programming, and real-time control. The EMX-1 melds a drum machine with a synth and sequencer, and adds enough knobs and buttons to make any gearhead happy.

The Roland MC-909 Sampling Groovebox ($1,600) is a self-contained, retro-styled, dance music sequencer with expandable synthesis and a professional sequencer and effects.

Sampling workstations

Akai Professional (www.akaipro.com) has the gold standard of sampling workstations, its MPC line. Because Akai has such cachet in dance and hip-hop circles, it has successfully bucked the current trend toward software samplers. The MPC series has several entries, from expensive pro models to more affordable units.

The top of the line is Akai's MPC4000 Plus ($3,500), which has a 128-track MIDI sequencer and a 64-voice, 24-bit stereo digital sampler. The series continues through the MPC2500 ($3,000), the MPC1000 ($1,500), and the MPC500 ($1,300).

Another, sampling workstation, the Roland MV-8800 ($2,700), is used by many of the top hip-hop and R&B producers. It's a one-stop beat production studio, from full drum sampling to CD mixing and burning.

Computer recording systems

Computer recording systems are a fairly old technology that have, for the most part, been replaced by DAWs in the digital music world. However, some manufacturers still make computer recording systems that are designed to be completely integrated music production studios. Although some long-revered products — like the Yamaha DSP Factory — have bit the dust, other products are still kicking.

The Soundscape recording and editing system for PCs has been around for a while. Originally developed by Mackie, it's now owned by Sydec Audio Engineering of Belgium (www.sydec.be). The latest version of Soundscape, the Soundscape 32, runs from $3,800 to $10,000, depending upon the package and bundled features. Soundscape has always been renowned for the stability of its PC recording systems and has a dedicated following of musicians and composers.

Lexicon's (www.lexiconpro.com) older digital recording products (like its Core or Studio) have been discontinued and replaced with three products called the Omega, Lambda, and Alpha. These products aren't technically self-contained music production centers, because they're designed to attach to your computer. But they're essentially complete desktop recording studios, with software, VST plug-ins, and a full-function MIDI and digital interface included. The prices for all three models are quite reasonable; the differences among the three models primarily have to do with functionality. Omega ($280) is the flagship product with all the bells and whistles; Lambda ($210) has fewer features than the Omega; and Alpha ($140) is a small, portable MIDI interface designed for laptops. Like most computer interfaces, they use the USB port to connect to your PC.

Bring in the MIDI traffic cop!

When you start to get several pieces of MIDI hardware, you're going to need to figure out how best to connect them and manage the communications flow among them. If you have several MIDI devices connected by a local area network (LAN) in your studio, a great utility for controlling MIDI communications and reducing latency is MIDIoverLAN CP from MusicLab (www.musiclab.com).

You install MIDIoverLAN CP on your DAW computer and on each of your network-connected MIDI computer workstations. It uses the network to send and control the MIDI message data, making MIDI cables and hardware MIDI interfaces unnecessary.

MIDIoverLAN CP is dual-platform, so it connects Macs and PCs seamlessly. It eliminates tortuous MIDI cable and interface setup, and uses the network cabling to synchronize sequencers and operate synthesizers at a much faster data speed than regular MIDI communication speeds.

MIDIoverLAN CP costs $169 for a two-computer license or $369 for an eight-computer license.

Super MIDI Modules

A zillion MIDI gadgets are out there — from electronic drum machines to tone modules, audio effects machines, and even weird MIDI controllers that look like they came out of someone's nightmare. I don't recommend mortgaging your house to get all this stuff, but some of these products can be really useful additions to your music studio.

Sound modules and modular synths

The principal function of a sound (or tone) module is to produce sound, whether by synthesis or sample playback. The hardware devices can emulate various synthesizers and acoustic instruments, and they can integrate into a MIDI production system to create new and unique sounds.

The rack-mountable sound and tone module market was cornered by Roland's JV series of sound modules, and my old JV-880 is still cranking out pro-quality tones.

Roland has moved beyond the JV series into modular synths, with its XV series of sound modules and the V-Synth XT (shown in Figure 5-2). The V-Synth XT ($2,500) is a rack-mounted version of its keyboard V-Synth. Roland uses built-in and expansion tone cards, called *VC cards,* to add sound banks and convert the V-Synth XT into a digital sound production unit with powerful capabilities, such as vocal processing and synthesizer emulations.

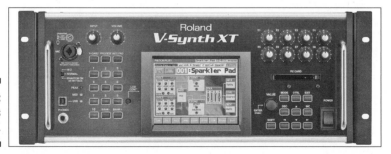

Figure 5-2:
Roland's
V-Synth XT.

Creamware (www.creamware.com) is a German company that, in addition to its software music products, makes a line of desktop synthesizers called Authentic Sound Box (ASB; http://asb.creamware.com), which replicate older, analog synths. For example, Creamware's Prodyssey ASB ($1,000) replicates the legendary ARP Instruments Odyssey synthesizer. Creamware also has emulations of a Minimoog, a Prophet-5, and a Hammond B-3 organ box that weighs 5 pounds, instead of the Hammond's 400 pounds!

Drum machines and weird controllers

MIDI is a simple computer protocol that just tells MIDI-compliant hardware or software to do something, like play a sound or turn an effect on or off. But this simplicity makes it really versatile, and almost any type of instrument (or any computerized machine, for that matter) can be rigged up to respond to MIDI commands. This includes MIDI drum machines, which play most of the commercial music you hear on the radio and CDs. It also includes a host of odd controllers, like the Samchillian.

Drum machines and electronic drum kits

Drum machines are MIDI-controlled devices designed to imitate the sound of drums or other percussion instruments. Stand-alone drum machines have become much less common these days, because they're being replaced with hardware samplers, software sequencers, and music workstations with integrated sequencing and looping drum libraries.

Most drum machines are sequencers that specialize in the reproduction of drum and percussion sounds. Drum machines also allow the adventurous composer to create unique beats and sounds, by editing the MIDI data.

Electronic drum kits attempt to simulate the look and feel of a real drum set. Models like the Alesis DM5 Kit ($500) and the Ion Audio iED01 ($500), are low-cost ways for a drummer to input his drumming into a MIDI system.

In an electronic drum kit, the drummer plays on pads, rather than a drum head on a traditional drum set. Then the drumming information (such as velocity of the hit, speed, and so on) is transmitted to the brain of the unit, the computer that formats digital data and sends it to whatever the drum kit is plugged into.

One great advantage of electronic drum kits is the volume control. Most of these kits have an audio out function, through which you can output the sound of the drums into an amp or public address (PA) sound system to pump up the volume. And most also have a headphone jack, so you can practice without disturbing the neighbors!

KORE Universal Sound Platform

Native Instruments (www.native-instruments.com) recently (as of this writing) released the second generation of its popular KORE Universal Sound Platform, called KORE 2. Intended for the studio as well as live performance,

KORE 2 ($500) is an integrated hardware/software MIDI controller that functions as an audio and MIDI interface, as well as a sound library and sequencer. Billed as "The Super Instrument" KORE 2 (shown in Figure 5-3) gives you tactile control over sounds and projects. It categorizes all your plug-ins and sound libraries into one easy-to-use interface, which operates as the command center for computer music production. It also works as a stand-alone concert device, allowing you to swap seamlessly between instruments and between presets while playing. You can bring up complex instrument and effect setups, all with the touch of a button.

Figure 5-3:
The Native Instruments KORE 2 with a laptop.

The Samchillian effect

The Samchillian (its full name is the Samchillian Tip Tip Tip Cheeepeeeee) is a keyboard MIDI controller (www.samchillian.com).

The brain-child of inventor and musician Leon Gruenbaum, it's a MIDI keyboard controller based on changes of pitch rather than fixed pitches. This design gives you the ability to perform very quick, melodic lines in any key or scale, without having to learn new fingering. Leon's contribution as the Samchillian's inventor is the software and his concept of playing musical tones in a relative manner.

The Samchillian (shown in Figure 5-4) has a very odd-looking but ergonomic computer keyboard designed and made by Kinesis (www.kinesis.com) and painted by legendary graffiti artist Pistol (Lonnie Heller).

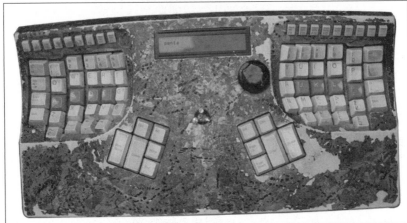

Figure 5-4:
The
Samchillian
MIDI
keyboard
controller.

Chapter 6

The World of Music Software

In This Chapter

▶ Finding out what notation software is and does

▶ Getting up to speed on the latest digital audio workstations

▶ Getting the lowdown on sampler products and instrument sounds

▶ Looking at some great plug-ins to make your music sizzle

*N*o matter how great your hardware is, you still need software to compose digital music. Some of the stand-alone digital audio workstations that I show you in Chapter 5 can do practically everything, but you're going to need one or more good digital music creation packages to really make your music heard.

Identifying the Main Types of Digital Music Software

There are two main types of software programs used to input digital music into your computer and compose digitally:

> ✔ **Musical notation software:** Sibelius and Finale are examples of musical notation software. Notation software is very easy to use and has lots of features that allow it to work and play well with other types of music programs. I use Sibelius for the templates and examples in this book because I'm more familiar with that software, but either package is great.

> ✔ **Digital audio workstations:** Sequencing programs, today often called digital audio workstations (DAWs), are, after plug-ins, probably the fastest growing area of music software. Programs such as Logic, Digital Performer, SONAR, ACID, and Cubase are the biggest sellers in the music business, and every year the DAW software vendors come out with more ways to make music easier and better, with features you can't live without.

The DAWs have a big advantage over the notation programs: You don't have to know how to read music to use them. Most DAW software has a modified notation function, but you don't have to know everything there is to know about music notation before you use it.

Choosing the software that's right for you will depend upon several factors. Mostly it comes down to how comfortable you are with the program, how easy it is to understand what it does, and how easy it is to make it do what you want it to.

How complex the music is that you'll be composing, and how much music training you've already had are also big factors. If you're a music student, you're familiar with music notation, or you want to be able to print out parts for other musicians, the notation software will probably be the best choice. But if you're just looking to add a drum or piano part to a nifty guitar ditty you wrote, sequencing DAW software will surely fill the bill.

Your history with composing digital music may also help you make your decision. If you've had experience with either a DAW or a notation package, you'll probably want to continue working with the same type of product.

The great thing is, all the software I cover here is MIDI-compatible. None of these packages is an isolated island, unable to interact with packages from other companies. Some are even designed to interact with as many software products as possible, like plug-ins. This takes some of the pressure off of your choice, because you don't have to pick something that's the final and perfect choice forever. In fact, if you're like me, you'll be adding new software to your arsenal for a long time.

Throughout this chapter, I list prices for most of the software. Use my price as a guideline only — you can probably get a better price by searching, and the prices will always vary from month to month.

Composing with Musical Notation Software

Musical notation is simply the musical notes on a sheet of music. If you're a schooled composer, you probably learned to compose with a score pad and a pencil. Now you're graduating to a music notation program. A *musical notation program* (also called a *scorewriter*) is software used to automate the task of writing and engraving sheet music. Musical notation software is to written music what a word processor is to written text.

Musical notation programs let you enter notes into the program using your computer keyboard, your mouse, or a MIDI controller connected to your computer (see Chapter 5 for more on MIDI controllers). You can play one note at a time or a whole song at once, and the software translates what you've played into musical notation.

And when the music is in the program, you can do a whole lot with it. You can

✔ Edit the notes and rhythms to make them more accurate

✔ Change keys or tempos

✔ Add or subtract different instruments

You can also use predesigned score templates and create full scores for any combination of instruments and voices, and have the program transpose and print the parts out for the musicians.

The two major music notation programs are Sibelius and Finale. Some other notation packages are available, some free, but these two have features that make them head and shoulders above the rest. Both packages have their supporters and detractors, but either one will do the job. I use Sibelius because it has a very easy-to-use interface and I learned how to use notation software with it. But Finale has a great pedigree and is used by many big-time music schools, like the New England Conservatory of Music and Juilliard.

If you're in an educational environment that uses one more than the other, by all means, use the one your school recommends. If your instructor wants you to use one package instead of another, please do. The goal of all software is to get your musical ideas out of your head as easily and clearly as possible, without fussing with the computer or technology. The tool isn't as important as your comfort with it.

In the following sections, I offer up a closer look at these two music notation software packages.

Finally Finale

The original big dog of music notation software was Finale ($350 for the academic version, $600 for the retail version; www.finalemusic.com/finale). Now owned by MakeMusic, Finale is still the premier notation software for Microsoft Windows and Mac OS X, although Sibelius is close on its heels.

There are several versions of Finale and, like Sibelius, if you're in music education, as either a student or a teacher, be sure to check out the educational pricing — it's a great deal cheaper. Like Sibelius, Finale has a lot of instrument libraries to draw upon, with a huge list of available plug-ins, to enhance functionality.

Figure 6-1 shows a screenshot of Finale 2007, with the score of Beethoven's Fifth Symphony loaded.

Listen to the Finale 2007 clip of Beethoven's Fifth Symphony on the accompanying CD, at Author/Chapter 06/Audio Examples.

Figure 6-1:
Finale 2007
and
Beethoven's
Fifth
Symphony.

Sibelius: It's not just a Finnish composer

Sibelius ($300 for the educational version, $600 for the professional version; www.sibelius.com) is an easy-to-use and powerful musical notation program. Even though it came along after Finale, it's growing in popularity.

It's available in several versions, from Professional to Student. It also comes with:

- ✔ The KONTAKT Player 2 sampled instrument set
- ✔ Sibelius Sounds Essentials, a new collection of over 150 pitched and hundreds of unpitched sounds
- ✔ PhotoScore Lite, a program that uses your scanner to digitize printed sheet music

A really nifty feature with Sibelius is the sound library options you can buy separately. These sound sets start to make your Sibelius output sound comparable to a DAW, with varied sampled sounds and instruments, which help make your music score come alive.

Figure 6-2 shows Sibelius editing Mendelssohn's *The Hebrides Overture.*

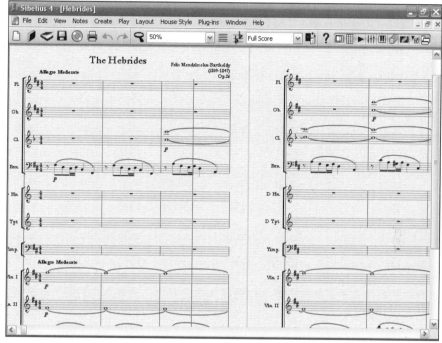

Figure 6-2:
Sibelius
editing
Mendels-
sohn's *The
Hebrides
Overture.*

Listen to an audio clip of this Sibelius score on the accompanying CD, at `Author/Chapter 06/Audio Examples`.

I use Sibelius for the examples in this book. You'll get very familiar with the program as you load the demo software from the CD and progress through the chapters.

Digital Audio Workstations

Maybe you're not into music notation. Maybe you find the process of writing out each note and rhythm tedious. Or maybe you want to start creating other-worldly sounds with effects plug-ins. Either way, if you're going to get into digital music seriously, you're going to want to use a sequencing program.

The term *sequencer* hearkens back to the days when stand-alone hardware sequencers were used instead of the computer. Now they're more commonly known as digital audio workstations (DAWs).

Most DAWs also can record digital audio as well as sequence MIDI data, and some have some pretty amazing features. In this section, I fill you in on the most popular DAW software packages.

Cross-platform software: Windows or Mac

If you like the flexibility of software that can run on both Windows and Mac, read on.

Cubase

Steinberg (`www.steinberg.net`) is a real powerhouse in the digital music field. It's been building MIDI interfaces and the software to go along with them since the advent of the MIDI standard in 1983.

Steinberg developed the immensely successful VST plug-in, and, with its flagship DAW software package Cubase ($499 for Cubase Studio 4, $999 for Cubase 4), Steinberg offers five product lines:

- ✔ Music Production with Cubase and the new Sequel
- ✔ Media Production with Nuendo
- ✔ Audio Editing with WaveLab
- ✔ A large selection of sampler products, called its VST Instruments line
- ✔ A couple of hardware products: a controller and a MIDI interface

Cubase has been around in various forms since 1989 and is dual-platform. It's had a lot of makeovers through the years, and has a ton of features, like full digital audio recording capabilities in addition to MIDI sequencing.

Sequel

Steinberg's Sequel ($100) is a fairly new package that is aimed at the lower end of the market. Sequel is an all-in-one package, with simple digital recording, editing, mixing, and live performance features.

Sequel includes a large collection of up-to-the-minute loops and sounds, and is designed to get the user up and running with a minimum of hassle. Figure 6-3 shows the main work screen of Sequel, with both MIDI and digital audio tracks.

You can check out the sound of Sequel on the accompanying CD, at `Author/Chapter 06/Audio Examples`.

Windows-only software

If you're on a PC and you know you'll never need to work on a Mac, this section is for you.

Figure 6-3:
Steinberg's
Sequel.

SONAR

Although Cakewalk (www.cakewalk.com) offers several products, SONAR ($139–$699; www.cakewalk.com/sonar) is Cakewalk's flagship DAW. It only runs on a PC, so it's pretty much had the market to itself for quite a while, making it the best-selling Windows DAW in the United States. It provides a very powerful digital music production environment, and supports a lot of formats, like Virtual Studio Technology (VST) and DXi instruments — turn to Chapter 8 for more on both.

Cakewalk offers three versions of SONAR: The top of the line version is SONAR Producer; the middle-of-the-road version is SONAR Studio; and the most affordable is SONAR Home Studio.

I've been running SONAR Home Studio XL through its paces and it has all the SONAR features you'll probably need. It's much less expensive than the Studio or Producer versions and includes over 1GB of instrument sounds, Boost 11 Peak Limiter, Dimension LE soft synth, and the Session Drummer 2 drum instrument.

Figure 6-4 shows the SONAR Home Studio 6 main editing window, called the Track view.

Figure 6-5 shows the same piece of music in Sonar's Console view, which lets you access the mixing controls more easily.

Figure 6-4:
The SONAR
Home
Studio 6
Track view.

Figure 6-5:
The SONAR
Home
Studio 6
Console
view.

ACID Pro

ACID started out as a loop-based music production software owned by Sonic Foundry, the company that also owned the Sound Forge digital audio recording tool. But after it was sold to Sony (www.sonycreativesoftware.com), ACID became a much more complete music product with the addition of multitrack recording and MIDI sequencing.

Now ACID Pro 6 ($375; www.sonycreativesoftware.com/acid) is a professional music workstation for composing, recording, mixing, and arranging audio and MIDI tracks, featuring full digital multitrack recording functionality (24-bit, 192 kHz) and advanced MIDI sequencing, in addition to its original looping capability. ACID has a cool audio-editing tool that can stretch or shrink sound without altering its pitch.

Figure 6-6 shows an ACID Pro project's main sequencing window, called the Track view, with several satellite windows, such as the Groove Pool and Mixer windows.

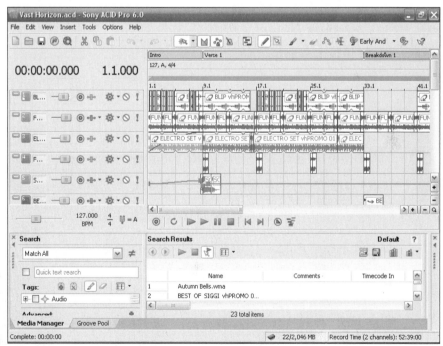

Figure 6-6:
ACID Pro 6
Track view.

Mac-only software

Because the Mac platform was used exclusively by the originators of digital music for the masses, as well as most professional music production studios, it makes sense that the Mac-only software is the most mature and seasoned. Windows is really a Johnny-come-lately to the arts and music scene.

In this section, I give you a look at some of the digital music software that makes its home only on the Mac.

GarageBand

GarageBand (www.apple.com/ilife/garageband) is a multifunction audio and music creation program from Apple (www.apple.com) developed for Mac OS X. It's only available as a part of the iLife suite (iPhoto, iMovie, iDVD, iTunes, and iWeb) and it's included on new Macintosh computers.

Although GarageBand is designed as a starter digital music product (it's not aimed at professional musicians), it has a lot of useful features packed into a small space, including:

✔ Audio recording via a DAW which can record and play back multiple tracks of audio, like guitar.

✔ A loop-based music sequencing tool, which comes with 1,000 prerecorded sampled and sequenced loops. Additional loops are available in five GarageBand Jam Packs.

✔ Virtual software instruments for creating songs or playing music live using 50 sampled or synthesized instruments. These instruments can be played using a MIDI keyboard controller connected to the computer, or using an on-screen virtual keyboard. Additional instruments are also available in the Jam Packs.

Because GarageBand is made by the company that brought you the iPod and iTunes, one of the great advantages of GarageBand is the ease with which you can make podcasts. It has a host of built-in tools that you can use to make professional-sounding podcasts.

Even though it isn't thought of as a professional-level digital music tool, GarageBand has its aficionados, and GarageBand files often find their way into mixes, from such groups as Nine Inch Nails, Brand New, and Limp Bizkit, and TV shows like *24*.

GarageBand uses Logic's audio engine. (See the following section for more on Logic.)

Logic Pro

Logic Pro ($999; www.apple.com/logicpro) is a Mac OS X MIDI sequencer and software DAW. Originally cross-platform (written for both Windows and Mac), it became a Mac-only software package when Apple bought out Emagic in 2002. A cut-down version, Logic Express, is also available from Apple.

Logic may be the most popular MIDI sequencer among music professionals. Although Digidesign's Pro Tools is used in practically every studio, Logic has more advanced MIDI functionality, and is free from the hardware commitments of Pro Tools (see "Pro Tools," later in this chapter). Logic can work with all MIDI controllers and control surfaces and supports real-time scoring with musical notation, guitar tab, chord symbols, and drum notation.

Logic Pro has many built-in synthesizers and software instruments and has very advanced audio effects like distortion, dynamics processors, equalization filters, and delays. One excellent feature of Logic is that it can seamlessly integrate your GarageBand pieces. So when you're ready to move up to a real pro DAW, you can import your existing GarageBand projects and immediately start working on them in Logic. Logic can record digital audio as well.

Digital Performer

One of the most powerful professional DAW packages for the Mac is Digital Performer ($795; www.motu.com/products/software/dp), made by Mark of the Unicorn (MOTU; www.motu.com). MOTU has a thriving MIDI and audio hardware business, in addition to publishing Digital Performer. Digital Performer is favored by serious (or not so serious) composers of large works, and is often used by composers of film scores, as well as other professional composers and arrangers.

Digital Performer is one of the best DAWs around, with a massive number of features composers can use for song writing, studio production, film scoring, live performance, remixing, post production, and surround mixing. It has unlimited tracks, unlimited undo, support for surround sound, 64-bit mastering tools, sample-accurate editing of audio and MIDI, automatic tempo calculation for film scoring, and many more bells and whistles.

Pro Tools

Pro Tools ($450–$2,000) by DigiDesign (www.digidesign.com) is the main professional tool for digital recording. It's been around longer than any of the software DAWs, and although it's just starting to play catchup in the MIDI sequencing race, it still has the largest base of professional music studio installations of any type of digital music product.

Pro Tools is both a hardware and software product — it runs on its own proprietary hardware. You can use Logic or Digital Performer with your Pro Tools hardware, if you want, but some incompatibilities may result if you do this. Your best bet is to use Pro Tools software with its hardware.

Other Great Software

Some software doesn't fit neatly into a specific category. This especially holds true for the latest generation of digital music software, programs that take the ideas of tempo, sound, and compatibility into new, uncharted territory. The following group of products are currently the best and brightest of the bunch.

Reason

Reason ($499) is a very popular music software program developed by Swedish software developers Propellerhead Software (`www.propeller heads.se`). Reason is a virtual studio that emulates a traditional studio's rack full of rack-mount equipment, with mixers, samplers, synthesizers, effects, and sequencers. These modules can be controlled from Reason's built-in MIDI sequencer or from other sequencing applications, such as Pro Tools, Logic, Cubase, and GarageBand, via Propellerhead's proprietary ReWire protocol.

Reason is one of the coolest programs ever. One of the reasons for the coolness is the fact that it has an interface like no other. It has a graphic replica of a studio rack, into which you can insert virtual devices (such as instruments, effects processors, and mixers) and build a complex music production studio, right on your computer screen. Figure 6-7 shows a loaded Reason virtual rack from the front.

A totally sick feature of Reason is how the virtual devices are connected. By pressing the Tab key, you see the rack from behind. Here you can click and drag the animated virtual cables to connect the devices. Figure 6-8 shows the same loaded rack from the rear, with the patch cables visible.

Reason to ReWire

Because Reason doesn't interface with plug-ins, it's often used with another program, such as Ableton (see "Ableton Live," in this chapter). Reason has a feature called ReWire, which gives it the ability to transfer audio data in real time between two computer applications. Using ReWire, you can output your audio tracks from Reason into Ableton, which then lets you use all the cool Ableton features to modify your sound. It's like ReWire is an "invisible cable" that streams audio from one computer program into another. Several software applications from different manufacturers now support ReWire transfer.

Figure 6-7:
A loaded Reason virtual rack.

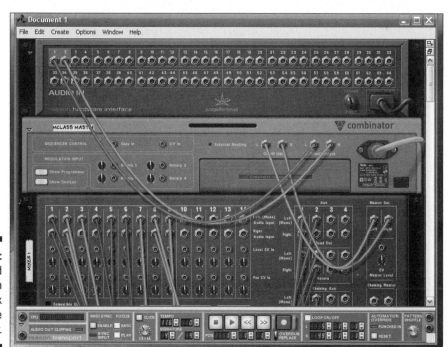

Figure 6-8:
A loaded Reason virtual rack from the rear.

Another great feature of Reason is that you can have two copies of the software running concurrently, which means you can have a version installed on your desktop and another copy installed on your laptop, for one price.

When using any software, be sure to find out if your software license allows you to install and run the software on more than one computer, or just one at a time. Some software packages, like Sibelius, let you install the software on two computers, but ask that you run only one copy at a time. Other software manufacturers only allow one licensed copy installed on one computer at a time and won't let you install and run a second copy.

Listen to a Reason 3 clip on the CD at `Author/Chapter 06/Audio Examples` on the CD.

Ableton Live

Ableton Live ($599; `www.ableton.com/live`) is an amazing program from the German company Ableton (`www.ableton.com`). Ableton Live provides real-time track editing, arranging, and sequencing, primarily for live performances. It's a loop-based software music sequencer for Macintosh and Windows, which, unlike other sequencer software, allows you to jam and create on-the-spot arrangements with your samples and prepared tracks. In addition to Live, Ableton also makes two other products, Operator ($149; `www.ableton.com/operator`) and Sampler ($199; `www.ableton.com/sampler`), which are used as audio synthesis instruments.

Figure 6-9 shows an Ableton Live Set with several windows open, such as a mixer and a browser.

One feature of Ableton Live that's very popular is its ability to warp the tempo of tracks, called its Elastic Audio feature. This feature lets you match audio and MIDI input from various sources to the tempo of your project, even in real time. You can fix timing errors in audio and use tracks with unrelated tempos in your new file.

Sound Forge

Sony Sound Forge ($320; `www.sonycreativesoftware.com/soundforge`) is a digital audio editing and creation suite which includes a real-time sample level wave editor, stereo, and multi-channel recording in very high-resolution, video support, VST and DirectX plug-in support, and a wide variety of file formats that can easily be burned to CD directly from the software.

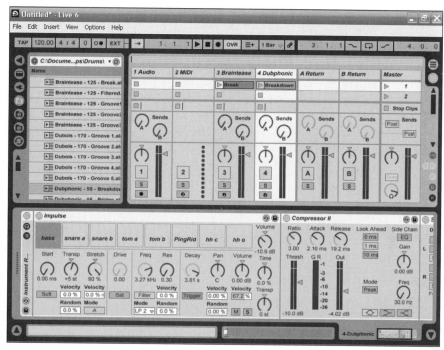

Figure 6-9:
An Ableton
Live Set.

Originally owned by Sonic Foundry, Sound Forge was purchased by
Sony in 2003 and is now part of its music software suite, which includes
the music production software ACID Pro and the video editing tool
Vegas.

I use Sound Forge a lot for creating high-quality audio files. I like the wealth
of effects plug-ins, such as equalization, normalization, reverb, and delay.
The ease with which you can cut and paste audio fragments makes it really
versatile and reliable.

A cut-down version, previously known as Sonic Foundry's Sound Forge LE, is
called Sound Forge Audio Studio. It's a very useful and inexpensive entry-
level audio editor.

Figure 6-10 shows Sound Forge with a digital audio file loaded.

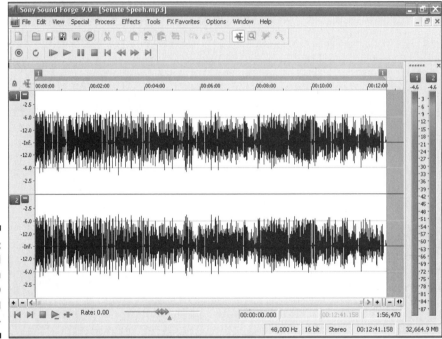

Figure 6-10:
Sound
Forge's main
audio
editing
window.

Software Samplers

Software samplers are programs that allow the composer to use small prerecorded digital audio recordings (samples) of various instruments. These instruments can be traditional acoustic instruments (like the violin, tuba, or tympani), or they can be totally made up, spacey electronic sounds. The samples can then be edited with a DAW for a music production project, or played by a MIDI controller in a live setting.

At one time, all samplers were hardware. Many big companies (such as Roland, Yamaha, Akai, and others) built very successful hardware-based samplers that were the standard in digital music production. But over the last several years, with the exponential increase in processing power of the Mac or PC, software samplers have matured to the point where they can provide the features, capability, quality, and number of samples to challenge the hardware samplers.

There are pros and cons to both software samplers and hardware samplers. Hardware samplers are generally more expensive than software samplers. Hardware samplers store the samples on a hard drive, and load the sample when requested, often fairly slowly. The size of the hard drive also limits how many different samples the hardware sampler can hold.

One big benefit of hardware samplers is that, if you're on a gig, a dedicated hardware sampler can be set up and is generally much more reliable than a computer or laptop on the road. You just load the sample set and you're off.

But in general, the music production industry is leaving large, expensive hardware samplers, and embracing software samplers. One reason is that the source material available for a particular software sample program is unlimited, and great new sample libraries are being created every day. And with the Internet, the software can easily be updated with bug fixes and enhancements.

All the samplers mentioned in the following sections are cross-platform — they support both Mac and Windows.

GigaStudio

TASCAM's GigaStudio ($599; www.tascam.com) is the granddaddy of all samplers. It was the first to develop streaming sample technology, which allows the composer to use extremely large sample libraries. GigaStudio set new standards for the quality of samples, establishing software sampling as a viable option when compared to hardware sampling.

KONTAKT

KONTAKT ($449; www.nativeinstruments.com/kontakt), made by Native Instruments, is a very powerful, easy-to-use software sampler. It has a massive number of features, such as real-time pitch shifting, time-stretching, and precise drum loop slicing.

KONTAKT is compatible with a large number of formats and is the default instrument sample library for many digital music software programs, such as Finale and Sibelius. It also supports streaming technology, for use with very large samples. I use Sibelius KONTAKT plug-in instruments for many of the sounds in this book.

HALion

HALion ($399) is Steinberg's software sampler that can be used as a VST2 or DXi2 plug-in or as a ReWire slave-device for Reason.

The current version, HALion 3, provides a great sampling and synthesis engine, a huge number of included samples, and easy-to-use interface, and supports 5.1 surround sound, very high-quality (384 kHz/32 bit) audio engineering.

Steinberg uses a USB key as a copy protection device for some of its products, which means that, unless you already have one for other Steinberg products, you need to purchase the Steinberg Key ($29) to run HALion. Fortunately, the same Steinberg Key copy protection device is then used for all Steinberg products that require it. Cubase 4, Nuendo 4, and WaveLab 6 have the Steinberg Key already included in the product package. The Steinberg Key is also required to run Steinberg VST instruments but is not included in the product boxes and must be purchased separately if no Steinberg Key is already present on your system.

REAKTOR

REAKTOR ($449; www.nativeinstruments.com/reaktor), by the amazing company Native Instruments, is the mother of all digital music creation programs. Like Reason, it's a very versatile, modular software music studio.

REAKTOR's value is that it's actually a laboratory for creating unique and exotic sound shapes, textures, and ambiences. It also has a very open plug-in support architecture, which allows you to easily use it with a lot of other sequencers.

It's got a ton of built-in instruments and effects, from emulations of classic synthesizers to sci-fi sound designs, to help musicians and engineers design and build their own software instruments and tools.

REAKTOR is sort of the Radio Shack of digital music studios: All the parts you need to build your own sound devices are enclosed. You can download more than 2,000 free instruments from the growing User Library, and its instruments can be freely used, examined, or altered.

Figure 6-11 shows a project during development in REAKTOR. Unlike DAWs, every project will have a different view, based on what tools are being used to create the sound or instrument. Therefore, REAKTOR doesn't have a default Track or Arrange view, like the other software I mention.

Figure 6-11:
A REAKTOR
project
under
develop-
ment.

SampleTank

SampleTank (www.sampletank.com) comes in two flavors: SampleTank 2 L ($300) and the larger SampleTank 2 XL ($500). Although it doesn't have the flexibility of HALion, KOMPAKT, or REAKTOR, it has a ton of great samples, and the easy user interface makes it a great choice for someone who just wants to use a sample and doesn't want to spend the rest of his life tweaking every parameter of a sound.

Playing with Plug-ins

The big news of digital music software is the plug-in. There's a plug-in for every kind of instrument sound and futuristic instruments that haven't even been invented yet.

A *plug-in* is a piece of software designed to function in conjunction with a sequencer or DAW, and provide extra features and sounds not included with the original DAW software. The biggest growth in the digital music software industry is with plug-ins.

A ton of great plug-ins — from vintage guitar and amp sounds, to different types of drum setups, to weird esoteric ambiences — are available. Plug-ins are distributed by all types of companies, too — from the major software vendors, to little two-man outfits that make a few plug-ins for a very specific type of sound.

The greatest feature of plug-ins is their compatibility, but there are a few different plug-in formats. On the Mac side, formats include

- ✔ Steinberg's VST and VST instruments (VSTi)
- ✔ MOTU's MAS
- ✔ Digi's TDM, HTDM, AudioSuite, and RTAS

Apple has also introduced the new Audio Units (AU) for OS X format.

On the PC side, the VST and VSTi formats dominate, with DirectX and DXi formats also very popular.

You probably won't buy a DAW because of which plug-ins it supports. Most DAWs support most popular formats, and, unless you're looking for a really specific instrument or sound for a project, you'll use whatever plug-ins you have for your platform. Fortunately, most plug-ins are dual-platform, because that's the real reason for the popularity of plug-ins — compatibility.

All Steinberg products support VST and VSTi (because Steinberg invented them) on both platforms. Logic and Digital Performer support the Mac format plug-ins. Sony and Cakewalk products support both VST and DirectX, and SONAR and Sound Forge come with a bunch of sounds and effects plug-ins.

In the following sections, I show you a few third-party plug-ins with instrument libraries and samples.

ABSYNTH

ABSYNTH ($340; www.nativeinstruments.com/absynth) is one of a series of excellent plug-ins by Native Instruments. Native Instruments makes the industry standard for add-ons, including soft synths, drum samples, guitar emulators, and DJ software.

ABSYNTH 4 is the latest version of the Native Instruments software synthesizer, which can function as a stand-alone synthesizer sound generator for your controller, or as a plug-in for other DAWs. It has a large library of sounds and instruments, and features three main synthesis modules, which can be customized to fit almost any particular synthesis type, and can be used to modulate a wide range of parameters. What this means is that you can create organic, evolving soundscapes that range from sublime pads to complex sonic textures.

You can chose from 1,200 prebuilt instruments, and alter the sound easily to fit your needs. Figure 6-12 shows ABSYNTH 4's Browser view, where you select either the individual sounds or a preconfigured instrument. Figure 6-13 shows ABSYNTH 4's Patch view, which is one place where you can modify your sound.

You can listen to a cool MP3 clip of some ABSYNTH sounds on the CD at `Author/Chapter 06/Audio Examples`.

BATTERY

BATTERY ($299; `www.nativeinstruments.com/battery`) is a Native Instruments drum kit plug-in that comes with a huge drum sample library. You can load the preconfigured drum kits based on genre (like '80s electronic, acoustic jazz, or ethnic percussion), and then edit each piece of the kit to your liking.

The user interface is very simple to use, and with a 12GB sample library, you'll be old by the time you've tried every sound. I especially like the performance articulations (roll, flam, buzz, right hand, and so on), which help make it sound like a real drummer is playing.

Figure 6-12:
The software synthesizer ABSYNTH 4 in Browser view.

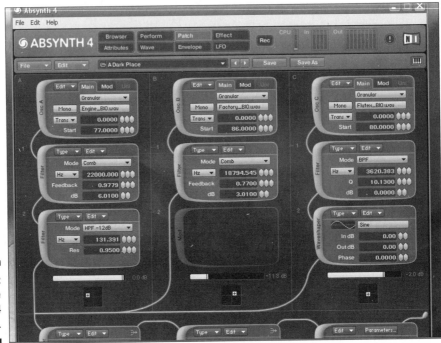

Figure 6-13:
The
ABSYNTH 4
Patch view.

In Figure 6-14, you can see an '80s electronic drum set loaded into BATTERY 3. Each separate part of the drum kit is identified as a distinct instrument, (like Crash Cymbal) so you can edit elements or add elements to (or subtract elements from) each part of the kit.

FM8

FM8 ($340; www.nativeinstruments.com/fm8) is another great Native Instruments plug-in. FM8 emulates and expands upon the famous FM synthesis that was introduced in the '80s with the ground-breaking Yamaha DX7.

FM8 is updated from FM7 and has a tone of beautiful sounds in an easy-to-use interface. With almost 1,000 sounds included, some of its best features are the *arpeggiator,* which lets you build repeating passages into a single sound, and a visual *morphing tool,* which lets you change or combine sounds by dragging the mouse.

Figure 6-15 shows FM8's instruments attribute screen, where you can find and select the instrument sound you want based on your criteria, such as timbre, articulation, or genre.

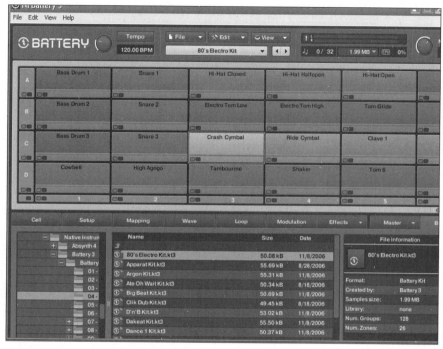

Figure 6-14: BATTERY 3 with an '80s electronic drum kit loaded.

Kinetic

Cakewalk's Kinetic ($80; www.cakewalk.com/products/kinetic/default.asp) is a totally cool beat-looping groove machine. You can make hip beats with an easy point-and-click interface and even tap beats with your mouse, computer keyboard, or MIDI controller. It has thousands of instrument patches, and exports to all file formats.

Kinetic 2 includes tempo-syncing ACID-format loops and MIDI Groove Clips so that drums, basses, keyboards, guitars, and other tracks will automatically lock to the tempo of the project.

A *Groove Clip* is an audio clip that lets you stretch its tempo without changing the pitch. You can also assign a reference pitch to a Groove Clip, so when your song changes pitch your clip will follow it automatically.

Kinetic uses the bundled DropZone sampler to provide instruments for the grooves, and bundles Dimension LE as a synthesizer plug-in. Dimension LE is a scaled-down version of the dual-platform Dimension Pro software synthesizer. Figure 6-16 shows Kinetic 2 with a groove set loaded.

You can listen to a short sample of a Kinetic groove set on the CD at Author/Chapter 06/Audio Examples.

Figure 6-15:
The FM8 sound selection attributes screen.

Figure 6-16:
Kinetic 2 Rhythm Beat Groove Production.

Part III
The Basics: Building Your First Tune

The 5th Wave   By Rich Tennant

"Where's the audience track? You know, where I can put in coughs, throat clears, and drink orders?"

In this part . . .

This is the part of the book where you start to get your hands dirty with building a real piece of music. In Chapter 7, I introduce you to the templates on the accompanying CD and get you started working with them. Chapter 8 shows you how to save a tune in different formats for different types of digital music players, print it out, or burn it on a CD to play in an audio CD player.

And because the greatest part of writing music is sharing it with others, Chapter 9 shows you where to publish your music on the Internet (and provides some background on copyright issues so you don't get burned).

Chapter 7

Instant Music: Using the Templates

In This Chapter

▶ Installing the music software

▶ Opening and playing your first tune

▶ Adding notes and building your tune

▶ Adding the guitar and drum parts

*I*n this chapter, you start making your own music. I make it easy for you at first — all you need to do is open my template files on the CD that comes with this book, and make changes to them. In later chapters, you're more on your own, but for right now, I show you, step by step, how to build a tune.

Setting Up Your Composing Software

The CD that comes with this book has Sibelius templates I've created that you use to follow along throughout this book. You download the template from the CD, follow my instructions about changing them, and then play them back.

Installing the demo software

The first thing you need to do is install the Sibelius 5 demo software. For your convenience, it's included on the CD, or you can download it from the Sibelius Web site (www.sibelius.com).

One advantage of downloading it from the Web site is that you know you're getting the most up-to-date version of the software.

If you prefer to download the Sibelius 5 demo software from the CD, turn to Appendix B, and follow the directions on loading the software.

Starting Sibelius

Make sure your audio is working before you start Sibelius. Try it out on a video from the Web, for example, or play a CD of music on your computer. Most times, if the audio works fine before you load Sibelius, it'll work fine when you get into Sibelius.

You can start Sibelius by clicking on the new Sibelius icon on your desktop, or choose Start⇨Programs⇨Sibelius Software⇨Sibelius 5 Demo (if you're on a Windows PC) or double-click your hard drive icon, navigate to the Applications folder, then double-click the Sibelius 5 Demo program icon (if you're on a Mac). You'll see the Sibelius 5 startup screen (shown in Figure 7-1). A nice Sibelius composition will play, which helps verify that your computer's audio system is working correctly.

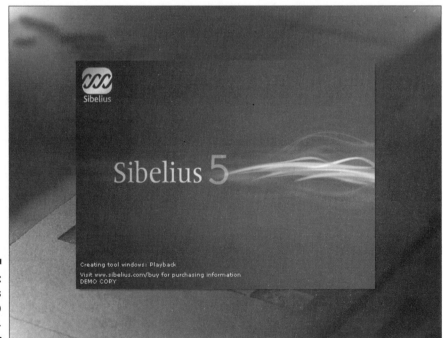

Figure 7-1:
The Sibelius
5 startup
screen.

Setting your playback

In order to hear the audio files on the CD and listen to Sibelius play your opus as you work on it, you need to have an audio device working on your computer. You can, of course, use the templates and write your music without having to hear the output of the music, but hearing each part after you write it, and then listening to the whole composition, is one of the great advantages of using music notation software.

You probably won't have to go through manually setting up your playback device — Sibelius usually does that automatically. But you may need to go to Play ➪ Playback Devices and set your audio outs, if you didn't do it during installation. Figure 7-2 shows the Playback Devices dialog box, where you can set your options.

Every computer has a different set of playback devices listed, depending upon what audio software and hardware are installed. If you're on a Windows PC, the Microsoft GS Wavetable device, which has some general sounds for all the instruments, is probably the device you'll use to start. It's nothing to write home about, but it gets the job done. When you get the full version of Sibelius, you can add extra sounds and make the playback sound much more realistic. The Mac has a full complement of built-in sounds using Apple's default MIDI sound set, its DLSMusic device.

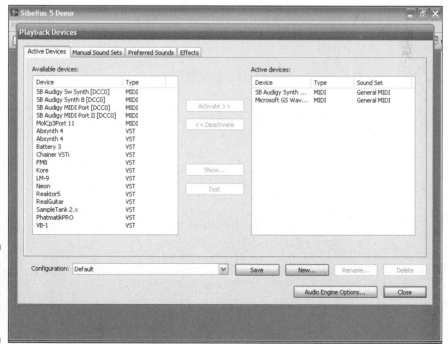

Figure 7-2:
Setting the audio playback device.

If your playback isn't working right, the Sibelius Web site has a Help Center (www.sibelius.com/cgi-bin/helpcenter/search.pl?com=main) with a lot of information. If your audio is not working at all (even before you start Sibelius), refer to the troubleshooting recommendations that came with your audio card or computer or contact your computer manufacturer.

Using the music templates

The CD that comes with this book has lots of files on it, and Appendix B has a thorough description of them. Some of the files are MP3 audio files to help you hear what the templates are supposed to sound like.

The files on the CD you'll use the most, however, are Sibelius score files, which have the filename extention of .sib. You'll use these templates to write your music, and you can find them in the My New Tune folder.

Don't worry about messing up the templates — you can't. You can alter them any way you want, or get the tune hopelessly fouled up, and it's not a problem. You can always open a nice, clean Sibelius template from the CD and start over. So feel free to experiment and try anything you want — the weirder the better!

You can open the Sibelius files by clicking on your CD icon in My Computer (on Windows) or by clicking on the CD icon on your desktop (on the Mac), or you can drag them to a new folder on your computer.

Opening My New Tune

When you start Sibelius, the music will play and the Quick Start dialog box (shown in Figure 7-3) appears. Here you can choose to open the last file you worked on, to open another file, or to start a new score.

For right now, select the Open Another File radio button and click OK. The Open dialog box appears. Click on your CD drive letter (on many computers, it's D:) and open the My New Tune-07-01.sib file.

When you open some of the templates, you may see an Update Score dialog box, telling you that the template was saved in an older version of Sibelius. I created some of these templates using Sibelius 4, and Sibelius 5 is just asking if you want to upgrade to a new House Style (see Chapter 10 for more on House Styles). Just click OK and the score will open.

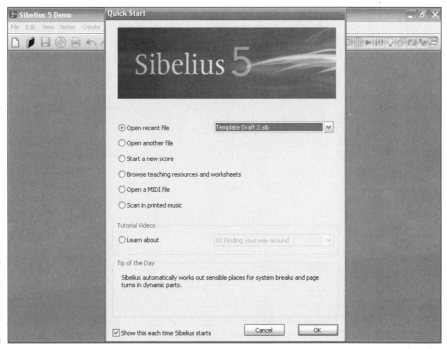

Figure 7-3:
The Sibelius
Quick Start
dialog box.

If you're already in Sibelius, you can open a Sibelius file without using the Quick Start dialog box. Just choose File➪Open.

My New Tune-07-01.sib has the first two bars of the bass line already created for you, and has staves for the lead guitar, rhythm guitar, bass guitar, and drums, as shown in Figure 7-4.

Here you're going to add all the notes for the other parts, and play your tune. First, change the View Size of the score paper, so you can get a better look at the music. Click on the drop-down list (see Figure 7-5), and select 50%. This gives you a better view of the whole page of music.

To play back the music at any time, press the space bar. Pressing the space bar again stops the playback. You can rewind the playback from the beginning at any time by pressing Ctrl+[(⌘+[).

Figure 7-4:
"My New Tune."

Figure 7-5:
Changing
the score
view size.

Building Your Tune

When you have your first tune open (see the previous sections), you want to add some music and hear what it sounds like. You can start by copying the two bars of the initial bass guitar part to the rest of the tune. Here's how:

1. **Highlight the bass guitar part by selecting the first bar with your mouse.**

    Sibelius puts a blue box around the bar.

2. **While holding down the Shift key, click the second bar with your mouse.**

    This highlights both bars in blue, as shown in Figure 7-6.

3. **Press Ctrl+C (⌘+C) to copy those two bass guitar bars.**

4. **Click the third bass guitar bar (the first bass guitar bar without any notes in it).**

    This highlights the bar in blue, as shown in Figure 7-7.

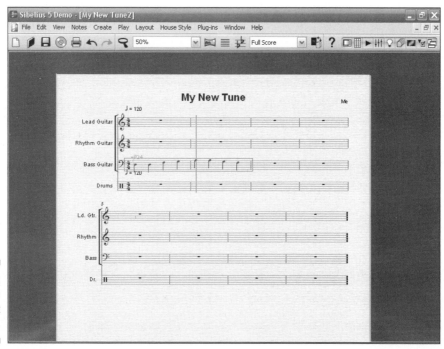

Figure 7-6:
The bass guitar part highlighted.

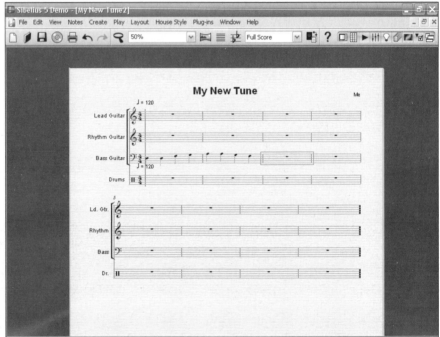

Figure 7-7:
The empty
bass guitar
bars
highlighted.

5. **Press Ctrl+V (⌘+V).**

   The two bass guitar bars are now also in the third and fourth bars.

6. **Click your mouse on the fifth bar to highlight it, and press Ctrl+V (⌘+V).**

   The two bass guitar bars are now repeated in the fifth and sixth bars.

7. **Click your mouse on the seventh bar to highlight it, and press Ctrl+V (⌘+V).**

   You should have a complete bass guitar part consisting of a two-bar phrase played four times in total, and it should look like Figure 7-8.

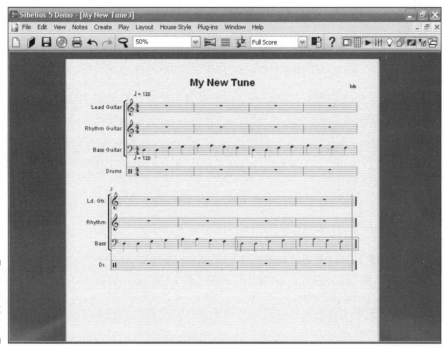

Figure 7-8:
The bass
guitar part
filled in.

If you didn't get it, don't worry: You can open My New Tune-07-02.sib, where I've put in the rest of the bass guitar notes for you.

If you're like me, you want to hear right away what your new part sounds like. One way to play it back is by opening the Playback window. Click on the black arrow button on the right side of the toolbar, and a floating Playback window appears. From this window, you can start or stop the playback, and rewind the playback to the beginning of the piece.

Press the first button (the Rewind button) to be sure the tune plays from the beginning, and then press the Play arrow, shown in Figure 7-9.

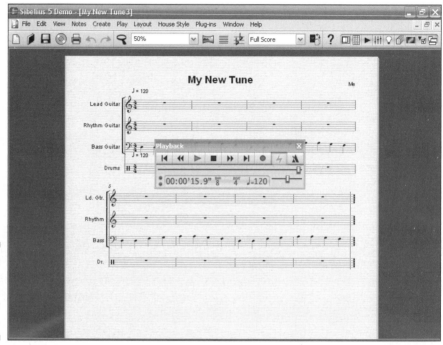

Figure 7-9:
Playing
back the
bass guitar
part.

Listen to "My New Tune" on the CD at `Author/Chapter 07/Audio Examples/My New Tune-07-02.mp3`.

If you don't hear the part, check out your playback device, and be sure your headphones are plugged in or your speakers are turned on. You may need to troubleshoot your playback device from the Play menu.

Depending upon what type of sound sets you have with your computer, playback will probably sound quite different from the MP3 audio file on the CD. For this example, I used the Sibelius Sounds Rock & Pop collection add-in. It provides more lifelike instrument sounds than the standard KONTAKT Silver sound set that comes with Sibelius. Sibelius sells lots of extra sounds, like the Garritan Personal Orchestra and ethnic World Music instruments (see Chapter 6 for descriptions).

Adding the rhythm guitar part

As scintillating as the bass guitar part is, it doesn't really make much of a tune. To flesh things out, you want to add the rhythm guitar part. I've built a nice '60s-style rhythm guitar part for you. Open the `My New Tune-07-03.sib` file. It should look like Figure 7-10.

Figure 7-10: "My New Tune" with rhythm guitar and bass.

Listen to "My New Tune" on the CD at Author/Chapter 07/Audio Examples/My New Tune-07-03.mp3.

Here I have you do the same thing you did with the bass part (see the preceding section) — copy the first two bars of the rhythm guitar part and paste into the other blank bars. To do this, follow these steps:

1. **Highlight the rhythm guitar part by selecting the first bar with your mouse.**

   Sibelius puts a blue box around the bar.

2. **While holding down the Shift key, click the second rhythm guitar bar with your mouse.**

   This highlights both bars in blue, as shown in Figure 7-11.

3. **Press Ctrl+C (⌘+C) to copy those two rhythm guitar bars.**

4. **Click the third rhythm guitar bar (the first rhythm guitar bar without any notes in it).**

   This highlights the bar in blue.

5. **Press Ctrl+V (⌘+V).**

   The two rhythm guitar bars are now also in the third and fourth bars.

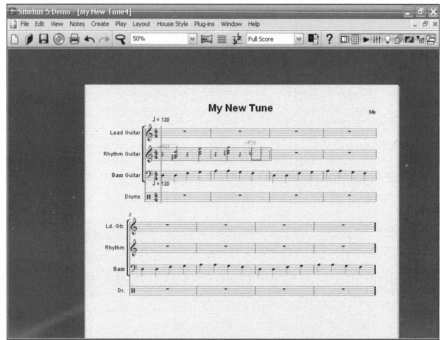

Figure 7-11:
The rhythm
guitar part
highlighted.

6. **Click your mouse on the fifth bar to highlight it, and press Ctrl+V (⌘+V).**

   The two rhythm guitar bars are now repeated in the fifth and sixth bars.

7. **Click your mouse on the seventh bar to highlight it, and press Ctrl+V (⌘+V).**

   You should have a complete rhythm guitar part consisting of a two-bar phrase played four times in total, and it should look like Figure 7-12.

Listen to "My New Tune" on the CD at `Author/Chapter 07/Audio Examples/My New Tune-07-04.mp3`.

You can hear your new part by opening the Playback window. Press Ctrl+[(⌘+[), and then press the space bar to start and stop the playback. If you need to load the filled-in file from the CD, it's `My New Tune-07-04.sib`.

Figure 7-12:
The rhythm
guitar part
filled in.

If you're using the demo version of Sibelius, and can't save each step, I saved the tune at each stage on the CD. Just load the file I indicate before the start of each section. You can also listen to MP3 audio tracks of each of the Sibelius files, so you can compare what your tune sounds like with the template each step of the way.

Adding the lead guitar part

Now that you have your rhythm guitar and bass parts finished (see the previous two sections), you can add a simple melody and have it played by the lead guitar. I've created the melody for you — I show you how to change the notes to your liking in Chapter 11.

Open the My New Tune-07-05.sib file. It should look like Figure 7-13, with the first four bars of the lead guitar part filled in.

Figure 7-13:
The lead
guitar part.

Fill in the rest of the lead guitar part the same way you did the rhythm guitar and bass guitar parts (in the previous two sections). Because I've already done four bars of this eight-bar ditty, you only have to copy and paste it once.

1. **Highlight the lead guitar part by selecting the first bar with your mouse.**

   Sibelius puts a blue box around the bar.

2. **While holding down the Shift key, click the fourth lead guitar bar with your mouse.**

   This highlights the first four bars in blue, as shown in Figure 7-14.

Figure 7-14:
The lead
guitar part
highlighted.

3. **Press Ctrl+C (⌘+C) to copy those four lead guitar bars.**

4. **Click the fifth lead guitar bar (the first lead guitar bar without any notes in it).**

   This highlights the bar in blue.

   The fifth bar may be on the second page of your score, so you may have to scroll down to find the open lead guitar bar.

5. **Press Ctrl+V (⌘+V).**

   The four lead guitar bars are now also in the fifth through eighth bars.

   You should have a complete lead guitar part consisting of a four-bar phrase played two times in total, and it should look like Figure 7-15.

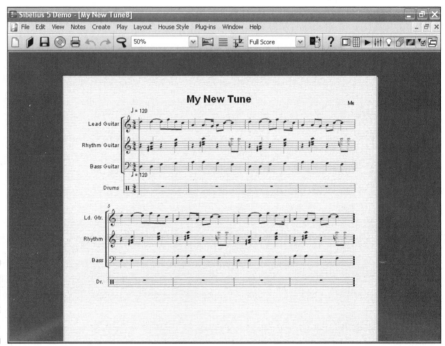

Figure 7-15:
The lead guitar part filled in.

Press Ctrl+[(⌘+[), and then press the spacebar to play it back and rock out!

If you want to compare what you have with the template, open the `My New Tune-07-06.sib` file.

Listen to *My New Tune* on the CD at `Author/Chapter 07/Audio Examples/ My New Tune-07-06.mp3`.

Thumpin' the drums

One thing that's really missing from this piece is the back beat of the drums. You can't have a retro '60s-sounding tune without a big beat! In this section, I show you how to add the drum part.

Open `My New Tune-07-07.sib`. It should look like Figure 7-16, with the first bar of the drum part filled in. Fill in the rest of the drum part the same way you did with the three guitar parts (in the previous sections). Because I've only done one bar of this eight-bar song, you have to copy and paste it seven times:

1. **Highlight the drum part by selecting the first bar with your mouse.**

   Sibelius puts a blue box around the bar.

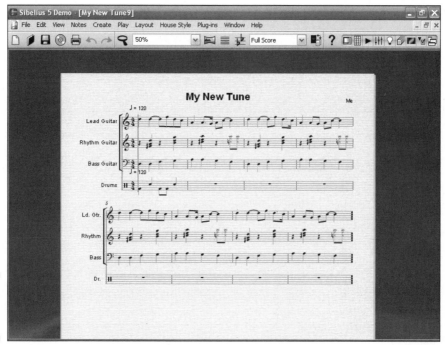

Figure 7-16:
The drum
part.

2. **Press Ctrl+C (⌘+C) to copy the first drum bar.**

3. **Click the second drum bar.**

   This highlights the bar in blue.

4. **Press Ctrl+V (⌘+V).**

   The first drum bar is now in the second bar.

5. **Repeat Steps 3 and 4 for the remaining six bars of the drum part.**

   You should have a complete drum part, and it should look like
   Figure 7-17. You can play it back to hear what it sounds like, or play
   the MP3 file from the CD. Your file should be the same as My New
   Tune-07-08.sib.

Listen to "My New Tune" on the CD at Author/Chapter 07/Audio
Examples/My New Tune-07-08.mp3.

The computer keeps good time, but the drum part isn't too interesting. You
can make the part a little better. First open the My New Tune-07-09.sib file
on the CD. It should look like Figure 7-18. I've gone ahead and added a cymbal
part and a little change to the drum rhythm in the second bar.

Figure 7-17:
The drum
part filled in.

Figure 7-18:
The drum
part altered.

Listen to "My New Tune" on the CD at `Author/Chapter 07/Audio Examples/My New Tune-07-09.mp3`.

You can make the rest of the drum part like the first two bars. Copy the first two bars from the drum stave and paste those two bars into bars three, five, and seven, to fill in the rest of the drum part. Here are the steps to follow:

1. **Click the first drum bar.**

2. **While holding down the Shift key, click the second drum bar.**

   This highlights the first two bars in blue, as shown in Figure 7-19.

3. **Press Ctrl+C (⌘+C) to copy those two drum bars.**

4. **Click the fifth drum bar.**

   This highlights the bar in blue.

5. **Press Ctrl+V (⌘+V).**

6. **Repeat Steps 4 and 5 twice more, clicking on the seventh and ninth bars.**

   You should have a complete drum part, and it should look like Figure 7-20. This matches up with the `My New Tune-07-10.sib` file on the CD.

Figure 7-19:
The drum part highlighted.

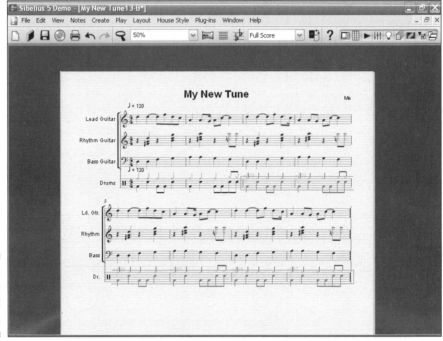

Figure 7-20:
The drum
part
changed.

Listen to "My New Tune" on the CD at `Author/Chapter 07/Audio Examples/My New Tune-07-10.mp3`. Play it back to hear your new drum part with the rest of the band!

Changing the notes

You can change the notes on the page very easily, in a variety of ways. You can change a note by:

- ✔ Clicking on the note and dragging it up or down to change its pitch

- ✔ Opening the Keypad and changing the duration of the note, as well as its pitch or articulation

- ✔ Highlighting a note, a group of notes, or a group of measures and choosing Notes⇨Transpose⇨Interval.

You can easily delete a note by clicking on it and just hitting the Delete key. You can also empty a measure of all its notes and rests by just clicking anywhere on the bar to highlight it and pressing the Delete key.

Undo is your best friend!

I often paste something in the wrong place, or cut something I shouldn't, or just generally mess up the score. No problem! I just press Ctrl+Z (⌘+Z), and my last action is magically removed, as if I went back in time. And if I need to reverse a series of goofs, I choose Edit⇨Undo History, and I can see my last several keystrokes. I can go back and undo a series of bad decisions. You can choose Edit⇨Redo if you change your mind.

Have fun changing the notes any way you want! You can always open My New Tune-07-10.sib from the CD and start over at any time. And of course, press Ctrl+Z (⌘+Z) to undo your mistakes.

You can't save your creation if you have the demo software, but you can open a new template at any time from the CD to continue forward.

Try odd things, like copying the lead guitar part and pasting it to the drums, or copying the bass part to the guitar. Then play it back to hear your very odd composition.

Chapter 8

To Live and Burn in L.A.: Output 101

In This Chapter

▶ Exporting the audio of your tune to CDs, podcasts, or ringtones

▶ Making your tune into a MIDI file for use by other music programs

▶ Printing your tune for others to play

Your new tune looks very nice sitting in Sibelius, and hearing it play back is fun. But if you want others to enjoy it, or even other musicians to play your tune, you're going to have to get it out of Sibelius and into a format other people and other programs can use.

In this chapter, I show you how to export the audio of your tune to different formats, like CDs and ringtones. I explain how to change it into MIDI format, so you can expand the tune with all the great MIDI sounds and tools available. And I show you how to print the score and parts so musicians can play and enjoy it, too.

Like the save function, the export functions of the Sibelius 5 demo are disabled. This means you'll need to get a full version of Sibelius to be able to take advantage of all the steps I describe in this chapter.

Outputting Your Audio

One of the first things you may want to do after you've completed your tune, is output the audio to a file. This will allow your music to be heard away from the Sibelius software, on CD, on the Web, or even as a ringtone! Different audio formats allow you to play your tune in various ways and reach more people with your music.

Before you try to save an audio file, make sure that your score plays back satisfactorily. If you haven't been able to play back your tune yet (see Chapter 7), nothing will come out when you try to save it as an audio file. The Sibelius site has all kinds of information to help with troubleshooting audio output.

To export your audio to a file, follow these steps:

1. **Choose File➪Export➪Audio.**

   If you're using the KONTAKT Player that comes with Sibelius, a warning box appears, telling you to carefully set up the player before you try to export your audio (see Figure 8-1). If you're not using the KONTAKT Player or you've already set up everything, you can ignore this.

   If playback is not rewound to the beginning of the tune, you may get another warning box (see Figure 8-2). In this case, click No to exit, and press Ctrl+[(⌘+[)to rewind the audio to the beginning. Then start the process again, starting with Step 1.

   When everything is all right, the Export Audio dialog box appears, asking where you want to save the audio file (see Figure 8-3).

2. **Click Choose Folder, and select the folder where you want the file to be saved.**

3. **If you want the screen to always show you where the recording is in the score as it progresses, select the Follow Score during Recording check box.**

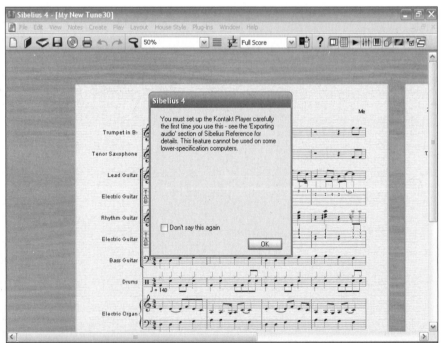

Figure 8-1:
The
KONTAKT
Player setup
warning.

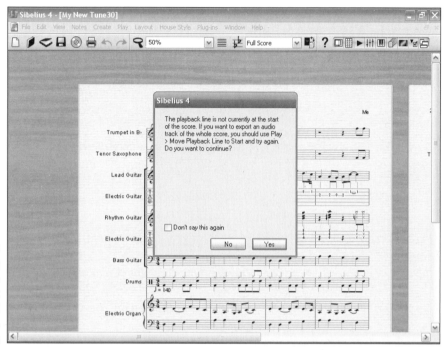

Figure 8-2:
The
playback
rewind
warning.

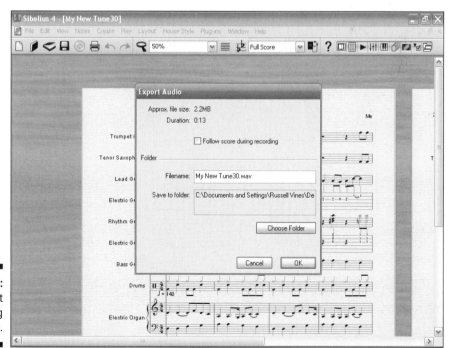

Figure 8-3:
The Export
Audio dialog
box.

4. **Click OK to start the recording.**

   When the recording starts, a box will appear, showing you the recording's progress (see Figure 8-4).

   When the export is finished, you'll have a WAV file (Windows) or an AIFF file (Mac), which can be opened by any digital music recording, playback, or burning software (like Windows Media Player or Mac's built-in iTunes).

In the following sections, I fill you in on three ways you can share your music after you export it.

Burning CDs

You may want to record your Sibelius files to a CD so that they can be played back through any audio CD player. In order to record CDs (called *burning*), you need a CD drive that records. All recent PCs and Macs have drives that record, so unless your computer was built before about 1999, chances are, you're covered.

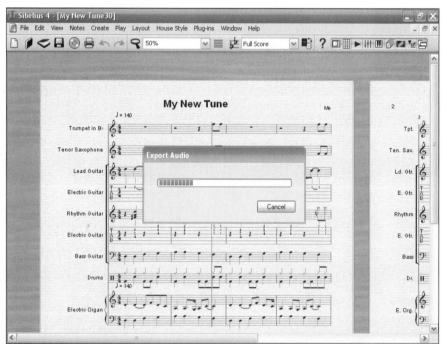

Figure 8-4: The progress of the export.

CD alphabet soup

The array of acronyms for CD players, recorders, and the discs they use can be confusing. Basically, there are three different CD drive types:

- **CD-ROM:** Only reads or plays CDs

- **CD-R (sometimes called CD+R):** Lets you write (copy data to) a CD only once

- **CD-RW:** Lets you write to the disc more than once

Add DVD capability to the mix, and it gets even more complicated. A DVD drive can hold much more data, but has essentially the same three functions:

- **DVD-ROM:** Read-only

- **DVD-R:** Write once

- **DVD-RW:** Write many

The DVD+R is a write-once disc that, in some configurations since 2004, has a much higher capacity than the DVD-R. DVD+R and DVD-R drives are not compatible, but may be both used in a DVD+-RW hybrid drive.

As a rule, if your computer has a DVD burner (that is, it can record on DVD-R or DVD+R discs), it can burn on a CD-R disc.

If you're on a PC, your digital audio will be exported in the WAV format. You can record WAV files to CDs, but you need some software to do so. An excellent piece of software that does a myriad number of things with CDs and DVDs is Roxio's Easy Media Creator 10 (available from www.roxio.com). Creator comes with a host of applications, and it can do practically anything with CD audio and DVD video, including record and clean up old LPs and tapes or capture live video from your camera or TV.

Apple makes it easy for Mac users: All the software you need to burn your new AIFF file is built into the system — there's nothing more you need to do. (Go ahead and gloat — you know you want to.)

Podcasting

Apple makes podcasting easy for Mac users, especially with GarageBand (www.apple.com/ilife/garageband), a multifunction audio and music creation program developed by Apple for Mac OS X as part of its iLife suite. Because Apple invented the iPod and iTunes, it's a natural that the Mac OS X platform would be the easiest way to make podcasts. Just use the Export MIDI function (see the "MIDI" section, later in this chapter), and then open the file using GarageBand. Making the podcast is a snap.

The complete process for making your own podcasts is a little involved for me to get into here, but if you want more information, check out *Podcasting For Dummies,* by Tee Morris, Evo Terra, Dawn Miceli, and Drew Domkus (Wiley). Also, Apple has some great tutorial videos on its site that help you step through the process. Its iLife Multimedia Tutorials series (www.apple.com/support/ilife/tutorials/index.html) covers every product in the iLife series, including GarageBand, iPhoto, iMovie, and iTunes. The tutorial video that shows you how to use GarageBand to create your own podcast is at: www.apple.com/support/ilife/tutorials/garageband/gb3-1.html. (And if you still get stuck, Apple has a lot of help at www.apple.com/support/ to help you figure out where you went wrong.)

If you open your tune with another software, you won't have the same sampled sounds, so it may sound quite different. For example, if you export from Sibelius to GarageBand, you won't hear Sibelius's KONTAKT sampled instruments — you'll automatically be using Apple's GarageBand instruments. This usually isn't a problem, unless you use a very specific instrument set, such as ethnic or unusual instruments for your sounds.

If you're on a PC, never fear: You can still make podcasts. Open the WAV file you just made with a sound editing software like Sound Forge (www.sonycreativesoftware.com/products/soundforgefamily.asp), or use the Export MIDI function (see the "MIDI" section, later in this chapter), and then open the file using a music software like SONAR (www.cakewalk.com) or Cubase (www.steinberg.net). Then you can save the file in the proper MP3 format for use with MP3 players (such as the iPod), Web browsers, and practically any audio product out there today.

A great Web site for locating free podcasting creation software is the Podcasting Software section (www.podcastingnews.com/topics/Podcasting_Software.html) of Podcasting News (www.podcastingnews.com). It has a great selection of free Windows and Mac podcasting software for publishing podcasts.

Making your own ringtones

Buying ringtones is expensive. The cell companies, online stores, and record companies all want to keep it that way, because the extra revenue from these bits of tunes adds up to big-time bucks, a multibillion dollar industry. But you don't have to pay to have your music tracks or legally acquired MP3s become ringtones. Putting a slice of a digital music track on your phone is actually very simple (and free, especially if you wrote the song).

Basically, you need four things:

- ✔ A cellphone that has MP3 ringtone support

- ✔ The digital track you want to use as the ringtone — either a CD you own, an MP3 you legally acquired, or a ditty you wrote yourself

- ✔ A way of transferring the ringtone from your computer to the phone — instant messaging (IM), e-mail, Bluetooth, USB, and so on

- ✔ Audio editing software that lets you export your clip to MP3 format

In addition to the audio software programs I mention in this book, like Sound Forge, free sound editing programs like Audacity (`http://audacity.sourceforge.net`) do this as well. Audacity works on Windows, Mac, and Linux. But if you use Audacity, you need to get the LAME library (`http://lame.buanzo.com.ar`). LAME is a free downloadable MP3 codec that allows Audacity to encode in the MP3 format. The commercial sound software packages, like Sound Forge, already have all the encoding you need.

If you created your future ringtone as a score in Sibelius, export it to audio by choosing File⇨Export⇨Audio. Then you need to use audio editing software to convert it to MP3 format — Sibelius won't do that.

If you're creating your ringtone from a CD, rip the song you want as a WAV (Windows) or AIFF (Mac) file, then use your audio editing software to convert it to MP3 format.

Then transfer the MP3 to your phone. If your phone has Bluetooth capability or a USB connection it may be just as simple as connecting to your phone from your computer and putting the ringtone on your phone, perhaps in the `Audio` folder (if it has one). Then just select the new ringtone in the same way you'd change your ringtone, using your Tools or Options menu.

If you don't have USB or Bluetooth, you may be able to e-mail or text the file to your phone as an attachment. Then change the options of your phone to use the attachment as your new ringtone.

If you don't have these options, or can't figure it out, there are Web sites that do it for you, sometimes for a fee, and sometimes for free. Some of the more popular sites are

- ✔ **MyxerTones (`www.myxertones.com`):** Free to use, but gives you a bunch of extra features if you sign up.

- ✔ **Mobile17 (`www.mobile17.com`):** Offers compatibility with a lot of different types of cellphones, but the signup and configuration section take a little time.

✔ **Fun For Mobile (www.funformobile.com/pages/ringtone/ uploadRingtone.php):** Has a free ringtone uploader that works well, plus a lot of funny ringtone pix, voices, and sounds available. (Be sure when you type the URL into your Web browser that you follow the capitalization exactly as I've listed it. If you don't, the page may not load.)

An extra bonus of Roxio's Easy Media Creator (see earlier in this chapter) is that it's bundled with Xingtone (www.xingtone.com), software to create your own personal ringtone using your new tune. And if you get fancy, you can even build and sell your ringtone creations through Xingtone's Web site (www.xingtone.com/mstoresamples/creator).

Be careful about which sites you give your cellphone number to, and be sure to read the fine print. Some free ringtone sites get your cell number to sell to spammers and advertisers. And there's nothing more irritating than paying phone charges for cellphone spam.

Many cellphones aren't able to download homemade ringtones. Check the model numbers listed in the ringtone software documentation to make sure your phone qualifies. Also, confirm that your phone can access the Internet — if it doesn't, you won't have any way to send your ringtones to your phone.

Outputting Your Music to Other Formats

You can output your score into other formats, such as ASCII tab, graphics, and MIDI. Outputting to other formats is a great way to get your tune out of Sibelius and into the music world.

ASCII TAB

ASCII is a computer format that's as old as the computer itself. It's a bare-bones file format that doesn't use graphics but is universally recognized by every kind of computer and software out there. In music, *ASCII TAB* is a file format used for writing guitar and bass guitar tabs using ASCII numbers, letters, and symbols.

To export your guitar and bass part to ASCII TAB, choose File⇨Export⇨ASCII Tab. Select where you want to save it, and you'll end up with a no-frills text file that looks like the one shown in Figure 8-5. ASCII TAB is the only universal file format for representing guitar tablature. It's primarily used for sharing tab via the Internet. It's ugly, but it works.

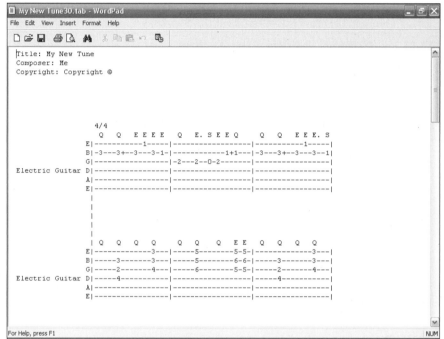

Graphics

Having a copy of your score in a graphics format is very useful. For example, sometimes I export a part to JPG or PDF, and then e-mail it to a musician who wants to look over his part before a gig or recording session. Graphics formats are also very useful for publications, such as books, magazines, or newspapers.

If you want to save your score or a part in a recognized digital graphics format, choose File⇨Export⇨Graphics. The Export Graphics dialog box (shown in Figure 8-6) appears. Here you indicate where you want to save the file and whether you want every page or just some pages formatted.

If you're not sure what graphics format to save your score in, pick the one with the highest resolution, as shown in the Dots per Inch drop-down list in the upper-right corner. As a general rule, the higher the resolution, the better quality the graphic output will be. Most computer systems will read most of these formats, but JPG, TIFF, and PDF are the most common and accessible graphics formats.

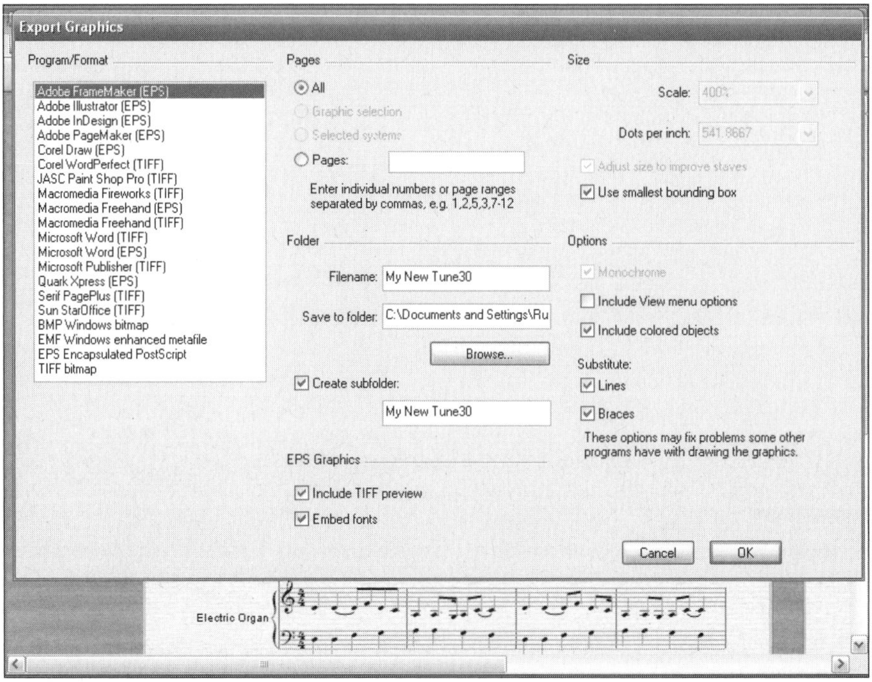

Figure 8-6:
The Export
Graphics
dialog box.

MIDI

In Chapter 16, I give you some great tips and tricks on how to sync your tune with MIDI programs to make it really start to shine. In this section, I show you how to export your opus to MIDI.

To export your tune into standard MIDI format, choose File➪Export➪MIDI. The Export MIDI File dialog box appears, letting you choose where to save the MIDI file (see Figure 8-7).

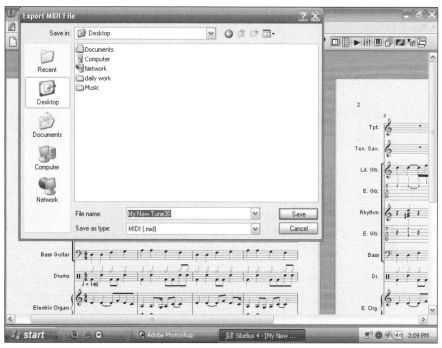

Figure 8-7:
The Export
MIDI File
dialog box.

This export procedure saves your file in simple MIDI format, which can then
be opened by DAW or music creation software (like SONAR, ACID Pro, or
Cubase). When you've opened the tune in one of these (or other MIDI) creation applications, the alterations you can do to the tune are limitless. You
can use all the plug-in sounds, instruments, and sound effects I describe in
Chapter 6, then output the file again to digital audio, for burning to a CD.

In Figure 8-8 you can see a MIDI output opened by SONAR Home Studio 6.

Figure 8-8:
A MIDI
output in
SONAR
Home
Studio 6.

After your tune is in MIDI format and opened by a real MIDI music creation program, you can change the sound of the instruments or add special sounds, like VSTi synthesizer plug-ins, to spice up the tune and make it sound more like a professional recording. In most DAW/sequencing programs, you can even record a vocal track directly into the program.

VST stands for Virtual Studio Technology, which is an interface standard developed by Steinberg for connecting audio synthesizer and effect plug-ins to audio editors and hard-disk recording systems. And VSTi stands for Virtual Studio Technology instruments, which were also developed by Steinberg, but the *i* stands for "instrument," like a softsynth or sampler to distinguish it from a plug-in processor effect, like a compressor, reverb, or delay.

After you make alterations to the MIDI file, you can save it to be used by a digital audio program for burning to a CD (see "Burning CDs," earlier in this chapter).

Manuscript paper

In Chapter 10, I go over the ins and outs of using the Sibelius manuscript paper formats (score paper). If you've created a tune that you'll be using as template for a lot of other works in the future, you can save that tune as manuscript paper. Then that tune will show up as a listed type of score paper when you begin to build a new composition.

To save your tune as manuscript paper, choose File➪Export➪Manuscript Paper. The box shown in Figure 8-9 appears. Click Yes.

I don't recommend using the Export➪Manuscript Paper function a lot. It clutters up the Sibelius-supplied score-paper formats and makes it harder to find the paper you want.

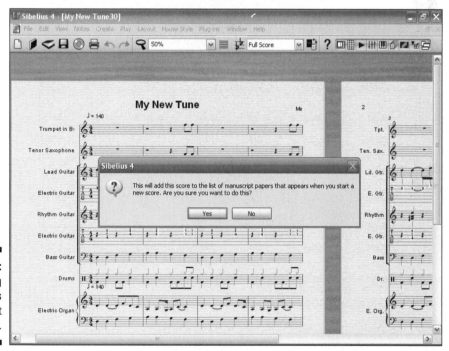

Figure 8-9:
Exporting
your tune as
manuscript
paper.

Printing Your Music

Long ago — long before the CD, podcasting, or the Internet — music was communicated from one musician to another via the printed page. Music notation evolved to allow this communication to develop and flourish. One musician in another town or village could play the music written by the great Beethoven by reading a piece of music.

You may not need or want to print your tune. But if you want others to play it, or if you're writing a piece for a band or student ensemble, you need to print parts out for each member of the band.

The demo version of Sibelius 5 included on the CD only prints out the first page of your score or part. If you need to print out more than one page, you'll need to get a full version of Sibelius, the educational version, or G7 (the tablature version of Sibelius).

Make sure you have a printer hooked up and ready to go.

Printing the score

To print a score, start by opening My New Tune 15 on the CD. You can print the score right away by clicking on the printer icon in the upper-left of the screen (see Figure 8-10).

A word about paper stock

Everyone wants to save money, and with the price of paper these days, you may be tempted to buy the cheapest printing or copy paper you can find — like the 20-pound stock on sale.

Don't.

Musicians are used to parts that are written on heavy, large-format manuscript paper, and although you may not be able to afford a large-format printer just for printing your music (they can run anywhere from $1,200 to $5,000), the least you can do is print the part on heavier paper stock.

Get a copy paper that has a weight of at least 32 pounds — this information is on the label. If your printer can handle it, you may want to go with a 67-pound cover stock in a light cream or Bristol color. The off-white helps reduce the glare of the page in stage lights, and if your music is used by a school band or is good enough to be inserted into the library of a working orchestra, a stiffer paper stock will help the music last longer.

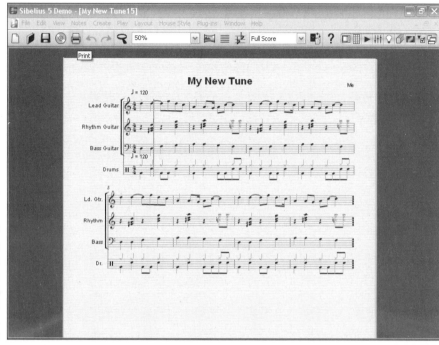

Figure 8-10:
Click the
printer icon
to — you
guessed
it! — print.

You can also print by choosing File⇨Print. The Print dialog box (shown in Figure 8-11) appears. This dialog box is handy if you're connected to multiple printers, or if you have a specific way you want it to print out. (If you click the printer icon [refer to Figure 8-10], you don't get the Print dialog box — the document just prints.)

If you have a big score that would be more readable if it were printed sideways on the page (called *landscape*) rather than the normal, vertical way (called *portrait*), you can change the direction of the printing. Just choose Layout⇨Document Setup, and click the Landscape button. A preview pane will show how the document will look. Click OK if you're happy with it. You can always change it back to portrait layout at any time.

Extracting the parts for others to play

The real benefit of a software notation system is its ability to print out the parts to a tune in the right keys for all the instruments. You can print out individual parts one part at a time, or all at once.

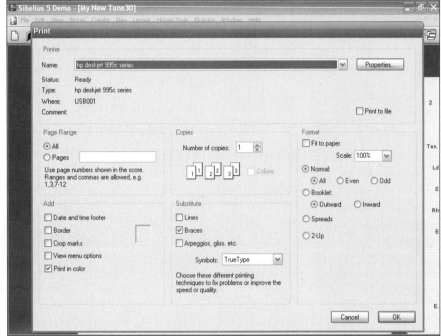

Figure 8-11:
The Print
dialog box
gives you
options.

To print out one part:

1. **Open the My New Tune 15 file.**

2. **Select the drop-down list that says "Full Score" and select "Lead Guitar," as shown in Figure 8-12.**

   The lead guitar part is now selected (see Figure 8-13). And you can print it just as you did the full score (see the preceding section).

To print out all the parts at once:

1. **Open the My New Tune 15 file.**

2. **Choose File➪Print All Parts.**

   The Print dialog box (refer to Figure 8-11) appears.

3. **Select your printer and whatever options you prefer, and click OK.**

   All the parts print individually.

When you select an individual part for printing, any changes you make to that part will be reflected on the full score. That way, if you see something you want to change on the part that you didn't catch on the score, you can change it and not have to worry about going back to the full score and duplicating the change.

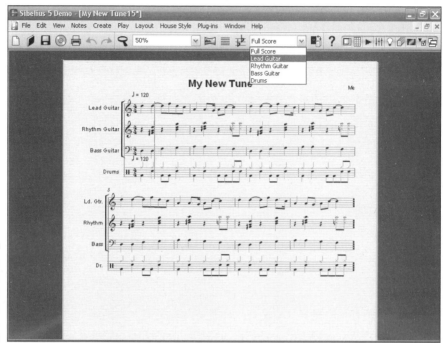

Figure 8-12:
Select the
lead guitar
part from
the menu.

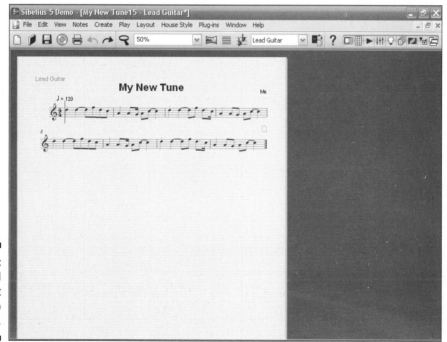

Figure 8-13:
The lead
guitar part
ready to
print.

Chapter 9

Sharing the Love: Internet Publishing

In This Chapter
▶ Publishing your music on the Internet
▶ Finding indie artist sites that distribute music
▶ Copyrighting your music

So you're writing your own original music, and you want others to share the fruits of your labor of love. You can keep burning CDs and emailing MP3s, but soon you're going to get bitten by the mass audience bug. Internet publishing may be the thing for you.

Publishing your music is very exciting. And with the Internet, scores that have been created with music notation software can easily be posted and disseminated. But publishing your music online does have some pitfalls, so in this chapter, I fill you in on the pros and cons of publishing on the Web.

Weighing Your Publishing Options

Along with everything else that changed in the music business with the advent of the computer, the music publishing business changed, too. It still exists in its original form — sheet music is created and sold in music stores, and orchestra, band, and choir folios are printed and distributed. But now nonprofessionals have the chance to expose their music to a much wider audience than was possible in the past.

Many free, composer-participant Web sites have been springing up to provide a forum for composers to share their works. Free public domain music sites allow a budding composer to reach a wider audience than ever before, and independent Internet distribution of music gives unknown artists the chance to share in the commercial rewards of their music.

In the following sections, I show you some of your options for publishing your music online.

Scorch

Sibelius has a very cool way to share your music on the Internet called Scorch, and it's free! Scorch is a free Web browser plug-in that allows you to view, play back, change keys and instruments, and even print scores directly from the Internet — whether you have Sibelius or not.

Used in conjunction with its online sheet music store, SibeliusMusic (www.sibeliusmusic.com), you can sell your Sibelius scores online (or give them away free, if you want). Anyone with the Scorch plug-in can read your music right on the site.

You can get the Scorch plug-in at www.sibelius.com/products/scorch. Scorch requires that you have the following:

- ✔ **On Windows:** Windows XP Service Pack 2 or Windows Vista; Internet Explorer 6 or later, Mozilla Firefox, or Netscape 7 or later; and 20MB of available hard drive space

- ✔ **On Mac:** Mac OS X 10.4 or later; Safari, Mozilla Firefox, or Netscape 7 or later; and 20MB of available hard drive space

When you have the Scorch toolbar plug-in installed, you can access any Sibelius score on the Sibelius Music site — view it, print it, even listen to it in the background while you work.

Sibelius has two sites for publishing music, SibeliusMusic and SibeliusEducation (www.sibeliuseducation.com). SibeliusMusic is primarily for music, and SibeliusEducation is used for distributing teaching materials and resources.

You can easily publish your score on SibeliusMusic.com or SibeliusEducation.com right from your Sibelius software. Just choose File⇨Publish on SibeliusMusic.com or File⇨Publish on SibeliusEducation.com.

Please don't self-publish "My New Tune," the Sibelius tune you create using my templates on the CD. Although I've had fun building it, it's copyrighted by Wiley Publishing.

You can also build your own eBay-like Web music store, using Sibelius Music Stores (www.sibeliusmusic.com/cgi-bin/mystore.pl). People visiting your site will be prompted to download Scorch, and then they'll be able to see and hear your music online, and purchase it if they want.

What's so great about independence?

In a regular record deal or distribution deal, musicians only make $1 to $2 per CD, if they ever get paid by their label. Often the record companies deduct all the expenses that were incurred in producing and distributing the CD before the artists get their share. This means that the musicians are usually the last in line to get any money from their project. Independent record labels and distributors commonly sell many fewer units than their bigger counterparts, but musicians make more per CD (up to $12 per CD) and have a say as to how the music is used.

Indie publishing

When you've gone over to the "dark side" and become a professional composer, the Internet offers even more potential. Independent music publishers are creating cooperatives and profit sharing sites that try to break free of the rigid record company control of the past. These sites offer downloads to purchase and CDs to order, and at the same time afford the artist greater control of the product and its distribution than the record companies did.

In the following sections, I show you how some of the indie publishers work, and what differentiates them.

artistShare

artistShare (www.artistshare.com) was founded in the fall of 2000 by musician and computer consultant Brian Camelio. It's intended to be a place where fans fund the projects of their favorite artists in exchange for the privilege of "participating" in the creative process.

Particularly popular with jazz musicians, artistShare allows artists and fans (called *participants*) from all over the world to connect with each other directly, by paying artists upfront for their projects. This allows the fans to experience the excitement of the creative process, and helps independent composers and performers secure the funding to create new works and distribute them.

For a small charge, often the price of a CD, the participants receive the work when it's completed, as well as extra content (such as rehearsal and performance videos, copies of the sheet music, and access to streaming videos).

CD Baby

CD Baby (www.cdbaby.com) is a very popular online record store that sells CDs by independent musicians. Founded in 1998 in Portland, Oregon, it's now the largest seller of independent CDs on the Web.

CD Baby says that its employees listen to every CD the site sells before it sells it. By eliminating the distributor, CD Baby sells CDs that come directly from the musicians — warehousing them, selling them, and paying the musicians directly.

Other indie distributors

Numerous commercial independent distributors are popping up with different business models — and they often come and go quickly. Some resell CDs from small or unknown artists. Some specialize in a particular genre of music (for example, ethnic music). Others are strictly online distributors that provide streaming audio/video or MP3 downloads only.

IDN Music (www.idnmusic.com) is an online catalog of music by independent bands. It offers both CDs and MP3s of several thousand bands of all genres, and that list is growing rapidly.

A good site that keeps up with the tides of indie music is Indie Music (www.indiemusic.com). Also, Indie-Music.com (www.indie-music.com) maintains a directory of current independent labels and artists.

Looking at Copyright Issues

No issue is hotter or more controversial in this era of digital expression than the issue of copyright. Huge teams of lawyers are gainfully employed representing companies that want to protect the copyrights owned by their client companies, and stop free downloading and illegal distribution of music.

The Authors Guild (www.authorsguild.org) and Electronic Frontier Foundation (www.eff.org) are two organizations created to help preserve the rights of authors, musicians, and digital artists.

You need to be aware of what your rights and responsibilities are as a composer when you begin to distribute your music on the Internet. This is important, because, as soon as you give your tune away or you post it for the public to download, it's gone.

Keeping legal control of your tune may not be that important to you. If any of the following describes you, you can ignore the issue of copyright (but I recommend reading this section anyway, just to know what you're giving up):

- ✔ You know you're not going to be a professional composer/songwriter in the future.
- ✔ You feel that your music should be free to all, shared by anyone who will enjoy it.
- ✔ You think your tunes aren't good enough.

If you're seriously turning pro

If you're really considering becoming a professional composer or songwriter, you can take advantage of some excellent resources to get up to speed on issues like fair use and copyright infringement. When I was studying music business at the Berklee College of Music, I used Sidney Shemel and M. William Krasilovsky's *This Business of Music,* which was one of the first nonlegal texts to describe what a working musician (or composer) needs to know about agents, contracts, recording deals, and so on.

Now in its tenth edition, it's still the definitive reference source for the music industry.

Another source for advice is the good ol' musician's union. The American Federation of Musicians (www.afm.org) has been giving advice and protecting composers' rights for over 110 years. With over 250 local chapters in the United States, you can probably find a chapter in your area (the union's Web site lets you search by state).

If you might ever want to go pro, if you might ever want to make some money off your music, or if you might be wrong about how good you are, you need to retain control of your tune.

Volunteer Lawyers for the Arts (www.vlany.org) offers free and low-cost legal services and information to artists and arts organizations in every artistic discipline, including music. Access to VLA's pro bono legal services is available to low-income artists and nonprofit arts organizations.

Registering your music with the U.S Copyright Office

The U.S. Copyright Office (www.copyright.gov) is the original office of public record for copyright registration and deposit of copyright material. *Copyright* is the protection provided by the laws of the United States to the authors of "original works of authorship," which includes literary, dramatic, musical, artistic, and certain other intellectual works.

Copyright protection is available to both published and unpublished works, allowing a composer or a music publisher to reproduce the work in printed sheet music form and on tapes, CDs, or records, as well as to broadcast or Web-stream the music.

The process for registering copyright for a sound recording is a little different than the process of registering copyright for a published piece of sheet music. Sheet music (called a *performing arts work*) uses Form PA, whereas sound recordings use Form SR. But both cost the same ($45) to register. For complete details on the different steps, go to www.copyright.gov.

International copyright

There is no such thing as an "international copyright" that automatically protects a composer's work throughout the world. Protection depends on the national laws of each country. However, copyright laws are standardized through international conventions that offer protection to foreign works under certain conditions.

International copyright treaties and conventions such as the Berne Union for the Protection of Literary and Artistic Property (Berne Convention)

and the Universal Copyright Convention (UCC) have greatly simplified the chore of registering copyright in multiple countries. Not all countries are signatories to these conventions, however. Copyright Witness (www.copyright witness.com) is a U.K. site that helps to answer questions about international copyright and has an automated self-assessment to assist you in determining if you need it.

Communing with Creative Commons

An innovative approach to the problems of copyright in the digital age is being pursued by Creative Commons (www.creativecommons.org), whose motto is, "Share, reuse, and remix — legally." A nonprofit organization, Creative Commons provides free tools that let authors, scientists, artists, and educators easily mark their creative work with the freedoms they want it to carry.

With a Creative Commons license, you keep your copyright but allow people to copy and distribute your work, as long as they give you credit — and only on the conditions you specify. You can specify your copyright terms and even offer your work free, with no conditions, to be placed in the public domain.

Anything in the *public domain* can be used freely by anyone whether for commercial or noncommercial purposes. Original works enter the public domain when the copyright has expired, such as is the case with music that is very old.

Making sure you don't infringe on someone else's copyright

With the use of samples and the ease with which music can be copied and pasted from other sources, you can pretty easily (and unknowingly) infringe upon someone else's artistic expression. If you're using purchased or downloaded samples in your work, you need to determine their copyright status.

If you distribute your tune with major parts copied from somewhere else, you could get in hot water with the original copyright owner. Most sample CDs are *free use,* which means you can use them in any project without having to pay a royalty or credit the source. If this applies to the music you want to use, the CD or download site may say *royalty free.*

If downloading samples or any music software from the Internet, always read the Terms of Use, which usually appear at the bottom of the page. After you cut through the legalese, you'll find information about how you can (or can't) use clips.

If you record music from another source (for example, a concert or a broadcast) and then use it for sampling, you could be in violation of copyright. You need permission from the artist to sample his music.

Part IV
Getting Fancy: Building Your Tune from Scratch

"Composing with this software is so much like composing with a band. Even the drum preset launches late and is usually a little buggy."

In this part . . .

In Part IV, you start to compose. Chapter 10 shows you how to build your own original piece of music from the ground up using digital music score paper, as well as how to change the parts of the score paper. In Chapter 11, you discover how to use the mouse and keyboard for basic note entry and editing, and find out how to create text information for your score.

Chapter 12 shows you how to compose music using your instruments — such as a MIDI keyboard, guitar, and bass — rather than just the mouse. Chapter 13 introduces you to the drum part and shows you how to add a funky back beat with drum samples.

Chapter 10

What's the Score? Creating Your Score Paper

*M*usic manuscript paper comes in many different forms. It can be a big score page with lots of orchestra instruments on it, a small score page for a combo with a singer, or individual sheets of music for each musician.

The composer uses manuscript paper to compose music, and it's called the *score paper.* The finished composition is called the *score,* and it can be any size, depending upon the size of musical group that the composition is intended for.

Back in the day, all composing was done with paper and pencil (and lots of erasers). Now with musical notation software, you compose right on the computer and can immediately see what you wrote on your computer screen. But digital composing still uses some old terminology. The terms *manuscript paper* and *score paper* are still used, but now they describe the area on your screen into which you input your notes.

The heart of the music composition project is the score paper. In this chapter, I explain why the score paper is important, how to choose the right paper for your project, and how to change the score to suit your needs, by changing the tempo, adding instruments, and transposing notes.

Choosing the Manuscript Paper

Your musical notation software will ask you what type of band or other group of instruments you'll be composing for before you write your first note. Having to make this decision upfront may seem like an unnecessary distraction, but it's designed to save you time in the end. You may be writing a piece for your school choir, a garage band, or a solo piano work.

If you take the time to pick the right manuscript paper before you start, you'll be ahead of the game, and more able to easily get your ideas into the computer. You can easily change your paper as you go, as you decide to add instruments or remove them. But anything that makes it easier to actually compose and be creative is a good thing, right?

Picking your score paper

As soon as you start Sibelius, you're asked whether you want to open a piece of music you were working on previously or start a new score. (Some other options you don't need to worry about right now are also presented.) When you have Sibelius open, you can close the tune you're working on at any time and start a new score by either clicking on the New Score icon, in the upper-right corner, or by choosing File➪New. The New Score dialog box (shown in Figure 10-1) appears.

The New Score dialog box is really made up of five screens. It guides you through the creation of your score. You can click Next to continue on to the next screen, or you can click Finish at any point along the way — you don't have to make all the decisions about your score at the very beginning if you don't want to.

In the following sections, I fill you in on each of these steps in more detail.

Instrumentation

The first decision you have to make when starting a new score is which instruments will play the music you're writing (known as the *instrumentation*). If you're writing for a standard ensemble, like a band or choir, use one of Sibelius's built-in manuscript papers. The Sibelius-supplied manuscript papers have a lot of helpful defaults (such as special instrument name formats, suitable staff sizes, and so on) already set up for you.

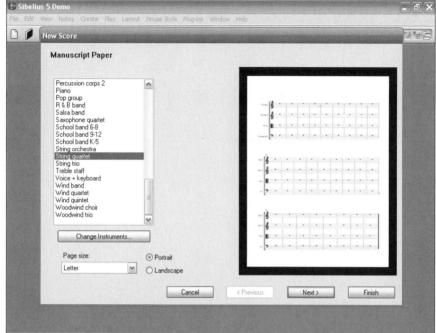

Figure 10-1:
The New
Score dialog
box is
where you
pick your
score paper.

If you're not sure yet what instruments you're going to write for, try to pick a manuscript paper that is closest to what type of music you're going to write. For example, if you're writing a piece for string orchestra, pick one of the String manuscript papers. If it's not exactly what you want, you can add or subtract instruments later (see the "Adding or deleting instruments" section, later in this chapter).

You can also select Blank as your manuscript paper, but then you'll be asked if you want to add your instrument at that time. If you say yes, the Instruments dialog box (shown in Figure 10-2) appears. The Instruments dialog box lists many types of instrumentation in alphabetical order. Just like selecting manuscript paper in a music store, you can choose between different shapes and sizes, or pick paper that is preprinted with standard groups of instruments.

You can add new instruments whenever you like — you don't need to decide what they'll be at the very start of your piece. But you need to pick at least one initial instrument when you create your manuscript paper. Otherwise, you'll have nothing to write your music for!

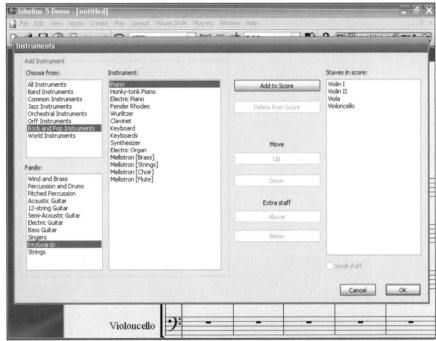

Figure 10-2: Selecting your instruments.

Because Sibelius knows about so many instruments (more than 460), the Choose From list at the top left of the Instruments dialog box shows you more convenient selections from the whole set. By default, Sibelius shows you Common Instruments, which number around 85. However, if you're itching to write for more obscure instruments, such as quint bassoon, ondes martenot, or hurdy-gurdy, select All Instruments to display the complete set. If you're writing specifically for band, jazz, or orchestra ensembles, choose the appropriate option from the Choose From list to see standard instruments used in these ensembles.

Don't worry if you can't find a particular or unusual instrument. Sibelius even lets you design your own instruments!

House style

The second screen of the New Score dialog box (shown in Figure 10-3) deals with house style — how a printed score looks is defined by its house style. You can think of the *house style* as the look or appearance of your score. Different publishers have their own house styles.

You can change the type of fonts you use, the size of the staves and notes, and even the thickness of the bar lines.

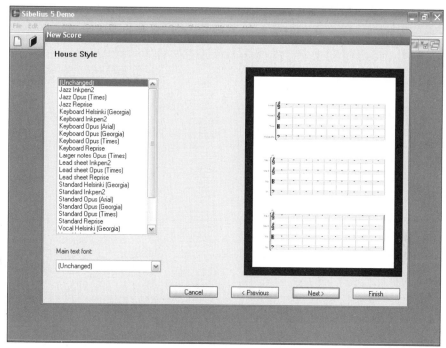

Figure 10-3:
Choosing
your house
style.

Time signatures

The third screen of the New Score dialog box (shown in Figure 10-4) allows you to choose a time signature and set the tempo of your new score. This is where you'll choose whether you want your tune to be in 4/4, 3/4, 19/8, or whatever.

Ninety percent of music is written in either 4/4 or 3/4. Sibelius defaults to 4/4, and that's what I have you use for *My New Tune.* You can change the time signature at other points in the score, but you need to set the time signature at the beginning of your tune.

Complex music often has several time signature changes within the piece of music. This screen just sets the *initial* time signature for your piece of music. You can change the time signature anyplace in your score, if you like, but you need to pick a time signature to start with.

Key signatures

The fourth screen of the New Score dialog box (shown in Figure 10-5) allows you to choose a key signature. The key signatures that appear at the start of each system are automatic. They're adjusted to suit the current clef, transposed for *transposing instruments* (instruments that don't play in the key of C, such as trumpets and saxophones) and omitted from those instruments that don't usually use key signatures (like percussion instruments).

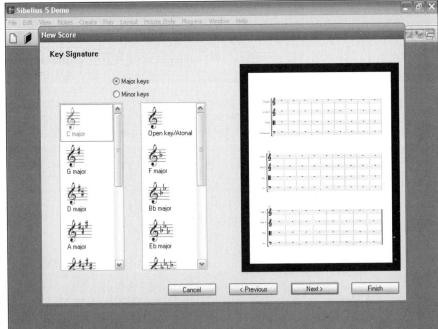

You can switch between major and minor keys using the radio buttons on the left-hand side of the dialog box. Like the time signature, you can specify the key signature at the start of the piece and change it anyplace within the tune.

You may know in what key your new opus will be, or you may not. Picking Open Key/Atonal may be a safe bet in that case. If you choose Open Key/Atonal, the software won't pick a key signature for your score.

You can go back later and change the starting key signature, when you've decided what key you want the piece to be in. To do this, hit Esc (to make sure you don't have anything selected by the mouse), choose Create⇨Key Signature, select the key signature you want (say, E Major), and then click at the start of your score. You can also use this method to create a key change anywhere in the score with the mouse.

Score info

The fifth and final screen of the New Score dialog box (shown in Figure 10-6) lets you enter some text, such as the title of your piece, the name of the composer and lyricist, and copyright information. This text is automatically added to the first page of the score. If you select the Create Title Page check box, Sibelius adds the title and composer to an extra title page that appears at the beginning of the piece.

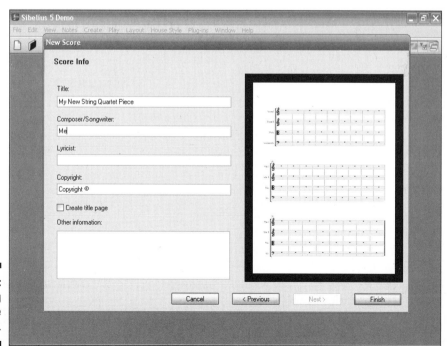

Figure 10-6:
Inputting
your score
information.

Working with ready-made formats

One of the greatest features about using music notation software is using the software's built-in score paper formats. Using their manuscript paper format is a lot easier than building one entirely from scratch, because everything is already set up for you — especially because all the instruments in the right keys are already laid out on the score. In the following sections, I introduce you to some of the formats for different types of music.

If you look in the Example Scores area of your Sibelius installation, you can find some of these examples. You can then load them into Sibelius and hear what they sound like.

Lead sheets

A *lead sheet* (see Figure 10-7) is another term for a piece of sheet music that contains just the bare bones of a tune. It usually has three parts: the song's melody written in traditional music notation, lyrics written as text below the staff, and the chord symbols placed above the staff. Sometimes a line of guitar tablature is added to the lead sheet.

The lead sheet is considered bare bones because all information about a particular arrangement or performance of a song has been removed. Lead sheets are often used by small jazz ensembles, because the musicians will improvise on the melody and chord progression (called the *changes,* in jazz).

The drum part, backup vocals, arranged harmonies — all these elements that make it a real piece of music — are not included in the lead sheet. It's intended to just capture the pure essence of a song.

If you decide to copyright your tune, a lead sheet is usually the form of a song to which copyright is applied. (You can find more information about copyright in Chapter 9.)

Because lead sheets are traditionally hand copies, they use somewhat different conventions from other musical scores. For example, lead sheets traditionally show the clef, time signature, and key signature only at the beginning.

Listen to *Jazz Lead Sheet* on the CD at `Author/Chapter 10/Audio Examples/Jazz Lead Sheet.mp3`.

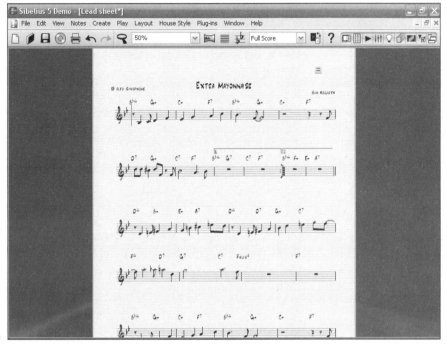

Figure 10-7:
A jazz lead sheet with melody and chord changes.

Jazz, rock, pop, and hip hop score paper

What you'll use for score paper for various small bands is quite varied. Most times you'll use a lead sheet, especially for jazz, rock, pop, or hip hop groups. Usually the parts aren't written out for every instrument or singer in a group like this. Often, commercial pop and hip-hop tunes are built in the studio layer by layer, using digital recording software and MIDI tools, without any written music at all.

But you may want to complete a full composition for a small or commercial group. Maybe you're going to have professional musicians at a recording session or performance of your work, and they need parts to play. Maybe you want a youth or school combo to play your tune or arrangement, and you want it to sound a very specific way.

In commercial music, sometimes the tune has already been recorded and a score with parts is created afterward. And here's another great feature of notation software: If you have access to the original composition, you can import the MIDI parts (like the bass line or the drum or guitar part) right into Sibelius or Finale, and build your tune from there.

Figure 10-8 shows the first page of a jazz combo arrangement of a Phil Woods composition called *Clinology*. You can see that there's a lot more detail in this score than a simple lead sheet. From this score you can print out all the parts for the instruments: the trumpet, alto saxophone, piano, keyboard synthesizer, bass, and drums.

Listen to a short clip of Sibelius playing *Clinology* on the CD at `Author/` `Chapter 10/Audio Examples/clinology.mp3`.

A blank rock/pop group score format is shown in Figure 10-9. This is the format I use to build the tune in this book, and it's a very useful and flexible format for rock, pop, funk, and hip-hop tunes.

School ensemble and choir scores

If you're writing for your school band or choir, Sibelius has a bunch of score formats that could work for you. One of the big advantages to using these built-in formats is the way the format automatically gives you the various instruments of a band in the proper transposition. This saves you from having to figure out what instruments you should write for and what keys they transpose into.

Figure 10-10 shows the start of the score for Todd Coleman's choir arrangement of Joyce Kilmer's poem *Trees*. It's written for traditional SATB voices — soprano, alto, tenor, and bass (or baritone) — with piano accompaniment.

Figure 10-8:
The jazz combo score to *Clinology*.

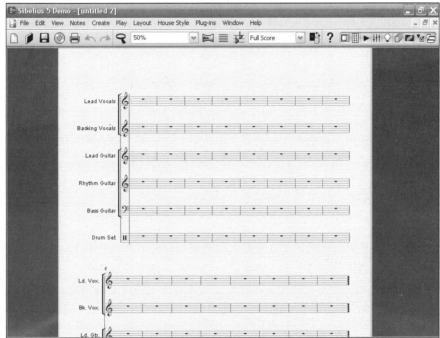

Figure 10-9:
A rock or pop group score format.

Figure 10-10:
Joyce Kilmer's *Trees* arranged by Todd Coleman for choir.

Listen to a short clip of Sibelius playing *Trees* on the CD at `Author/Chapter 10/Audio Examples/trees.mp3`.

Your school's marching or concert band may be just the venue for your new composition. Your notation software, whether it's Finale or Sibelius, will have several different band formats that you can use, including instruments specific to marching bands, like a glockenspiel.

The score paper format does a lot more than just give you a blank notepad on which to write your notes. It shows you the common instruments that play in this type of ensemble, what clef they use, and what keys they play in, if they're transposing instruments. This allows you to write a flute part, for example, and then copy and paste it to the clarinet, and the software will transpose it automatically for you. Just remember to pay attention to the range of the instrument (that the notes aren't too high or too low for the instrument to play); Sibelius will let you know by coloring the offending notes in red.

Jazz big band

Another common school ensemble is the jazz big band. Figure 10-11 shows the first page of the big band piece *In a New York Minute,* by composer Simon Wallace and arranged by James Pearson. It's scored for regular big jazz band instrumentation: five saxophones, four trumpets, four trombones, drums, guitar, vibes, piano, and bass.

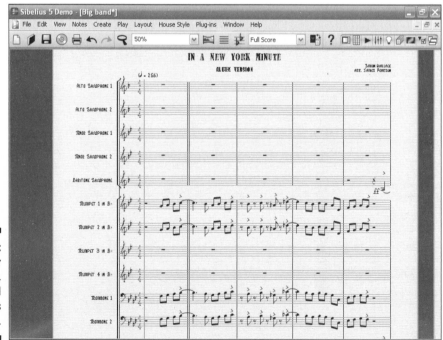

Figure 10-11:
In a New York Minute, arranged by James Pearson.

Listen to a short clip of Sibelius playing *In a New York Minute* on the CD at
`Author/Chapter 10/Audio Examples/nyminute.mp3`.

String and orchestral ensemble score paper

Similar to band instruments like trumpet and saxophone, string instruments
play in a variety of settings and ensemble types. The most common all-strung
setting is the string quartet. Earlier in this chapter, I show you how to use
five steps to build a new piece of music using the string quartet manuscript
paper. The score paper of my new piece, called *My New String Quartet Piece*,
is shown in Figure 10-12 as it appears after the final step. The common instrumentation for a string quartet is two violins, viola, and cello.

Strings are also a vital part of the orchestra. Figure 10-13 is an excerpt from
the score to *Hebrides* showing the string section parts. This screenshot only
shows a part of the full score, because there are so many instruments in a
large orchestra.

Although there are only five different parts listed — two violins, viola, cello,
and contrabass — usually several musicians play each part, making the
string section the largest of the orchestra.

Figure 10-12:
*My New
String
Quartet
Piece* score
paper.

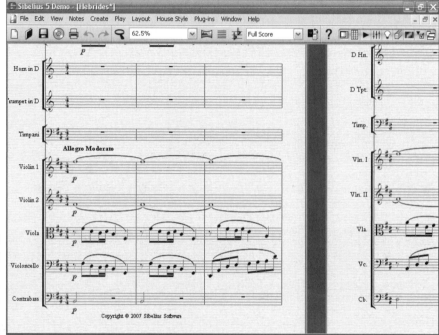

Figure 10-13:
String
section
parts to
Hebrides.

Changing Your Score

Even if you find the perfect score paper, you're going to eventually want to make changes to the score. This section gives you some good pointers on how to do it.

You can't mess up the templates. Do whatever you want to them, and if you're stuck, you can open a new Sibelius template from the CD and start over.

Changing the tempo

The tempo of a piece of music, how fast or slow it goes, is usually indicated by the metronome marking at the beginning of the score. Often, the metronome marking is accompanied by a word or description to help inform the player of how fast the piece should be played.

In this section, I guide you through changing the tempo of the music created in Chapter 7. Start by opening `My New Tune-10-01.sib` on the CD, and change the View to 100 percent.

If you look at the upper left of your score, just above the lead guitar part, you see a quarter note with an equal sign (=) and the number 120. This is called the metronome marking, and it means that the tune should be played at 120 beats per minute, a very common tempo for music. If you click on the number, it turns blue to indicate that it has been selected, as shown in Figure 10-14 (you can't actually see the blue color in this book, but you can see where the selected metronome marking is).

Say you want to make the tune a little faster, to perk it up a bit. After you highlight the metronome marking, double-click it, and your cursor changes to a small line after the 0 in 120. Press the Backspace or Delete key twice, leaving the 1 in place, and type **40** to change the tempo from 120 beats per minute (bpm) to 140 bpm, as shown in Figure 10-15. Press Escape to accept the change.

Listen to My New Tune on the CD at `Author/Chapter 10/Audio Examples/My New Tune-10-02.mp3`.

To hear what it sounds like at the new tempo, press Ctrl+[to rewind the playback. Press the space bar and the tune is now faster! You can open the Sibelius file `My New Tune-10-02.sib` to hear the new tempo, too.

Figure 10-14:
The selected metronome marking.

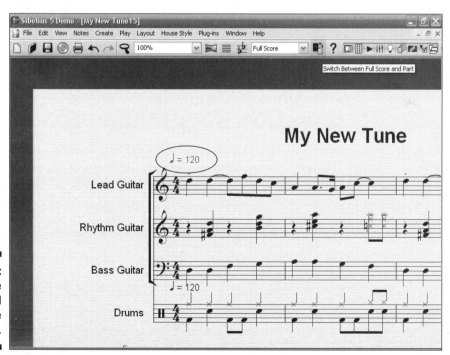

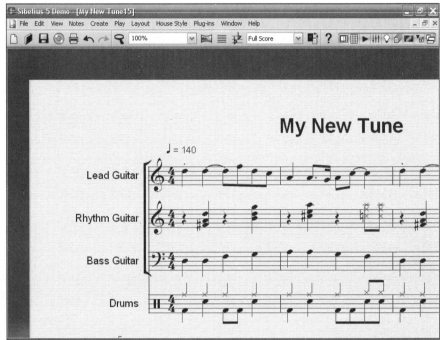

Figure 10-15:
Changing
the tempo
from 120
bpm to
140 bpm.

A metronome marking can also be placed anywhere in a piece of music to change the tempo anytime. But it's *always* placed above the first stave of music.

Adding or deleting instruments

Rarely will your score paper have exactly the instrumentation you want. Most often, you'll start out with a score paper that has just a few of the instruments you want, and then you'll add instruments to fit the type of band.

Adding an organ part

For the sake of illustration, say you want to add an electric organ part, like they used to have in early rock bands. Follow these steps:

1. **Open My New Tune-10-02.sib.**

2. **Choose Create⇨Instruments.**

3. **Under Family, select Keyboards.**

4. **Under Instrument, select Electric Organ.**

   After you double-click Electric Organ, you should see two new entries on the right in the Staves in Score box — one stave for each hand of the organ part (see Figure 10-16).

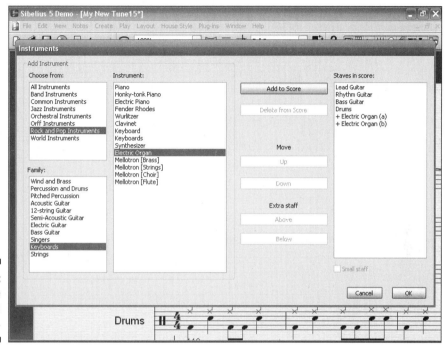

Figure 10-16:
Adding the
electric
organ part.

5. **Click OK.**

   You see your score with a new two-handed organ part added at
   the bottom, as shown in Figure 10-17. This is the same as My New
   Tune-10-03.sib.

6. **Now you need to put some music into the blank staves, so copy the
   bass part to the left hand part of the electric organ.**

   Check out Chapter 7 for detailed instructions on how to copy and
   paste bars.

You can always load My New Tune-10-03.sib and try again. I have the bass
part already copied in My New Tune-10-04.sib.

The organ needs more than just the bass part — this sounds a little boring.
You can copy the lead guitar part to the right hand part of the organ. This
time, highlight the Lead Guitar stave and copy it to the organ's right-hand
stave. (As usual, you can jump ahead by loading My New Tune-10-05.sib
from the CD.)

Figure 10-17:
"My New
Tune" with
the organ
staves
added.

Transposing the bass part

The bass part is a little too low for the organ, for this type of music. So you
may want to transpose the left-hand part of the organ up an octave, so it
sounds better. (I've already done this for you in `My New Tune-10-06.sib`,
if you want to jump ahead.)

1. **Highlight the organ's left-hand stave by clicking on the first bar
   to highlight it, and holding down the Shift key and clicking on the
   last bar.**

2. **Choose Notes⇨Transpose.**

   The Transpose dialog box (shown in Figure 10-18) appears.

3. **Next to Transpose By, select the Interval radio button.**

4. **Under Transpose by Interval, select the Up radio button; in the two
   drop-down lists, select Major/Perfect and Octave.**

5. **Click OK.**

   You see the organ part transposed up an octave, as shown in Figure 10-19.
   Now the left-hand organ part is in a little better-sounding range, and will
   sound nicer.

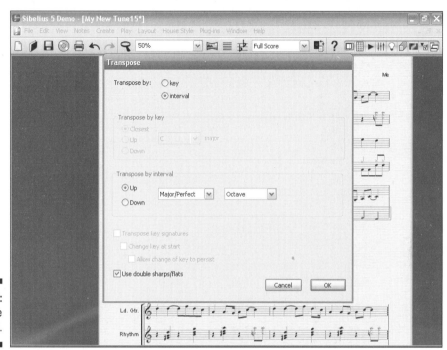

Figure 10-18:
Transpose
by interval.

Figure 10-19:
The organ
part
transposed.

You want to be sure the organ plays all eight bars. So follow these steps:

1. **Highlight the first four bars of the part by clicking on the first bar of the right-hand stave, holding the Shift key, and clicking the fourth bar of the left-hand stave.**

   It should look like Figure 10-20.

2. **While the bars are highlighted, press Ctrl+C (⌘+C).**

3. **Highlight the fifth bar of the right-hand part and press Ctrl+V (⌘+V).**

   This copies the first four bars of both organ staves to the fifth through eighth bars of the tune, as shown in Figure 10-21. (You can also look at the finished organ part by opening `My New Tune10-07.sib` on the CD.)

To hear just the organ part, highlight the organ staves (Ctrl+click/⌘+ click on each stave) and press P. This will play back just the organ part.

Listen to My New Tune on the CD at `Author/Chapter 10/Audio Examples/My New Tune-10-07.mp3`.

Figure 10-20:
Selecting
the organ
part.

Figure 10-21:
The finished
electric
organ part.

Adding horns

In this section, you add a trumpet and tenor saxophone part. I already did the hard part (which isn't so hard), and added the trumpet and tenor staves to the score, in `My New Tune10-08.sib`. If you want to add them yourself, you can do it the same way you add the electric organ part (earlier in this chapter), but this time, select a trumpet and a tenor saxophone, as shown in Figure 10-22 and Figure 10-23.

Simple playback

You can play back any single stave from the score by clicking on a bar and pressing P. The playback will start from that bar and only play the stave highlighted. This technique is very useful when you want to hear just the single part you're working on. If you hold Ctrl (⌘) and click more than one stave, and then press P, you can play back more than one stave. Be sure to hit Esc to unselect, so the next time you play back you'll hear all the instruments.

Figure 10-22:
Adding
the trumpet
and tenor
sax parts.

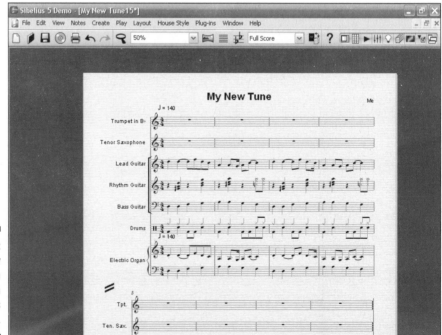

Figure 10-23:
"My New
Tune" with
the horn
staves
added.

You can open `My New Tune10-08.sib` to continue from here.

1. **Choose Window➪Keypad (Ctrl+Alt+K/Option+⌘+K).**

   The Keypad appears.

2. **Highlight the second bar of the trumpet part and click on the eighth note a couple of times until the bar is full of eighth note rests (see Figure 10-24).**

3. **Now put in two F notes at the end of the second trumpet bar.**

   If you're adventurous, try using the Keypad to add the two notes, as shown in Figure 10-25. I get into more detail about adding individual notes in Chapter 11 so if you're not so adventurous, for now just open `My New Tune-10-09.sib` on the CD and continue.

4. **Copy that bar from the trumpet part and paste it to the tenor sax part, as shown in Figure 10-26.**

   Again, you can try it yourself, or just open `My New Tune-10-10.sib` if you want to move on.

5. **Copy the first two bars of both parts and paste three times to fill out the rest of the trumpet and tenor parts, as shown in Figure 10-27.**

   When you're done, it should look like Figure 10-28. I've already done this for you in `My New Tune-10-11.sib`, if you want to open it and compare your version to my version.

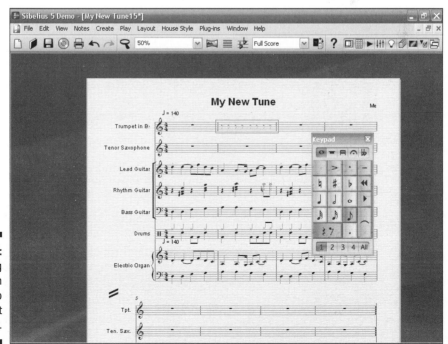

Figure 10-24:
Adding eighth note rests to the trumpet part.

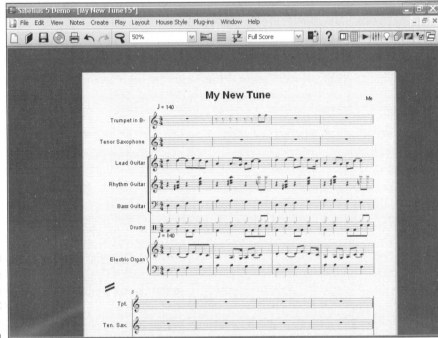

Figure 10-25:
Adding the
trumpet
notes.

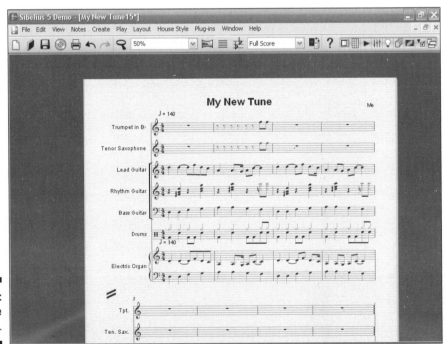

Figure 10-26:
Adding the
tenor notes.

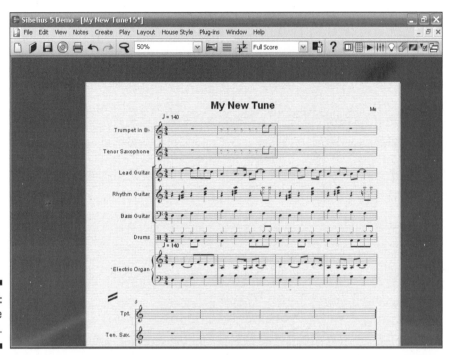

Figure 10-27:
Copying the horn parts.

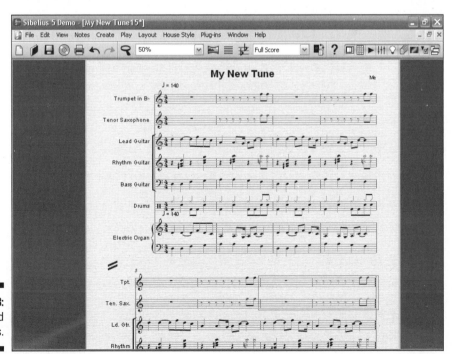

Figure 10-28:
The finished horn parts.

Transposing the tenor part into the correct range

The tenor part looks a little too high for the tenor player to play easily. You can tell by the red color of the note. This is Sibelius's way of letting you know that you wrote a note that's out of the comfortable range of the instrument.

Sibelius always tells you if you've written a note that's either too high or too low for the range of the instrument, by coloring the note red. If you want, you can turn this off in the View dialog box (choose View⇨Note Colors and deselect Notes out of Range), but this notification is very handy when you're first learning to compose to a varied group of instruments. (See Appendix A for more information on instrument ranges.)

You can transpose the tenor part down an octave to make it fit in the proper range of the saxophone:

1. **Highlight the tenor part by clicking on the first bar, holding Shift, and clicking on the last bar of the tenor's part.**

2. **Choose Notes⇨Transpose.**

   The Transpose dialog box appears.

3. **Next to Transpose By, select the Interval radio button.**

4. **Under Transpose by Interval, select the Down radio button, and in the two drop-down lists, select Major/Perfect and Octave, as shown in Figure 10-29.**

5. **Click OK.**

   You see that the tenor part is well within the playing range (see Figure 10-30), and the tenor player doesn't need to strain herself!

Listen to "My New Tune" on the CD at Author/Chapter 10/Audio Examples/My New Tune-10-12.mp3.

I've done this all for you, so you can open the My New Tune-10-12.sib file on the CD if you want to see the results. Press Ctrl+[(⌘+[) to rewind the playback, and then press the space bar to hear your tune with all the new instruments.

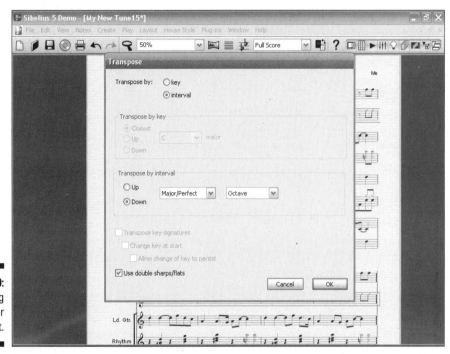

Figure 10-29:
Transposing
the tenor
part.

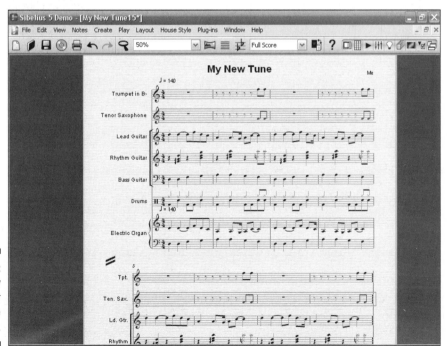

Figure 10-30:
The new
tenor
saxophone
part.

Chapter 11

No-Frills Notes: Basic Note Entry

*Y*ou can enter notes into music software in a number of ways. If you're using a digital audio workstation (DAW) that allows MIDI real-time and step-time entry, you can connect your MIDI keyboard to your computer and record your playing right into the software as the tune plays. Or you can enter each note, one at a time, using either your MIDI controller or your mouse and keyboard. The latter approach takes longer, but it lets you input musical passages that you probably couldn't play up to speed. Then you can edit each note using one of several views, such as the Piano Roll, Staff, or Event List views.

In music notation software, such as Finale or Sibelius, you can also enter music into your score a variety of ways. In Sibelius, there are five ways of creating and editing notes, chords, and rests:

- ✔ **Mouse input:** You can use the mouse to create notes, rests, and text, and use the mouse to edit, move, and copy them.

- ✔ **Alphabetic and step-time input:** You can use the computer keyboard alone, or use the computer keyboard with a MIDI keyboard.

- ✔ **Flexi-time input:** You can record music directly into Sibelius in real time using a MIDI controller.

- ✔ **Importing music files, like MIDI:** You can convert music from other formats, including MIDI, Music, Finale, and SCORE, into Sibelius.

- ✔ **Scanning printed music:** You can turn printed music into a Sibelius score.

In this chapter, I cover the first two options, and in Chapter 12, I cover the last three.

Entering Notes with the Mouse

Using the mouse is the most basic and easy way to enter notes into your score. In this section, I show you how to add a couple of notes for the horn players in "My New Tune."

1. **Open `My New Tune-11-01.sib` from the CD and press the Escape key to be sure you haven't selected anything.**

   Nothing should be highlighted on the screen.

2. **If it's not already open, open the Keypad by choosing Windows⇨Keypad (Ctrl+Alt+K/Option+⌘+K).**

   The little Keypad box should appear on your screen. You might need to drag the Keypad to one side, to get it out of the way of the score.

3. **To add some notes to the trumpet part, click on the whole note (o).**

   The note in the Keypad should turn blue, and the number 1 in the bottom of the Keypad should also turn blue, signifying that you've selected the whole note (as shown in Figure 11-1).

   Don't worry about messing up the notes, you can always reload the template `My New Tune11-01.sib` from the CD, and start over, or just continue on in the chapter.

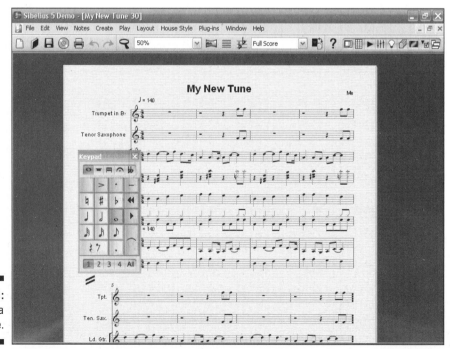

Figure 11-1: Selecting a whole note.

4. **Move your pointer to the beginning of the first bar of the trumpet part, and click on the D line (the second line down from the top), shown in Figure 11-2.**

Be sure to get the whole note right at the beginning of the bar; otherwise, Sibelius will think you want it someplace else. Sometimes getting the note right where you want it is a little tricky. You may need to increase the View size to get a closer look at it. If you put the note in the wrong place, it's not the end of the world — you can press Ctrl+Z (⌘+Z) to back out, or reload My New Tune-11-01.sib.

You see a blue line at the beginning of the second bar. This means you're still in Enter Notes mode.

5. **Press Esc to quit entering notes.**

6. **Copy this bar and paste it to bars three, five, and seven.**

Turn to Chapter 7 for complete instructions on how to copy and paste bars.

If you get messed up, you can load My New Tune-11-02.sib from the CD to see how it's supposed to look. It should look like Figure 11-3 when you're done.

Listen to "My New Tune" on the CD at Author/Chapter 11/Audio Examples/My New Tune-11-02.mp3.

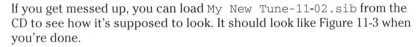

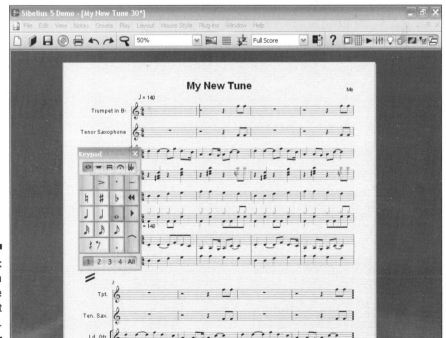

Figure 11-2:
Adding a note to the trumpet part.

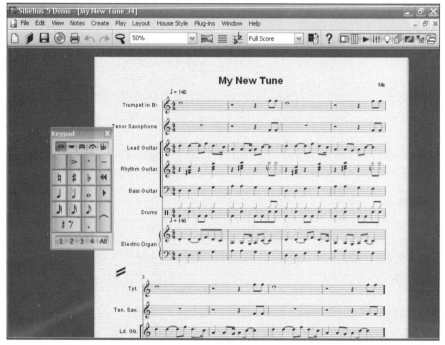

Figure 11-3:
Copying and
pasting the
trumpet
notes.

7. **Press Esc to unselect, press Ctrl+[(⌘+[) to rewind the playback, and press the space bar to start the playback.**

Now you want the tenor saxophone to play the same part as the trumpet.

8. **Click the first bar of the trumpet, press Ctrl+C (⌘+C), select the first bar of the tenor part, and press Ctrl+V (⌘+V) to paste the bar there.**

It should look like Figure 11-4.

Now the tenor's note is too high, because you copied it from the trumpet, which has a higher range than the tenor sax. When Sibelius finds a note that's out of range for the instrument — either too high or too low — it will color the notehead red.

So you want to move the note down an octave. In Chapter 10, you choose Notes⇨Transpose to transpose the note down an octave. In this chapter, I show you a different approach.

9. **Left-click on the D in the first bar of the tenor part with your mouse and drag it down an octave lower to the lower D, the space under the staff, as shown in Figure 11-5.**

If you get lost, you can open My New Tune-11-03.sib and continue.

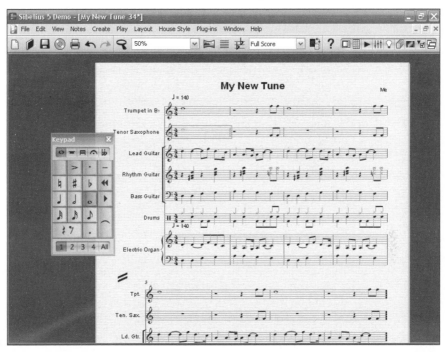

Figure 11-4:
Pasting into
the tenor
part.

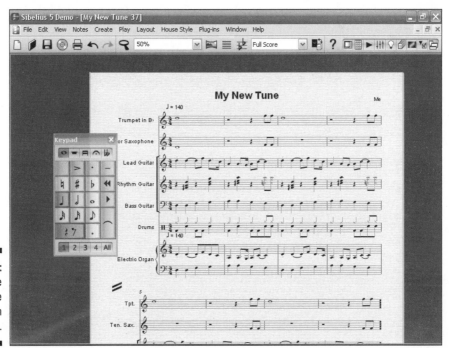

Figure 11-5:
Moving the
tenor note
down an
octave.

10. **Copy and paste this tenor note to the rest of this part by highlighting the first bar of the tenor part, pressing Ctrl+C (⌘+C), and pressing Ctrl+V (⌘+V) in bars three, five, and seven of the tenor part.**

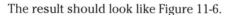

The result should look like Figure 11-6.

Listen to My New Tune on the CD at `Author/Chapter 11/Audio Examples/My New Tune-11-04.mp3`.

11. **To hear what the new horn parts sound like, hit Esc to unselect everything, press Ctrl+[(⌘+[) to rewind the playback, and press the space bar to hear the tune from the beginning.**

If you want to hear only the horn parts, without the other instruments playing, highlight the first bar of the trumpet part. Then, while holding down the Shift key, click on the first bar of the tenor sax part. The first two bars should be highlighted. Press P to hear just the horn parts. To hear only one stave, or a group of staves, you can select the part you'd like to hear, then press P to playback

To compare what you wrote to what it's supposed to look like, open `My New Tune-11-04.sib` from the CD.

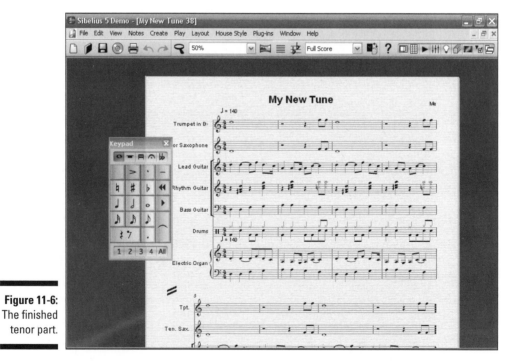

Figure 11-6:
The finished tenor part.

Using alphabetic input

You can type notes into your score using the letters on your computer keyboard. You can try it by following these steps:

1. **Press Esc to make sure nothing's selected.**

2. **Click on an empty measure with your mouse to highlight it.**

3. **Press Ctrl+Alt+K (Option+⌘+K) to open the Keypad.**

4. **Press N and choose the note's duration value on the Keypad with your mouse.**

5. **Press the letter A, B, C, D, E, F, or G on your computer's keyboard to insert the note you want.**

6. **Press 0 (zero) on the computer number pad to insert a rest.**

7. **Press Ctrl+Up Arrow (⌘+Up Arrow) or Ctrl+Down Arrow (⌘+Down Arrow) to change the octave of the note.**

8. **Press Esc when you're finished.**

Adding Text and Lines

Music is more than notes. If you're going to have a piece of music played by a musician, you need text to describe important concepts or directions about the piece. Lines and bar lines also play an important function in creating the final sound of your tune.

Getting fancy with bar lines

Bar lines do more than just separate a group of four beats. A *double bar line* is used to signal the start or end of a section, usually accompanied by a *rehearsal mark* (a letter or number that helps the musicians all start at the same place). And an *ending bar line* tells the musician that the tune is finished — there isn't any more.

A *repeat bar line* tells the performer to go back and repeat the section he just played, or just repeat the indicated section. A repeat barline can also give the performer different notes to play when he gets to the end of the repeated section; these are called *first and second ending bars.*

If you put a repeat in your tune, you can get it to play twice as long:

1. **Open My New Tune-11-05.sib and press Esc to make sure nothing is highlighted.**

2. **Click the very last bar line at the end of the tune.**

   You may need to change your View to 100 percent to get a closer look at it. Your selection should look like Figure 11-7.

Figure 11-7:
Selecting
the last bar
line.

3. Choose Create⇨Barline and click End Repeat.

This places an end repeat bar line at the end of the last bar (see Figure 11-8).

If you have trouble inserting the end repeat on the last bar, you can open `My New Tune-11-06.sib` to have it done for you.

Now the tune will play all the way through twice.

4. To hear it play back, press Esc, press Ctrl+[(⌘+[ ), and press the space bar.

The tune will play once, hit the repeat bar, and seamlessly start playing again from the beginning.

You may want to repeat a specific section, not the entire tune. To do that, insert a start repeat bar line at the beginning of the section you want to repeat, and an end repeat bar line at the end of the repeated section.

In Sibelius, as in real life, a section can be repeated more than once. Maybe a section needs to be repeated three, four, or more times. You can have Sibelius play back a section multiple times, by highlighting the end repeat barline, and choosing Window⇨Properties⇨Playback. You can click the box under Play on Pass to indicate how many times you want the section repeated.

Figure 11-8:
Creating an
end repeat
bar line.

If you're going to have live musicians play your piece, and you want a section repeated more than once, you need to enter text on the staves to indicate it. Otherwise, they'll just repeat the section once.

Here you'll put a Start Repeat in our tune, to make the tune play back just the last four bars, not the entire piece:

1. **Open My New Tune-11-06.sib, and press Esc to make sure nothing is selected.**

2. **Select the bar line at the beginning of bar 5, as shown in Figure 11-9.**

3. **Choose Create➪Barline➪Start Repeat.**

   A start repeat bar line is created. It should look like Figure 11-10.

   If you have trouble, you can open My New Tune-11-07.sib to see what it looks like.

   Listen to "My New Tune" on the CD at Author/Chapter 11/Audio Examples/My New Tune-11-07.mp3.

4. **Press Esc, press Ctrl+[(⌘+[), and press the space bar to hear it.**

   This time the playback will be a little different. The tune will play through once, but instead of going back to the beginning to repeat the whole piece, it will jump to the fifth bar, and only repeat the last four bars.

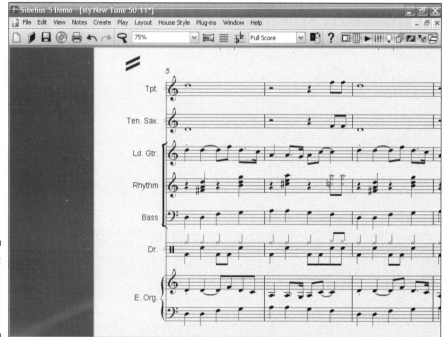

Figure 11-9:
Selecting
the barline
to start the
repeat.

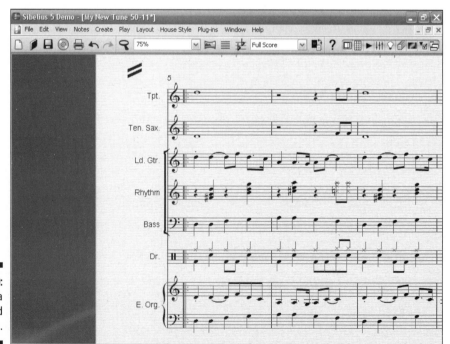

Figure 11-10:
Creating a
repeated
section.

Hairpins

In Chapter 14, I show you how to use dynamic markings to make changes to your tune. But while I'm describing text lines, I want to mention a specific line that affects the dynamics of the tune.

Hairpins (see Figure 11-11) are crescendo and decrescendo lines. These lines are written under the staff and tell the performer to either gradually increase loudness while playing (crescendo) or gradually get softer during the passage.

You can easily create a hairpin in Sibelius:

1. **Select the note where you want the hairpin to start, and press H to create a crescendo, or Shift+H to create a decrescendo.**

2. **Press the spacebar to extend the hairpin, and Shift+space bar if you go too far and want to make it shorter.**

Hairpins have handles on either end that can also be adjusted, and you can use your mouse or arrow keys to reposition the hairpin along the staff.

Figure 11-11:
Hairpins are crescendo and decre-scendo lines.

Entering Other Types of Text

You can enter lots of different kinds of text into your score. Besides dynamics and lines, such as *slurs,* music uses a lot of text to indicate the composer's intent. If you're writing for brass instruments, for example, you may have to tell the musicians which kind of mute to use. Or you may need to let the whole band know that a specific section is played four times, rather than one or two.

To see all the various types of text that you can use in your score, choose Create⇨Text. You'll come to a series of menu options that describe a lot of different links of text you can put into your score.

Don't go overboard with instructions, because the musicians primarily read the notes. Too much text can confuse the performer, and clutter up the page. Text instructions should be to the point and brief, and only used when necessary.

From the Create⇨Text menu, you can add or edit any type of text-related object, such as title and composer information, headers and footers, drum legends, metronome markings, and a ton of other information.

Free text

You can enter any free text anywhere easily, or use the Create⇨Text menu to create specific text, like chord symbols. In Chapter 14, you enter chord symbols, dynamic expressions, and lyrics from the text menu. But for now, just try entering free text. Open one of the templates, select a bar anywhere on the score, and press Ctrl+T (⌘+T). You see a flashing cursor waiting for you to enter your text. Just type whatever text you want, and hit Esc to end. Your text will position itself right above the bar (or note) you selected.

To instantly bring up a menu of all the lines you can use in Sibelius, such as hairpins, trills, and slurs, press L at any time. A box with two columns appears. The left column, Staff Lines, shows a list of lines that only affect the individual staff with which you're working, and the right column, System Lines, shows you lines that will affect the entire score.

Tempo text

The *tempo* of a piece of music is how fast or slow it goes. A lot of music stays in the tempo it starts with, especially if the tune is played by a band. But conducted music may change the tempo at different places in the score. The piece may slow down or speed up for dramatic effect, or a tempo change may be required to move the work from one theme to another theme.

Often words are used to tell the player or conductor to speed up or slow down. A gradual increase in tempo may be indicated by the term *accelerando,* and a gradual slowdown can be indicated with the term *ritardando.*

The tempo of a piece of music is usually indicated by the metronome marking at the beginning of the score. It's often accompanied by a word or description to help inform the player of how fast the piece should be played.

Sibelius has an easy way to add tempo text to your score:

1. **Press Esc to be sure nothing is selected.**

2. **Press the letter L to bring up the Lines menu.**

   Because ritardando, rallentando, accelerando, and other tempo text lines affect all the instruments, they're in the right-hand column, the System Lines list.

3. **Use the scroll bar to pick the one you want and click OK.**

   Your pointer changes to a big blue arrow.

4. **Click on the bar where you want the element to start.**

5. **While holding down your right mouse button, drag the element from left to right to make it as long as you need.**

System lines appear at the top of systems — that is, they affect the whole score. You won't see them on each individual staff in your score, but they will appear in the parts when you create them. Staff lines appear only on the stave on which they're placed.

Editing text

If you want to change existing text, lines, or symbols, you can do this several different ways.

To edit a piece of regular text, select it, choose Window➪Properties, and select the Text tab. You can change the text font, size, bold, underline, or even change it to a different element altogether.

To change the position of all the text and lines in your score, choose House Style➪Default Positions. In the Default Positions dialog box (shown in Figure 11-12), you can change the default positioning of all the text elements. This is very useful if, for example, you want to change the position of the lyrics written in a vocal part.

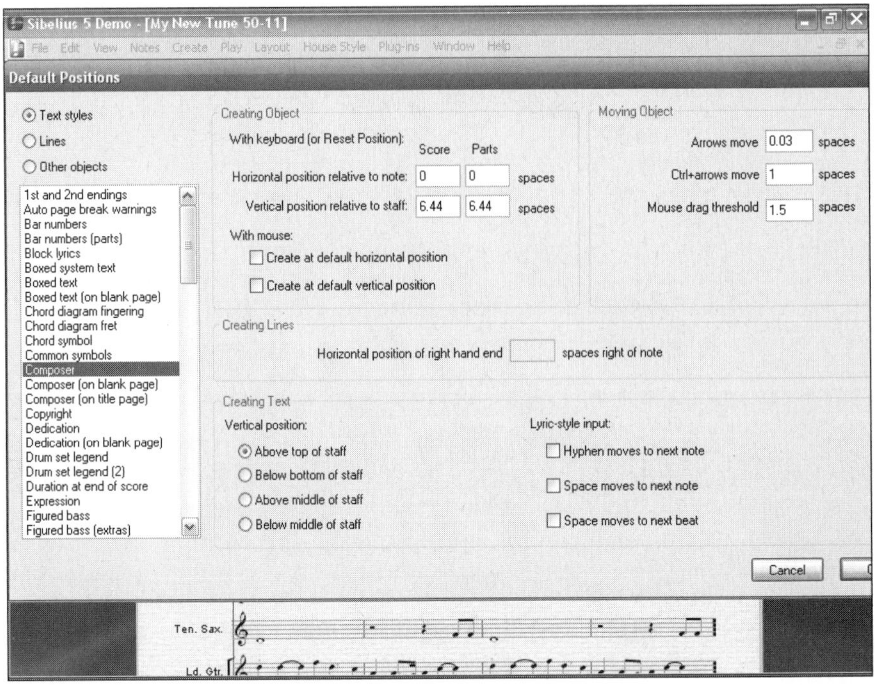

Figure 11-12:
Changing
the default
position of
the text in
the Default
Positions
dialog box.

You can also change the style of every instance of a specific text element in your score, by choosing House Style⇨Edit Text Styles. The Edit Text Styles dialog box is shown in Figure 11-13.

When you open the Edit Text Styles dialog box, you're asked which text elements of the score you'd like to edit, such as the chord diagrams, the lyrics, or the instrument names. For example, if you want to change the way your name as the composer appears on the score, highlight Composer in the Edit Text Styles dialog box, and click Edit. You can then change some elements of how your name looks on the score, including the font style and size, its horizontal or vertical position on the title page, or whether the composer's name appears only on the title page, or repeats on every page (see Figure 11-14).

Altering the look of any line element in your score, such as trills, slurs, and hairpins, is also very easy. Choose House Style⇨Edit Lines, and pick the staff line or system line you want to change (see Figure 11-15).

Use the same technique to edit musical symbols. Choose House Style⇨Edit Symbols, then pick the symbol you want to change in the Symbol dialog box (see Figure 11-16).

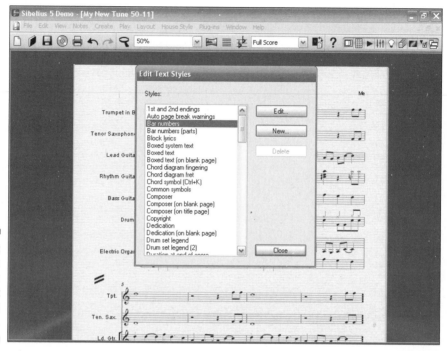

Figure 11-13:
Editing the text style in the Edit Text Styles dialog box.

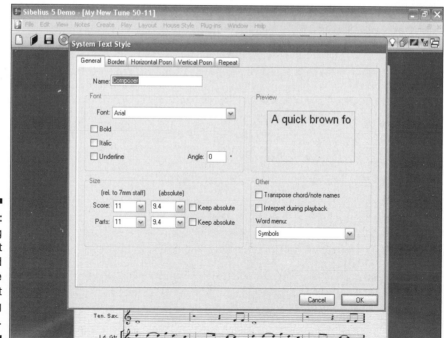

Figure 11-14:
Changing the font style and size in the System Text Style dialog box.

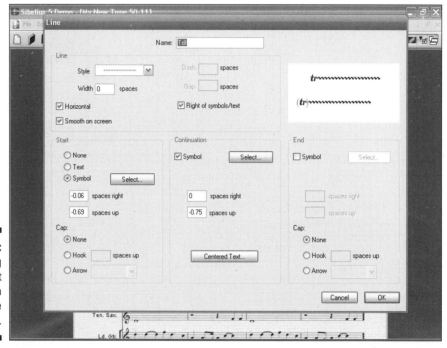

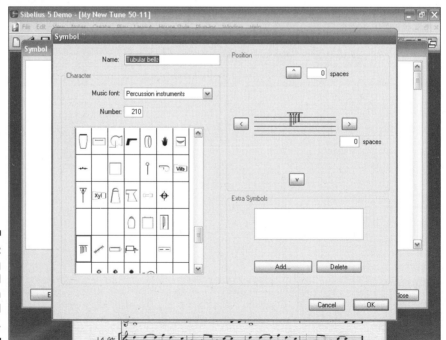

You can also change the main text and music fonts to a different pen style, to make it look more handwritten, for example. Choose House Style⇨Edit All Fonts, and select Inkpen 2 from the Main Music Font and the Music Text Font drop-down lists to give your score a jazzier, handwritten look.

Be careful about changing lots of default elements in Sibelius, other than the fonts. The default positions and font sizes of all the text, line, and symbol elements have been well thought out by the Sibelius folks, so you should rarely have a reason to change these.

Chapter 12

Composing with Your Instrument

* *

In This Chapter

▶ Using a MIDI keyboard controller to compose

▶ Digitally recording with your guitar or bass

▶ Scanning music into Sibelius

* *

*Y*ou can use your computer keyboard and mouse to get your notes into your software (see Chapter 11), but there are easier methods available, especially if you're experienced with a piano keyboard or guitar. All music production software lets you input music using a MIDI keyboard or other type of MIDI-compatible controller. You can also record your guitar or bass by playing into a digital audio workstation (DAW) program. You can even sing your part into the MIDI software, if you have a microphone connected to your computer.

In this chapter, I show you step-time input, flexi-time input, and scanning. I'll also show you the basic steps to record your guitar with digital audio software.

Entering Notes with a MIDI Keyboard Controller

The most common way to enter notes into digital music software is with a MIDI controller, usually a piano-like keyboard. In Sibelius, you can use your MIDI keyboard controller to enter notes one at a time or in real time, as the score is playing.

In Chapters 4 and 5, I show you the ins and outs of various MIDI controllers. Here, I tell you how you can enter notes into your score using one.

Attaching the controller

To make music with a MIDI keyboard controller, you obviously need to plug the keyboard into your computer. Three types of MIDI cables are commonly used:

- ✔ **USB cable:** A USB cable is the most common type of MIDI connection. In fact, almost every hardware peripheral made uses a USB connection to communicate with your computer. To use this type of connection, simply plug one end of the USB cable into the USB jack on your MIDI key- board controller and plug the other end into your computer's USB port. Couldn't be easier.

  Most hardware manufacturers include a USB cable with the controller. You may want to get a longer cable, though, if you need to position the controller a little ways away from the computer. You may also get a CD of USB drivers for your operating system.

- ✔ **Standard MIDI cable (see Figure 12-1):** For many years, a true-blue standard MIDI cable was the only way to connect a MIDI peripheral to a MIDI hardware interface or computer. A MIDI cable has a distinctive 5-pin connector on each end of the cable. You can buy one at a music or guitar shop.

  Some MIDI keyboards have jacks for these cables even if they have a USB connection, because not all MIDI hardware has a USB port to con- nect to — only MIDI In, MIDI Out, and sometimes MIDI Thru connectors. You need two of these cables, because you connect the MIDI Out jack on your MIDI controller to the MIDI In connection on your sound card or MIDI interface, and then you use another cable to connect the MIDI In jack on your MIDI instrument to the MIDI Out connection on your MIDI interface or sound card.

Standard MIDI cable—use this if your MIDI interface
has standard 5-pin input and output ports

Figure 12-1:
A standard
MIDI cable.

✔ **Game port connector (see Figure 12-2):** A MIDI game port, or joystick connector was the pre-USB way to connect a MIDI device to a computer. Early PC sound cards, like Creative Labs SoundBlaster cards, had a connection on the back to attach a joystick for game play. This became a convenient place to connect a MIDI device.

To attach a MIDI controller to your game port, first connect the 15-pin end of the MIDI game port connector to the sound card's joystick port. Then connect the cable labeled In to the MIDI Out jack on your keyboard. Then connect the cable labeled Out to the MIDI In jack on your electronic keyboard.

If you use a joystick, unplug it before attaching the MIDI game port connector. Then plug the joystick into the pass-through connector that's now attached to the game port.

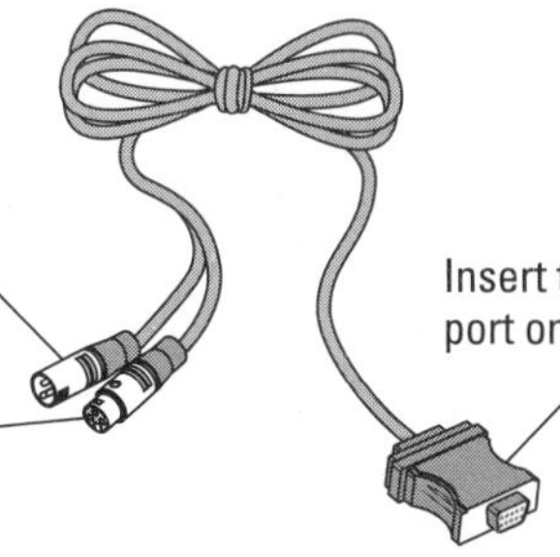

Joystick connector—use this if your MIDI interface is the joystick port on your sound card.

Insert this MIDI IN plug into the MIDI OUT port on your MIDI instrument

Insert this plug into the joystick port on your sound card

Figure 12-2: A MIDI joystick connector.

Insert this MIDI OUT plug into the MIDI IN port on your MIDI instrument

Step-time input: Inputting notes and chords into your score one at a time

Step-time input is what Sibelius calls inputting notes and chords into your score one at a time. Step-time is probably the best way to input your notes accurately.

Basically, you press a key on your MIDI controller to enter each note and use your computer's keyboard to change the note's corresponding value. You select a starting position in the score, either a rest or a note. Choose a note value on the keypad using the mouse or numeric keys, and then play the notes and chords on the keyboard.

Be sure to plug in your controller before you open Sibelius; otherwise, Sibelius may not know it's connected. If Sibelius doesn't see your controller, unplug the controller and shut down Sibelius. Then plug it back in, and start Sibelius. The Sibelius Help section also has a lot of info on resolving MIDI controller connection problems.

When your MIDI keyboard controller is hooked up and ready to go, follow these steps to try some step-time entry:

1. **Open a blank score, and select any manuscript paper.**

   You can click Finish, and skip all the steps of creating a new score, if you don't want to mess with that now. Check out Chapter 10 for more on how to create your score paper.

2. **Press Esc to make sure nothing has been selected.**

3. **Click on an empty measure (see Figure 12-3).**

4. **Press Ctrl+Alt+K (Option+⌘+K) to open the Keypad.**

5. **Press N, and choose a note value with the Keypad.**

   In Figure 12-4, I chose a half note.

6. **Play a note on your MIDI keyboard.**

   I played a middle C, as shown in Figure 12-5.

7. **Press Esc when you're finished.**

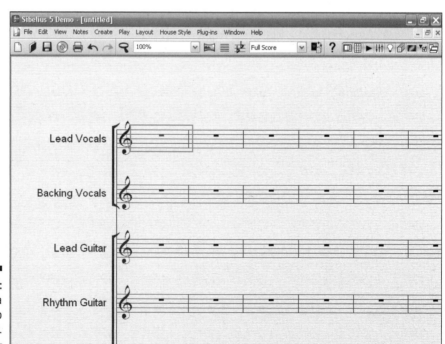

Figure 12-3:
Selecting a measure to input.

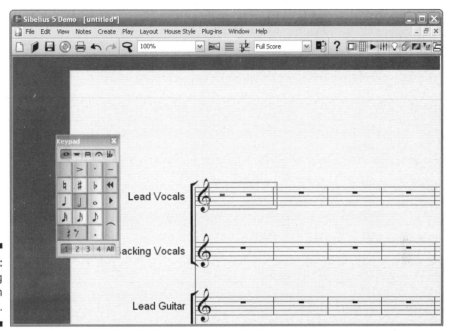

Figure 12-4:
Selecting
the duration
of a note.

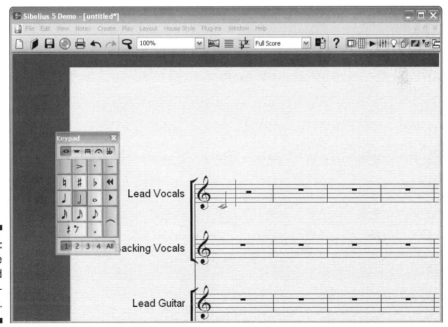

Figure 12-5:
A half note
entered
using step-
time input.

You can enter rests during step-time input by either selecting a rest value on the Keypad, or pressing 0 (zero) on the computer keyboard's number pad.

You can also enter chords using step-time input. In Figure 12-6, I selected the half note duration from the Keypad, and then played a major C chord.

Flexi-time input

With a MIDI controller, you can enter your notes into your Sibelius score in real time with a process it calls *flexi-time*. As opposed to entering each note one at a time, you can play along with your score, and Sibelius enters what you're playing into the score.

Using flexi-time to enter your music is easy:

1. **Click in an empty bar.**

2. **Press Ctrl+Alt+Y (Option+⌘+Y) to open the Playback window.**

3. **If you want a *count-in* (that is, if you want to hear a metronome click four beats before it starts recording), click on the metronome icon at the far right of the playback window (Figure 12-7).**

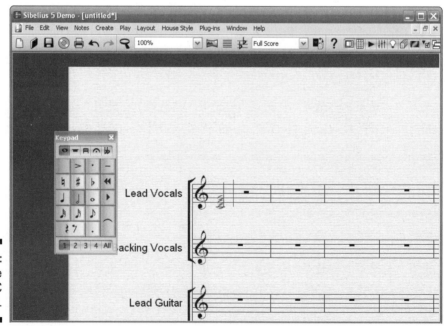

Figure 12-6:
Step-time
input of a C
chord.

Flexi-time latency

Entering music using flexi-time requires a fast computer with a lot of memory, otherwise it will start to slow down and the score will get way behind your playing. Also, if you have a lot of instruments in the score, it can slow down during flexi-time input.

Here are a couple suggestions for working with flexi-time:

✔ Use a good ASIO-capable sound card, with updated ASIO drivers, and set the latency setting as low as possible (perhaps around 10ms).

✔ Make sure you have the latest USB drivers for your keyboard. Cheaper USB MIDI connectors can have some latency.

✔ If your computer and MIDI controller can use a FireWire connection, use that. It's faster than a USB cable.

Remember: The Sibelius support forum (www.sibelius.com/community/index.html) is great place to find answers to your questions.

4. **To start recording, click the red button on the Playback window.**

   The metronome ticks a four-beat count-in before it start to record. In Figure 12-8, I played a C major scale.

5. **Play your part, then either click the stop button, or hit the space bar, to stop.**

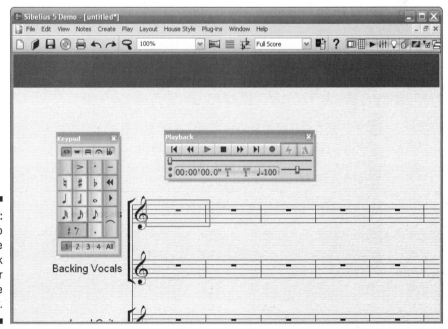

Figure 12-7: Setting up the Playback window for flexi-time input.

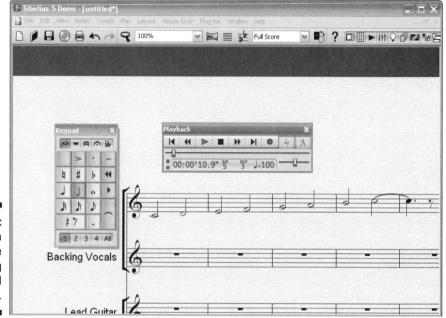

Figure 12-8:
Recording a
flexi-time
part using
your MIDI
keyboard.

If you're like me, and don't play exactly along with the metronome, very weird rhythms may get entered into your score. Sibelius may think you really want that half note $\frac{1}{32}$ of a beat before the bar, for example. You can choose Notes⇨Flexi-Time Options to tell Sibelius how exactly it should follow your tempo if you speed up or slow down. You can also tell it how many beats of the count-in there should be, whether to insert one voice or multiple voices (chords), and a few other nice details.

Entering Notes with a Guitar

If you want to enter MIDI information with a guitar, you need a MIDI guitar (see Chapter 4). A few companies make MIDI guitars, such as Brian Moore Guitars (www.iguitar.com). Starr Labs (www.starrlabs.com) still makes the Ztar, a guitar-like controller with keys, not strings, on the fretboard. But a true MIDI guitar is a rarity these days, as other types of controllers have been more commercially successful.

Most likely, you don't have a true MIDI guitar, but don't worry: You can record your guitar directly into most digital audio workstations (DAWs) and synchronize it with your MIDI file. Unfortunately, Sibelius is not a DAW; you can't record digital audio directly into your score. But you can record digital audio in a host of other programs, save the performance as a MIDI file, and import it into Sibelius.

Probably the most popular programs for directly recording digital audio recording are the Mac programs Digital Performer, and Logic Studio and the dual platform program Pro Tools.

For this example, I use SONAR Home Studio 6, which is available on Windows. You can get a 30-day trial version of the 32-bit version of SONAR 7 Producer Edition at `www.cakewalk.com/Support/kb/kb20061101.asp`. Other Windows-based products that can record digital audio include ACID Pro, Ableton Live (also Mac-enabled), Cubase, and Steinberg's Sequel.

SONAR 6 requires DirectX 9 or later to be installed on your system. If you don't have DirectX 9 installed, you can download it at `www.microsoft.com/windows/directx/default.aspx?url=/windows/directx/downloads/default.htm`.

Connecting your guitar

If your sound card has a ⅛-inch input jack (built-in sound cards that come with your PC usually do), plug your ¼-inch mono guitar or audio cable into a ⅛-inch stereo adapter, and then plug the ⅛-inch adapter into the microphone input or line input jack on your computer sound card. Figure 12-9 shows where to put the adapter.

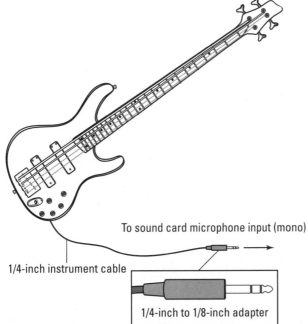

To sound card microphone input (mono)

1/4-inch instrument cable

1/4-inch to 1/8-inch adapter

Figure 12-9: Using a ⅛-inch adapter to plug in your guitar.

If you use a professional or prosumer sound card, there is probably a ¼-inch input jack on your sound card or audio hardware interface that you can plug your guitar cable or audio cable into.

You can also connect a mixer to the sound card like the setup shown in Figure 12-10. To get a good sound, a preamp will probably also be necessary, to boost the input signal.

Recording your part

To digitally record your axe into your DAW, follow these steps:

1. **Set the sampling rate.**
2. **Set the audio driver bit depth.**
3. **Set the recording bit depth.**
4. **Open a project file.**
5. **Insert an audio track.**
6. **Check the input levels.**
7. **Record the digital audio.**

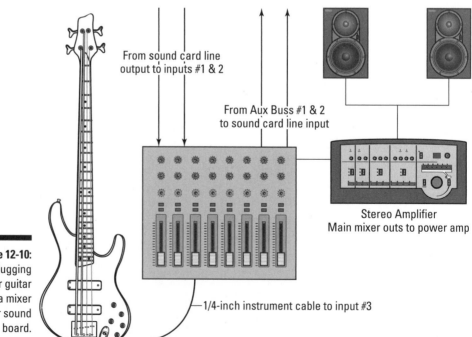

From sound card line output to inputs #1 & 2

From Aux Buss #1 & 2 to sound card line input

Stereo Amplifier
Main mixer outs to power amp

Figure 12-10: Plugging your guitar into a mixer or sound board.

1/4-inch instrument cable to input #3

8. **Listen to your recording.**

9. **Record another take, if you need to.**

I go into each of these steps in greater detail in the following sections.

I'm using SONAR Home Studio 6 for this example. Your DAW may use a slightly different process, but the general steps are the same for every DAW.

Setting the sampling rate

You should set the sampling rate before recording any digital audio. Most audio CDs sample at a 44,100 Hz rate.

The sampling rate, sample rate, or sampling frequency defines the number of samples per second taken from a continuous signal to make a discrete signal. For time-domain signals, it can be measured in hertz (Hz). The inverse of the sampling frequency is the sampling period or sampling interval, which is the time between samples.

To set the sampling rate in SONAR Home Studio 6, follow these steps:

1. **Choose Options⟹Audio.**

   The Audio Options dialog box (shown in Figure 12-11) appears.

2. **Select the General tab.**

3. **Under Default Settings for New Projects, select a sampling rate from the Sampling Rate drop-down list.**

   For CD-quality sound, use 44,100 Hz.

4. **Click OK.**

Lower sampling rates save disk space but result in lower-quality audio. Before embarking on any major project, consider what media your project will eventually be stored on, and what sampling rate is best for that media.

Setting the audio driver bit depth

You can record audio data at 16 or 24 bits. Recording and playing back at the same bit depth usually makes sense.

The drivers for most sound cards use anywhere from 16 to 24 bits to play back recorded data. CDs use 16 bits. You can possibly get better sound quality by recording at a higher bit depth and converting to 16 bits when it's time to master your project, but keep in mind that 24-bit audio takes 50 percent more memory than 16-bit audio, which may strain your computer's storage capability and speed of operation. Your sound card's documentation could have some advice on choosing an audio driver bit depth.

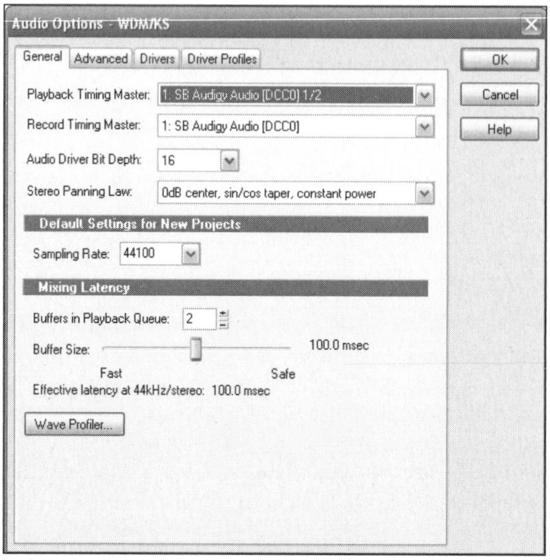

Figure 12-11:
Setting the sampling rate in the SONAR Home Studio 6 Audio Options dialog box.

In SONAR, you set the audio driver bit depth in the same place you set the sampling rate (refer to Figure 12-11). In the Audio Driver Bit Depth drop-down list, select 16 and click OK.

Setting the recording bit depth

To set the recording bit depth in SONAR Home Studio 6, follow these steps:

1. **Choose Options⇨Global.**

   The Global Options dialog box (shown in Figure 12-12) appears.

2. **Select the Audio Data tab.**

3. **In the Record Bit Depth drop-down list, select 16.**

4. **Click OK.**

Opening a project file

Open a new project file to input and save your recording. In SONAR Home Studio 6, follow these steps:

1. **Choose File⇨New.**

   The New Project File dialog box (shown in Figure 12-13) appears.

2. **In the Name field, enter the name of your project.**

3. **From the Template list, select the Normal template.**

4. **Click OK.**

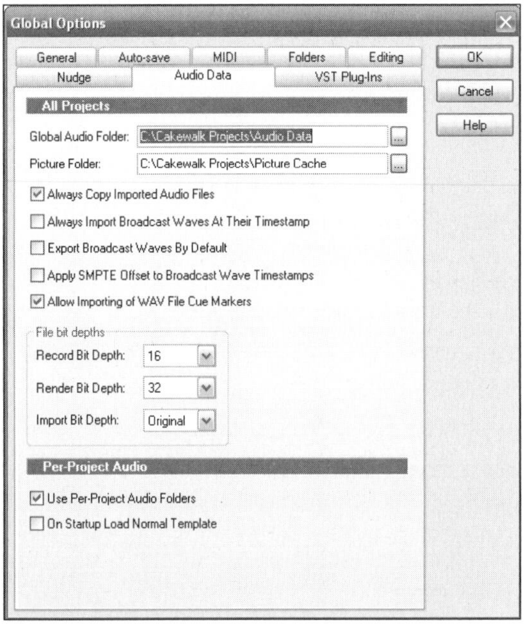

Figure 12-12:
Setting the
record bit
depth in the
SONAR
Home
Studio 6
Global
Options
dialog box.

Figure 12-13:
Opening a
new project
in the
SONAR
Home
Studio 6
New Project
File dialog
box.

Inserting an audio track

You may have to insert an audio track into your project file. This is the track you'll be recording directly into. In SONAR Home Studio 6, insert a new track by following these steps:

1. **Open the Track view (shown in Figure 12-14).**

   Most DAWs use this view as the default.

2. **Right-click wherever you want to insert the new track.**

3. **Choose Insert Audio Track from the pop-up menu.**

4. **In the track's Output field, click the drop-down arrow and select an audio output from the menu.**

5. **In the track's Input field, choose an audio input.**

   Usually you select the left channel of one of your sound card's inputs to record a mono track, or the stereo input to record a stereo track.

Most DAWs have a normal or default template that has several audio tracks in it already, so you may not have to insert a new audio track.

Figure 12-14:
The new project's Track view pane in SONAR Home Studio 6.

Checking the input levels

Be sure to check and adjust the recording input level before you record your tribute to the guitar gods. If your audio input is too low, it'll be lost in the background noise. If it's too high, it'll overload the input channel and be distorted or clipped. And I don't mean distortion in the good, head-banger, metal guitar sense — I mean just plain ugly and harsh distortion.

After all this prep has been done, you'll record your digital audio. When you finish recording, click the Stop button or press the space bar. Then play your performance back and listen to it to be sure it's what you want.

If you want to redo it, press Ctrl+Z (⌘+Z) to undo the recording, rewind the track to the beginning by clicking Rewind, and record another take. Then if it's what you want, save it for posterity!

Scanning Music Using PhotoScore

Composers have wondered over the years, "Wouldn't it be great if I could just scan my printed sheet music into my music software? Then the divide between the new digital world and the old paper music world would be bridged." The development and refinement of optical character recognition (OCR) software lets you input hard-copy sheet music into your musical notation program.

Sibelius comes with a free music OCR scanning program called PhotoScore Lite by Neuratron (www.neuratron.com), which scans and reads printed music into Sibelius. After the music is read, you can edit or transpose the score in Sibelius, play it back, extract parts and print — just as if you'd input it yourself.

In my experience, music software scanning by OCR programs is still really in its infancy and takes lots of fudging to get right. OCR programs have trouble especially with handwritten sheet music, because the hand style varies so much. But continual progress is being made with these programs, and it won't be long before composers will be able to scan almost any type of printed music into software.

A demo version of the scanning program PhotoScore is available from the Sibelius Web site at www.sibelius.com/cgi-bin/download/get.pl?com=sh&prod=psldemo.

If you don't own a scanner, you can still try out the PhotoScore's scanning functions with the PhotoScore Lite demo. It includes several pre-scanned images for you to play around with. Download and install the PhotoScore demo, and give PhotoScore a run through using a sample image:

1. **Start the PhotoScore demo.**

   It's either an icon on your desktop called PhotoScore Lite Demo Music Scanning, or you can choose Start⇨Programs⇨Neuratron⇨PhotoScore Lite Demo. On Mac, just double-click the PhotoScore Lite disk icon.

2. **Open the example bitmap image called `Bach Invention.bmp` (see Figure 12-15).**

   PhotoScore show you the scanned image (see Figure 12-16), with blue lines marking the staves it has found.

3. **Click Read This Page to turn the scanned image into a music file.**

   Reading the page will take a little while (depending on the speed of your computer) and a progress bar will show you how long you have to wait, as shown in Figure 12-17.

   When PhotoScore has finished reading the image, the main editing window (shown in Figure 12-18) appears.

   From this window, you can edit any errors in the scanning by using the keypad to change the pitch of any wrong notes, just as you would in Sibelius. Because this is an example score, there are no errors, so just go to the next step.

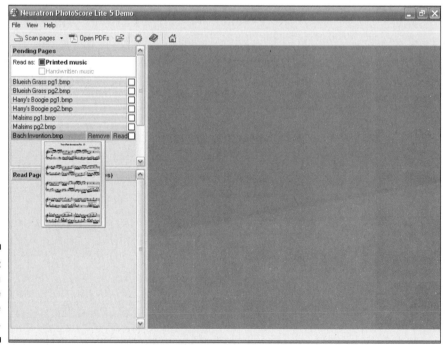

Figure 12-15:
Opening a
PhotoScore
sample
bitmap.

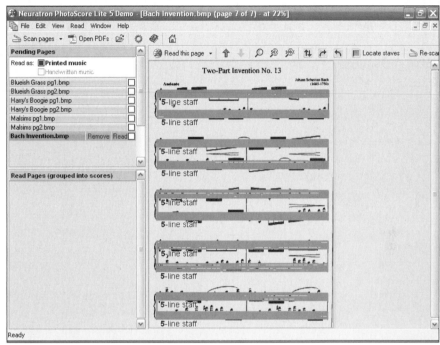

Figure 12-16:
The pre-
scanned
image.

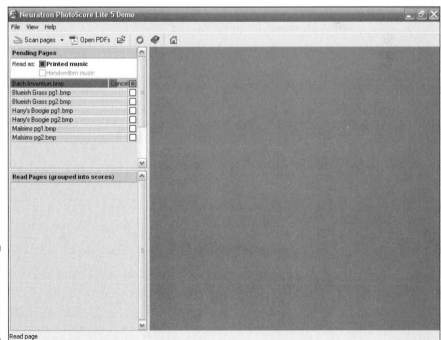

Figure 12-17:
PhotoScore
reading the
bitmap
image.

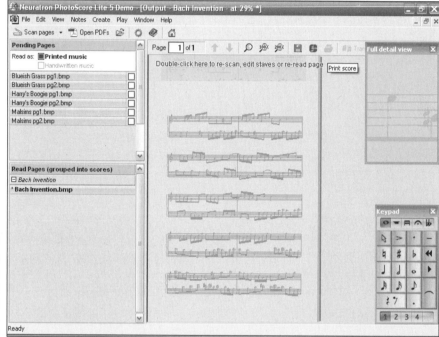

Figure 12-18:
The
PhotoScore
main editing
window.

4. Click the Sibelius icon on the PhotoScore toolbar (see Figure 12-19) to send the music to Sibelius.

If you don't already have it open, Sibelius starts. The Open PhotoScore File dialog box (shown in Figure 12-20) appears.

5. Leave the settings in the Open PhotoScore File dialog box, if you want, and just click OK.

After your file is imported into Sibelius, you can play it back, add instruments, or do everything you can do with Sibelius with your new score.

An advanced version of PhotoScore Lite called PhotoScore Ultimate is available for separate purchase. PhotoScore Ultimate can read more complex music (up to 32 staves), as well as more markings in the score (slurs, hairpins, and so on), text (such as titles and lyrics), and even handwritten noteheads. You can go to www.neuratron.com or www.sibelius.com for more details on purchasing PhotoScore Ultimate 5.

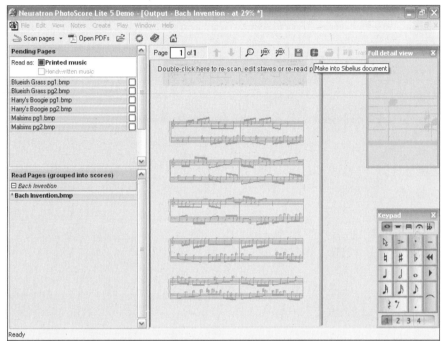

Figure 12-19:
Importing
the scanned
image into
Sibelius.

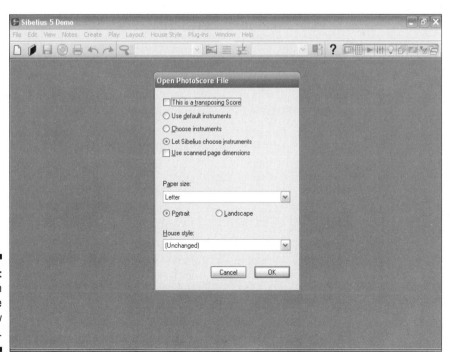

Figure 12-20:
The Open
PhotoScore
File window
in Sibelius.

Chapter 13

Keep the Beat: Adding the Drum Part

. . . .

In This Chapter

▶ Adding the funky back beat to your tune

▶ Getting great drum samples from the Web

▶ Recording a live percussion track

. . . .

*T*he drums are the booster rockets of hip-hop, pop, and R&B music. In the digital music world, the drum part is created by recording a live drum trap set in the studio, by playing a MIDI drum controller, or by playing an electronic drum kit. Some record producers even remove the drummer altogether, by using prerecorded samples, loops, and beats.

Writing a good drum part to your tune can be difficult. Often drummers don't read music as well as (or as poorly as) the other members of the band. Maybe the drummer *can* read music very well, but you don't know how to get your ideas in the score in a way that the drummer can easily understand.

In this chapter, I show you how drum parts are built, and then get you started putting some funky beats into your music.

Looking At the Four Ways to Write a Drum Part

There are four ways a drum part is usually written for a piece of music for a studio session or live performance:

- Bars containing slashes in every bar, similar to a chord progression written for a chordal instrument, such as a bass, guitar, or piano (see Figure 13-1): In this type of part, only the major elements of the tune are noted, such as the tempo and time signature, major ensemble rhythms, and a description of the style or idiom of the piece of music.

- A simplified part with some basic rhythms noted, but still fairly spare (see Figure 13-2): It has the major elements noted in the preceding bullet, as well as a description of the style of the music (rock, bossa nova, swing jazz, and so on).

- An extensively detailed part, with specific notes and rhythms, and an indication as to which part of the drum set the drummer is expected to play (see Figure 13-3): This is more common in educational music, or in parts intended for a less experienced drummer. Sometimes film music requires specific rhythms and sounds. Or maybe the composer has a very specific style that he wants, which can't be described well. Pitched percussion parts have to be spelled out exactly.

Figure 13-1:
A jazz drum part with slashes.

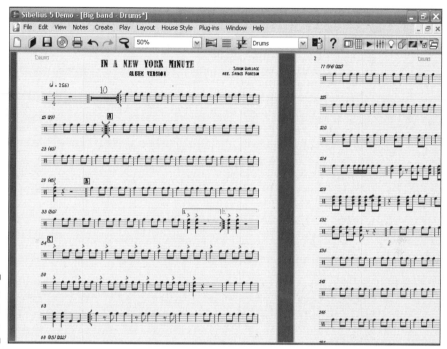

Figure 13-2:
A minimal
drum part.

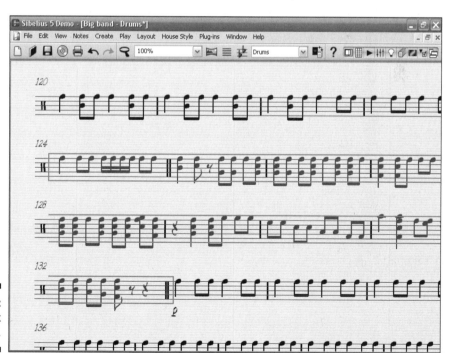

Figure 13-3:
A complex
drum part.

✔ **None:** You read that right: In bands such as small group jazz, rock, or pop, a written drum part is often not even used. In jazz, if the piece is a part of the standard jazz repertory (a *standard*), the drummer is expected to know how it starts and ends, as well as the rhythmic feel. In a garage band, the drummer makes up his own part, and creates something to go along with the other musicians. Or the composer of the tune describes the feel and rhythm to the drummer.

Percussion parts, especially in concert band or orchestra, are often notated using a single line, rather than the five-line stave musicians are used to seeing. Because the percussionist will most likely be called on to play multiple percussion instruments during the course of the piece, the single line uses text to indicate which instrument is to be played (see Figure 13-4).

Pitched percussion, such as the tympani or the vibraphone, is commonly notated with a five-line stave, because a definite pitch must be indicated. Check out the tympani part in Figure 13-5.

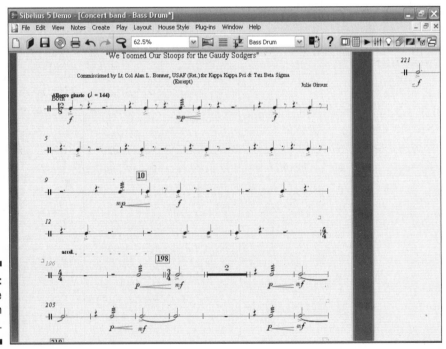

Figure 13-4:
A single-line bass drum part.

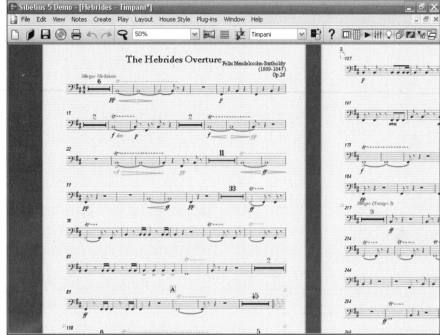

Figure 13-5:
The tympani
part to the
*Hebrides
Overture.*

Writing a New Drum Part

To get some practice, you can change the drum part of "My New Tune." I'll
have you use drum parts written by the drummer and percussionist Dom
Moio from the CD (see the nearby "Dom Moio" sidebar to find out more about
him). You're going to copy some of Dom's drum beats into the tune, and see
how they change the feel of the music.

Start by opening My New Tune-13-01.sib. Press Esc to be sure nothing is
selected, and change the view to 50 percent.

A composer usually writes text on the score to indicate which line of the
stave refers to which drum. The notation I'm using here, which is a fairly
common one, is shown in Figure 13-6. The examples in this chapter use primarily the closed hi-hat, the snare drum, and the bass drum.

All of Dom's drum patterns and fills can be found on the CD at Author/
Chapter 13/Templates/Drum Patterns.

Dom Moio

Dom Moio (www.dommoio.com) contributed the drum parts for "My New Tune," and I asked him to help because he's a drummer and percussionist extraordinaire. I've played with Dom off and on for over 30 years, in lots of different show, radio, TV, jazz, and rock venues, and I've always found him to be a consummate professional in every way.

Moio has played with jazz luminaries such as Mose Allison, Herb Ellis, Ahmad Jamal, and Clark Terry. He's also met and studied with legendary Cuban master percussionist Walfredo de los Reyes, Sr. When Moio was studying with Reyes, he developed what would become a lifelong passion for Latin rhythms.

Among his frequent record dates, Dom has recorded two CDs with jazz great Carl Fontana.

He also recorded with the Jazz Nonet with Chuck Marohnic and Greg Hopkins. In 1997, Moio did a re-recording of the Four Tops hits with the group's original singers, playing both drums and Latin percussion. Mel Bay has published two of Moio's books: *Latin Percussion in Perspective* and *Be-Bop Phrasing for Drums*.

Moio is currently teaching a Latin percussion class, "Music in World Cultures," plus private drum lessons at Mesa Community College, plus keeping a busy schedule at Arizona State University and traveling as a clinician for Trick Drums, Latin Percussion, Evans Drum Heads, Calato/Regal Tip Drumsticks, and Sabian Cymbals.

Common Drum Notations

Figure 13-6:
Common drum notations.

Dom Moio

Changing the basic beat

With `My New Tune-13-01.sib` open, open `Drum Set Beats #4.sib` from the CD. It should look like Figure 13-7. Change the View size to get all four bars on your screen if you need to.

Listen to `Drum Set Beats #4.sib` on the CD at `Author/Chapter 13/ Audio Examples/Drum Set Beats #4.mp3`.

To move back and forth between the two Sibelius scores you have open, go to the Window menu. At the bottom of the Window dialog box, you can pick the score you want to see.

Figure 13-7:
A drum set
template.

Follow these steps:

1. **Click on the first bar of Drum Set Beats #4.sib to highlight the whole measure.**

2. **While holding down the Shift key, click on the last bar to highlight all four bars.**

3. **Press Ctrl+C (⌘+C) to copy the four drum kit bars.**

4. **Choose Window⇨1 My New Tune-13-01.**

   My New Tune-13-01.sib should now be the score you see.

5. **Click on the first drum bar to highlight it, and press Ctrl+V (⌘+V) to paste the new drum kit part into the drum stave of My New Tune-13-01.sib.**

   It should look like Figure 13-8, with the new part in the score. If you want to open a template that already has it done for you, open My New Tune-13-02.sib.

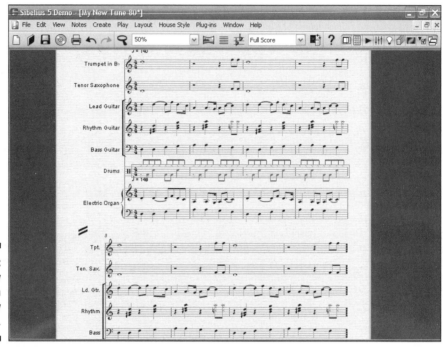

Figure 13-8:
"My New Tune" with the new drum part.

Listen to "My New Tune" on the CD at `Author/Chapter 13/Audio Examples/My New Tune-13-02.mp3`.

If you hit Esc, press Ctrl+[(⌘+[), and press the space bar, you can hear the tune from the beginning and check out your new drum part. You'll notice that starting on the fifth bar, the drums go back to playing the original drum part. You can paste the new drum part into the fifth bar of the drum stave to make the drummer play the new part all the way through, if you like. Or you can leave it as it is, with the drummer changing the feel halfway through the tune.

Adding a drum fill

All drummers like to add little beats and rhythms that signify the end of a phrase or section, making the music more interesting and propelling the band into the next section. These are called *drum fills,* and they help the musicians feel the natural musical divisions between these phrases.

In "My New Tune," each phrase is four bars long. So you can try putting a drum fill in the fourth bar. Close out of any files you have open. Reopen `My New Tune-13-01.sib` from the CD, and open `Sixteenth Note Fills #2.sib`.

This time you're only going to copy the first bar from `Sixteenth Note Fills #2.sib` and paste it into the fourth bar of the drum part of `My New Tune-13-01.sib`:

1. **Click on the first bar of `Sixteenth Note Fills #2.sib` to highlight it.**

2. **Press Ctrl+C (⌘+C) to copy it.**

3. **Choose Window⇨My New Tune-13-01.**

4. **Click on the fourth bar of the drum part to highlight it, and press Ctrl+V.**

   The sixteenth note fill should now be pasted into that bar, as in Figure 13-9.

Listen to "My New Tune" on the CD at `Author/Chapter 13/Audio Examples/My New Tune-13-04.mp3`.

If you also want to put the fill into the last bar of the drum part, go ahead and click on measure eight. Press Ctrl+V (⌘+V) to copy the fill into the last bar, and play it back to see if you like having the fill in both places. You can also open `My New Tune 13-4.sib` to check out the new drum fills.

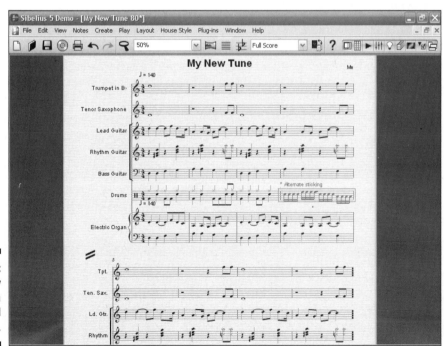

Figure 13-9:
"My New Tune" with a drum fill inserted.

There are eight different sixteenth note drum fill templates on the CD, so you can open My New Tune-13-01.sib as often as you like and copy a bar from any of the templates into any bar you choose. Or combine them, using one sixteenth note drum fill for bar four and a different one for bar eight.

Fills are most effective when used sparingly. That doesn't mean you can't copy the entire four-bar fill and use that as a drum part, just to see what it sounds like. But with a live band, you're going to wear out the drummer and turn the tune into a drum solo if you have the fill going all the time (not that it's a totally *bad* thing . . .).

On the CD, you find

- ✔ **Seven drum set beats:** These rock beats start out simple, but get progressively complicated.

- ✔ **Six basic rock figures:** These are a little more complicated, with a sixteenth-note rock feel to them. These six variations can be used with a lot of different types of rock. Experiment with cutting and pasting them into your score, and if you're a drummer, practice playing along with either the audio track or the Sibelius template.

- ✔ **Six basic rock figure combinations:** Here Dom has mixed things up a bit. In the previous examples, the third and fourth beat of each bar were the same as the first and second beats. In these examples, the rhythm is altered a bit to make the figure more interesting.

- ✔ **Eight sixteenth note fills:** These are intended to be used to add spice at the end of phrases, usually during the fourth and eighth bar of a four-bar phrase. Although the templates are four bars long, you normally would only use one bar of these fills.

  If you're playing these on the drums, play one of these fills at the end of the four-bar drum beat or rock figure example, to get the idea of how the fill should sound.

This makes a couple of thousand different drum beat combinations to put into your tune. And as you add more advanced drum beats to your library, you could eventually have tens of thousands of combinations to use in your compositions.

Experiment with moving the individual notes up and down, or in or out of the staff, to get a different drum sound. You can always open a fresh template from the CD and start over at any time.

Adding a Drum Pattern

You can use one of Sibelius's 24 predefined drum patterns, and have it inserted automatically in your score. You don't even need to create a drum kit staff first — Sibelius's plug-in will do it for you.

To use this plug-in, open `My New Tune-13-01.sib`, and choose Plug-ins➪ Composing Tools➪Add Drum Pattern. The Add Drum Pattern dialog box (shown in Figure 13-10) appears.

You're presented with several choices. You can:

- ✔ **Choose a style for the drum pattern.** You're shown a list of different musical styles, and you can pick the one suited to your tune.

- ✔ **Set the tempo of the pattern by selecting the metronome mark.**

- ✔ **Decide whether to create an intro bar, which starts the pattern off with an introductory fill.**

- ✔ **Decide when and how often the pattern should include a fill or break bar.**

- ✔ **Opt to end with an outro bar, which specifies whether the plug-in will end the pattern with a one-bar or two-bar concluding fill.**

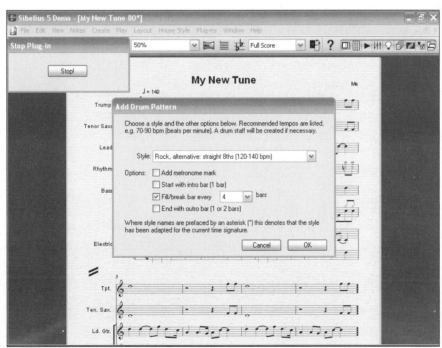

Figure 13-10:
Using the
Sibelius
drum
pattern
plug-in.

For now, in the Style drop-down list, select Rock, Alternative: Straight 8ths (120–140 bpm), and uncheck the Add Metronome Mark, Start with Intro Bar (1 Bar), and End with Outro Bar (1 or 2 Bars) check boxes. Leave the third box, Fill/Break Bar Every 4 Bars checked (and make sure 4 is selected in the drop-down list). Press OK, and the plug-in will take a couple of seconds to complete. When it's finished, you should have a completed drum pattern inserted into the tune, as shown in Figure 13-11. You can hit Esc and play it back to hear the tune with the new drum pattern.

If you want to try a different drum pattern, just choose Plug-ins➪Composing Tools➪Add Drum Pattern, pick another drum pattern, and it will automatically replace the old pattern with the new one you chose.

Try lots of patterns! Even slow or fast patterns can sound interesting, with fills or break bars in different places.

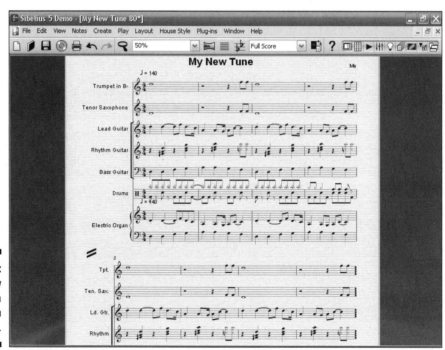

Figure 13-11:
"My New Tune" with a built-in drum pattern.

Getting a Drum Sample

Another way to get good drum sounds is by using free drum MIDI files from the Internet, or buying one of the commercial drum sample libraries that are offered on the Web or in music stores.

In Chapter 6, I discuss Native Instruments's BATTERY 3, which has thousands of drum kit samples. These samples can be used in virtually any type of music composition software that recognizes sample plug-ins.

There are tons of vendors and distributors of drum kit sounds on the Web. In addition to the major sample libraries, such as SampleTank (www.sampletank.com), KONTAKT (www.nativeinstruments.com/kontakt), and Studio Instruments (www.apple.com/logicstudio/instruments), some of the most popular are

- AbstractBeats.com (www.abstractbeats.com)
- Bangin-Beats (www.bangin-beats.com)
- DrumSamples.com (www.drumsamples.com)
- Drums On Demand (www.drumsondemand.com)
- ModernBeats (www.modernbeats.com)
- Silicon Beats (www.siliconbeats.com)

The price for these libraries varies a lot, but with a little searching you can find decent, well-made drum samples and groove loops for free or almost free on the Web.

One good way to get a MIDI drum sample into Sibelius, is to:

1. **Export the tune as a MIDI file from Sibelius.**

2. **Use a digital audio workstation program, like SONAR or Logic, to open the MIDI file.**

3. **Remove the old drum track, and use a drum sample plug-in to create a new drum track.**

4. **Save the file as MIDI, and then open it with Sibelius.**

You will need to tweak the drum notes, because different programs use different parts of the stave for the drum sounds. But this approach is a very good way to get good drum parts into your Sibelius score.

Part V
Beyond the Basics: Advanced Composing Tips and Tricks

The 5th Wave   By Rich Tennant

"Hey George, give it a rest. Let's have lunch. I picked up some bluefish. Man, I love bluefish. Do you love bluefish, George?"

In this part . . .

Here I give you some tips and tricks that will help your music advance beyond the basics. In Chapter 14, I show you the musical touches that really make a composition sound great, by adding expression, dynamics, phrasing, and backup parts.

Chapter 15 looks at even more advanced composing elements, such as harmonies, chords, countermelodies, and intros and outros. Chapter 16 shows you how to fine-tune your MIDI mix and make it sound its best, by tweaking your playback devices, changing the playback feel, and getting your MIDI setup to play nice with other MIDI devices.

Chapter 14

Spice Is Nice: Marking Up Your Score

· ·

In This Chapter

▶ Writing chord symbols and guitar tab

▶ Adding dynamics and articulations to your score

▶ Writing lyrics for the singer

· ·

*O*ne of the most difficult tasks music software has is to play a music passage with human feeling. Obviously the computer has no feeling toward the music and never will. A performer infuses the music with his thoughts, feelings, and personal history every time he picks up his instrument, but the computer doesn't know Beethoven from a spreadsheet.

In the previous chapter, you create some nice music. You use the templates to create notes, add instruments, and change the notes and rhythms. But what really makes music are dynamics, articulations, and chords. Tweaking the language of music and adding the important musical touches really make a composition stand out from the rest. And that's what you do in this chapter.

Writing Chord Symbols and Tablature

Chords are one of the three major elements that make up a tune — the other two are the melody and rhythm. Most popular, rock, jazz, and country music have a framework of chords called the *chord progression*. These chords are identified in the score using *chord symbols*.

Almost every singer/songwriter creates a chord progression in the early stage of composing a song. He may create the chord progression first, and then sing a melody to go with the progression. Or he may think of the melody first, and then create some chords to go with it.

Singing the blues

A common chord progression is one called the *blues progression*, also known as the *12-bar blues*. The 12-bar blues is one of the most popular chord progressions in popular music. As old as blues music itself, the 12-bar blues has had lots of variations over the years. It's the foundation of a large part of rock, pop, and blues music, and has even been considered one of America's greatest contributions to music. It's also the foundation for rock's common three-chord song style.

But the 12-bar blues is fundamentally three chords played in a particular order. If you studied music, you may recognize the chords as tonic, subdominant, and dominant. But to the rest of us jazz and rock players, the three chords are remembered by three numbers: one, four, and five, usually represented by the Roman numerals I, IV, and V7. (The number 7 is how the V chord is usually notated, to indicate that it's the dominant seventh chord.)

In the key of C, the most basic 12-bar blues progression would be four bars of C (the I, or tonic), two bars of F (the IV, or subdominant), two bars of C, one bar of G7 (the V7, or dominant seventh), one bar of F, and two bars of C. These 12 bars create one full blues progression, which is then repeated as needed.

The rhythm section likes changes

The phrase *Don't go changing* doesn't apply to the rhythm section — the guitars, keyboards, bass, and drums that supply the heartbeat of the band. *Changes* are the chord progressions of a tune. When jazz players get together to jam, they play the chord progressions to popular songs, called *standards*.

You can try entering chord symbols into the rhythm guitar part on "My New Tune." Start by opening the template My New Tune-14-011.sib from the CD. Press Esc to be sure nothing is highlighted, click on the first bar of the rhythm guitar part to highlight it, and increase the View size to 100 percent or more. It should look like Figure 14-1.

Creating a chord symbol in Sibelius is easy. Actually, there are several ways to create text that notates the chords to be played. But if you do it the way I explain, there's a very cool benefit: If you transpose the part for some reason (say the singer wants the tune in a different key, or you decide to copy and paste it to another instrument), the chord symbol will transpose along with the notes. You won't have to go back and change every chord symbol. Here's what to do:

1. **Select any note of the first chord of the first bar (the chord on the second beat) and press Ctrl+K (⌘+K).**

   You'll see a flashing vertical line above the chord.

2. **Right-click to bring up a submenu of chord symbols.**

   If you're familiar with building chord progressions, you may not need to do this step, because you probably already know the proper syntax to get the chord you want. But for the sake of this exercise, pick a chord name from the menu, as shown in Figure 14-2.

3. **Select the *D* on the left of the list of note names.**

   The letter *D* is now above the first rhythm guitar chord, as shown in Figure 14-3.

   If you get lost, you can reload `My New Tune-14-01.sib` and try again, or you can move ahead by opening the template `My New Tune-14-02.sib`.

4. **Without hitting Esc, and while remaining in Chord mode, press the space bar twice to move two steps to the next chord.**

   You should see the flashing vertical line over the next chord.

5. **Either right-click again to bring up the chord symbols menu, or just type** G **to enter the next chord.**

6. **Press the space bar two more times to get to the third chord, and type** A.

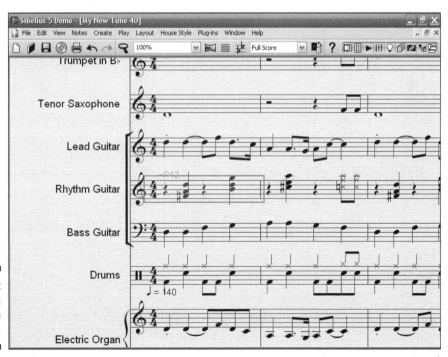

Figure 14-1:
Highlighting
the rhythm
guitar part.

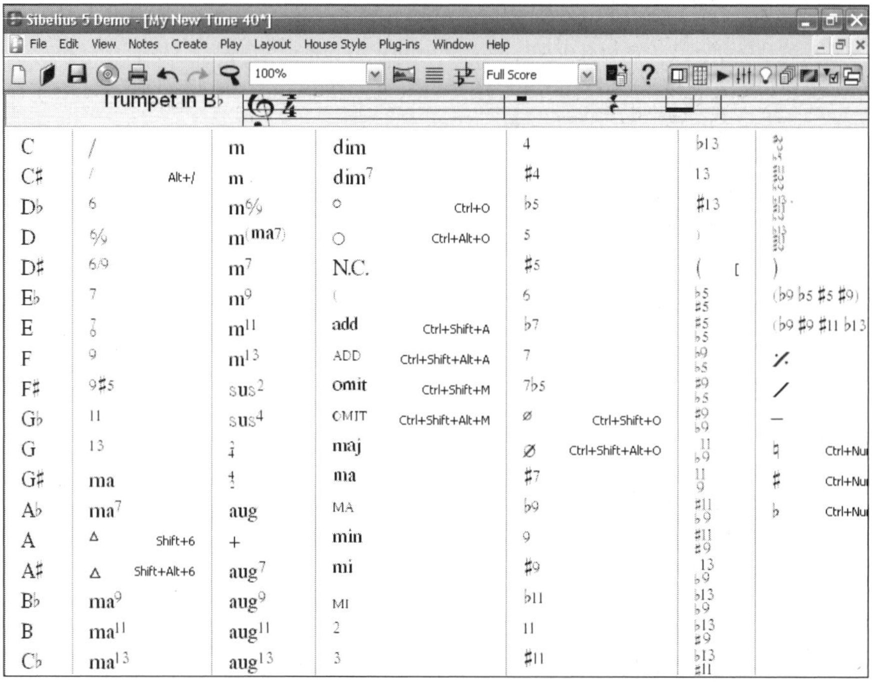

Figure 14-2:
The chord symbols submenu.

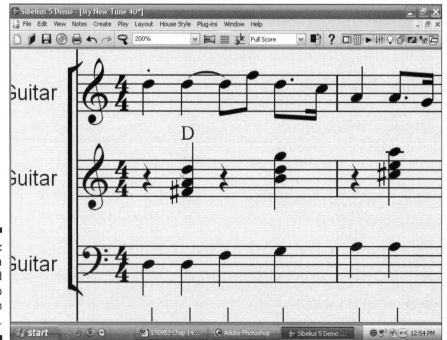

Figure 14-3:
Entering a chord symbol into the rhythm guitar part.

7. Press the space bar twice more and type F.

Your final two bars should look like Figure 14-4.

8. Highlight the first two bars of the rhythm guitar part, and copy and paste the two bars three times to fill out the rest of the guitar part.

It should look like Figure 14-5, with the chord symbols inserted in every bar of the rhythm guitar part.

If you're new to copying and pasting bars, check out Chapter 7, where I walk you through this step by step.

If you want to add guitar frames, instead of, or in addition to, the chord symbols, just press Shift+K instead of Ctrl+K (⌘+K) after selecting the note, to bring up the Chord Diagram dialog box (shown in Figure 14-6). Here you can pick the chord name, and then pick the diagram you want to show. The menu will give you a couple of common fingerings for the chord you picked — just pick the one you like.

If you get lost, you can either load the template My New Tune-14-02.sib and retry it, or load My New Tune-14-03.sib and continue on with the chapter.

Figure 14-4:
The rhythm guitar chords.

Figure 14-5:
The finished rhythm guitar part.

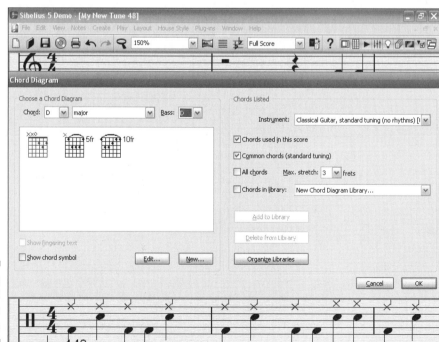

Figure 14-6:
The Chord Diagram dialog box.

The tablature back story

Tablature is one of the greatest advancements in sheet music. For decades, all sheet music offered for sale at your music store was created by piano players primarily *for* piano players.

Before the rock revolution, sheet music sales were a major part of the income for a popular song. Music stores and department stores had "song demonstrators" who would play the piece for prospective purchasers, so they could hear how it went before they shelled out their dime. Even after rock changed the music business, sheet music notation was still using traditional notes and chords, but sometimes adding a small guitar fingering chart to help the guitarist play the right chord. But the popular music wasn't being played on the piano anymore, and because the guitar was the predominant popular instrument, piano notation just wasn't a good fit.

One reason it *wasn't* a good fit is that traditional notation — just showing the melody, chords, and lyrics — couldn't accurately describe what the original performer was playing on the guitar (or bass). In modern music, rock especially, the performance style, string bends, chord voicing, and improvised solos were an essential part of the piece. And there was a growing audience of potential sheet music purchasers who didn't read traditional notation but still wanted to learn the piece of music.

A Sibelius plug-in will automatically calculate chord symbols in your score, as long as there are chords or multiple notes on the score itself. Go to Plug-ins⇨ Chord Symbols to use this plug-in.

All guitarists read tab

Tablature (called *tab* for short) tells the players of fretted stringed instruments (most often guitarists) where to place their fingers, rather than which specific notes to play. This type of notation lets the musician see more clearly exactly what the original performer of the tune is doing. (For more on how tablature came to be, check out the nearby sidebar.)

To enter the tablature parts for "My New Tune," start by opening My New Tune-14-03.sib from the CD. Press Esc to make sure nothing has been selected, and then follow these steps:

1. **Choose Create⇨Instruments.**

   The Instruments dialog box appears.

2. **Under Choose From, select Rock and Pop Instruments.**

3. **Under Family, select Electric Guitar.**

4. **Under Instrument, click twice on Electric Guitar, Standard Tuning [Tab].**

   Two tablature instruments are added to the Staves in Score box.

5. **Click on one of the new tab staves and move it up or down to position one tab stave under the Lead Guitar stave, and the other under the Rhythm Guitar stave, as shown in Figure 14-7.**

   You should now have two new staves in your score: one tablature stave for the lead guitar, and one new stave for the rhythm guitar, as shown in Figure 14-8.

   If you want to start from here, you can open -14-04.sib and continue from this point.

6. **Highlight the first four bars of the lead guitar part, and copy and paste them into the first electric guitar tablature part, as shown in Figure 14-9.**

   For step-by-step instruction on how to highlight, copy, and paste, turn to Chapter 7, where I describe the process in detail.

7. **Highlight the first four bars of the rhythm guitar part, and copy and paste them into the empty tablature stave below the Rhythm Guitar stave.**

   It should look like Figure 14-10.

8. **Copy the two new tablature parts to the second half of the tune.**

   It should look like Figure 14-11.

   You can open the template My New Tune-14-05.sib and compare it with what you've done.

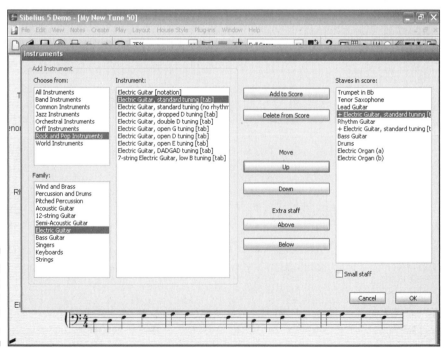

Figure 14-7: Adding guitar tablature staves.

Figure 14-8:
The new tablature guitar staves in the score.

Figure 14-9:
The lead guitar part in tablature.

Figure 14-10:
The rhythm guitar part in tablature.

Figure 14-11:
The completed tablature parts.

Adding Expression to Your Score

Music is much more than just notes and rhythms. How loudly or softly the note is played is called a *dynamic marking*. A dynamic marking is a letter or group of letters under the staff that tell you how softly or loudly you should play the musical passage. (Check out Chapter 3 for more about dynamic markings.)

To add some dynamic markings to your score, begin by opening the template My New Tune-14-06.sib from the CD. Press Esc to be sure nothing is highlighted, and change the view to 75 percent. Then follow these steps:

1. **Click on the first bar of the trumpet part to highlight the whole bar, and press Ctrl+E (⌘+E), Ctrl+P+P (⌘+P+P) — hold down the Ctrl (⌘) key while pressing the P key twice — and then press Esc.**

   You should have the pianissimo (*pp*) expression indicated under the first trumpet measure, as shown in Figure 14-12.

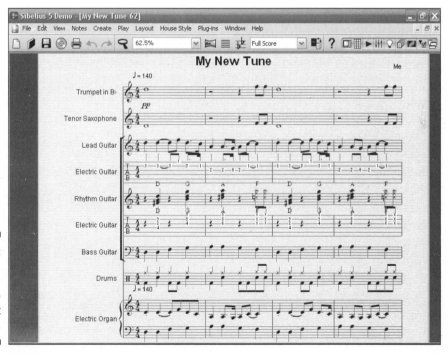

Figure 14-12:
Adding a dynamic marking to the trumpet part.

2. **Now highlight the *pp*, press Ctrl+C (⌘+C), click on the first bar of the tenor sax part to highlight it, hold down the Shift key while clicking on the first bar of each instrument, and press Ctrl+V (⌘+V).**

   The *pp* expression should now appear in the first measure of every instrument, all the way down to the second organ stave. It should look like Figure 14-13.

   This makes the tune play quietly. You can hit Esc, press Ctrl+[(⌘+[), and then press the space bar to hear it.

What if you want to make the tune get gradually louder. Repeat the preceding steps to put the mezzo-piano (*mp*) expression under every instrument's third bar, the mezzo-forte (*mf*) expression under the fifth bar of every instrument, and finally the forte (*f*) expression on every instrument's seventh bar. It should now look like Figure 14-14. You can open the My New Tune-14-07.sib file to see and hear what it's supposed to be.

Listen to "My New Tune" on the CD at Author/Chapter 14/Audio Examples/My New Tune-14-07.mp3.

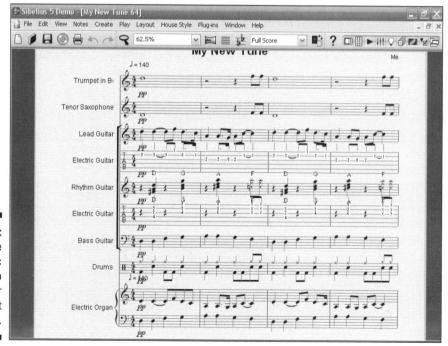

Figure 14-13:
Adding the dynamic marking to the other instrument staves.

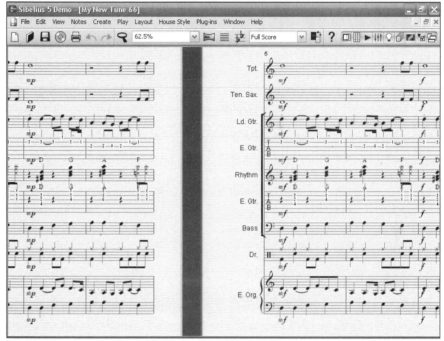

Figure 14-14:
Dynamics
entered for
the whole
tune.

Music notation software plays the dynamics you've notated in your score, but sometimes rather oddly. A computer doesn't "play" the dynamics the same way a musician would. So if you're writing a score to be played by live musicians, enter the dynamics you want *them* to play, but don't expect the dynamics markings in your score to sound exactly as you'd like them when you play your score on your computer.

Using Articulations

An *articulation* is another way the note is to be played. Sometimes a note is played very smoothly, or *legato,* and sometimes it's played detached and clipped, or *staccato.* You can indicate these articulations with marks above the notes — a line (≠) for legato or a dot (•) for staccato. An *accent mark* (>) above a note tells the player to make the note stand out and play it a little louder than the other notes.

Spicing up the horn parts

Say you want to enter some articulation marking for the horn players. Start by opening `My New Tune-14-08.sib`, pressing Esc, and changing the View to 100 percent. Press Ctrl+Alt+K (Option+⌘+K) to bring up the Keypad. Then follow these steps:

1. **Hold down Ctrl (⌘) and click on the two eighth notes in the second bar of the trumpet part.**

2. **While still holding down Ctrl, click on the two eighth notes in the tenor sax part.**

3. **Click on the little dot that looks like a period in the Keypad, called a staccato.**

   Sibelius should put a staccato dot over the top of all four notes, as in Figure 14-15. You can open the template `My New Tune-14-09.sib`, where I've it done for you.

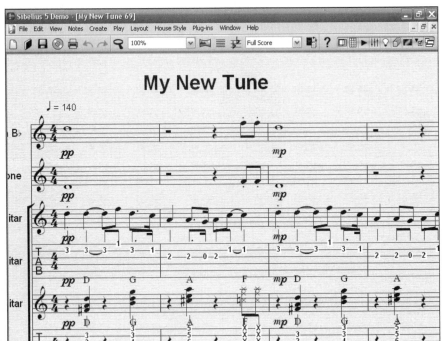

Figure 14-15: Placing a staccato in the horn parts.

4. Press Esc, copy the second bar of the trumpet and tenor sax parts, and paste them into the fourth, sixth, and eighth bars of the horns parts.

It should look like Figure 14-16, or like the `My New Tune-14-10.sib` file. You can highlight just the horn parts and press P to hear the difference.

You can experiment with different articulations for the horns. Repeat the process, but instead of using a staccato, use the accent, or tenuto. Or press F11 to bring up the Keypad's page of articulations, and experiment with them. *Remember:* You can't hurt anything — if you need to start over, open `My New Tune-14-08.sib` and start fresh!

Slurring your notes

A *slur* is a note that blends into another note. Usually the pitch changes with the second note, but the second note is not articulated, and becomes an extension of the first note.

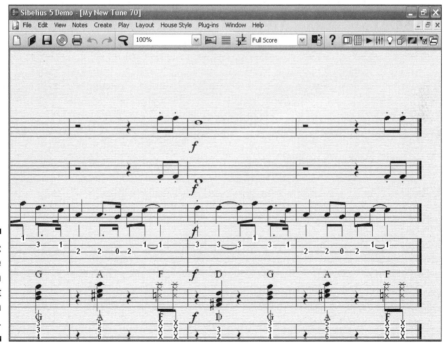

Figure 14-16:
Copying the articulation to the rest of the horn part.

A slur is notated by a special articulation mark, a curved line that connects two different notes, check it out in Chapter 3. It means that the player should move from one note to the other smoothly, without stopping the sound.

Adding Lyrics

You can't have a song without lyrics. Well, you *can,* but eventually the singers are going to get cranky singing "do-do-do" all day.

Try adding lyrics to a few bars of the familiar folk tune "Scarborough Fair":

1. **From the CD, open the `Scarborough Fair-01.sib` file.**

2. **Select the first note and press Ctrl+L (⌘+L).**

   You see a flashing cursor.

3. **Type Are and press the space bar to go to the next note, as shown in Figure 14-17.**

4. **Type you and press the space bar again to get to the next note.**

Figure 14-17:
Adding
lyrics to a
note.

5. **Repeat Step 4 three more times, entering** going, to, **and** Scar **under the next three notes.**

6. **Press the hyphen (-) key and type** bor **under the next note.**

7. **Press the hyphen again and enter** ough **under the next note.**

   The hyphen spreads the syllables of the word *Scarborough* over three notes.

8. **Press the space bar to get to the last note, type** Fair?, **and press Esc to finish.**

   Your melody and lyrics should look like Figure 14-18. You can open the template Scarborough Fair-02.sib to see what it should look like.

When you play back a vocal track in Sibelius, you hear a male or female voice (depending upon which one you picked in the Instruments section), singing a "doo" syllable for each pitch and rhythm. Unfortunately, entering lyrics won't make the computer sing the actual words, the software isn't that advanced yet.

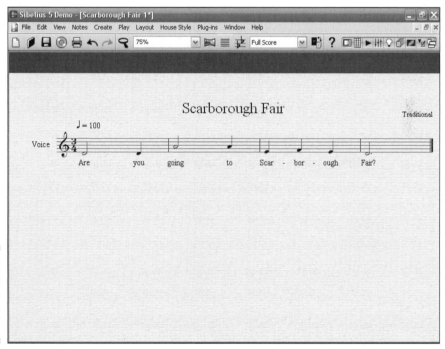

Figure 14-18:
The opening lyrics to "Scarborough Fair."

All in the phrasing

If you've played music for a while, or you've studied music in school, you've heard the term *musical phrasing.* It's a common term, but it can mean different things. A *musical phrase* is a series of notes or measures that complete a musical thought. It can be as few as eight notes, like the famous opening of Beethoven's Fifth Symphony, or a complete melody of many bars.

For example, the four bars in "Scarborough Fair" (refer to Figure 14-18) complete a musical phrase. Phrasing is used by composers to form a natural division of the melodic line, and create a degree of structural completeness. Like the communication of a written or spoken thought, a phrase gives the feeling of beginning and ending, a sense of completeness when it's played.

 Often, sheet music has more than one lyric, if the melody repeats. To enter second verses of lyrics on the same notes, select the note, and press Ctrl+Alt+L (Option+⌘+L), instead of Ctrl+L (⌘+L) as you did for the first verse. This places the second verse directly under the first verse in the score.

Making Your Score Pretty

A score that does more than just show you the notes, harmony, and rhythms is a good thing. The score can be a work of art just on its own, with a nice title page with colors and graphics.

Adding a title page

Sibelius lets you create a blank page at the beginning of your score, and you can use that page to insert text or graphics. This makes the score look good when printing out a copy for distribution. Published scores often have a title page, and if you're submitting a score for a contest, you may be required to create a page with your personal info on it.

If you want a title page, you can set that up when you're creating a new score. In the New Score dialog box, select the Create Title Page check box.

If you need to add a blank page after you've been working on your score for a while, select the first bar line at the start of the tune, and press Ctrl+Shift+Enter (Shift+⌘+Enter). The Special Page Break dialog box appears. For a title page, just select the Blank Page(s) check box, select the Number of Blank Pages radio button, and type **1** in the field to the right, as shown in Figure 14-19. You can add text or graphics to the blank page.

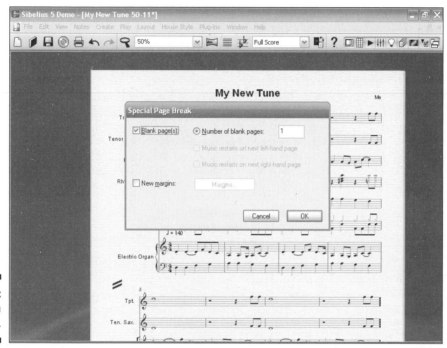

Figure 14-19:
Inserting a
blank page.

Getting fancy with colors

You can change the color of anything in the score — notes, rests, text, anything. Maybe you need to make sure a tempo change will be noticed by the
conductor, or you want rehearsal letters to stand out. Color can help you
make that happen.

Here's how to add color to your score:

1. **With your score open, press Esc to make sure nothing is selected.**

2. **Click to select the object, note, or anything in the score that you want
   to color.**

3. **Press Ctrl+J (⌘+J).**

   The Color window (shown in Figure 14-20) appears.

4. **Select the color you'd like for your object and click OK.**

   If you're not crazy about the color, and you want to delete coloring,
   select the colored element, and either choose Layout⇨Reset Design, or
   press Ctrl+Shift+D (⌘+Shift+D). This resets the color back to the original.

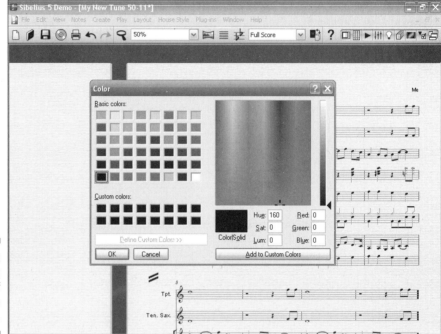

Figure 14-20:
Changing
the color of
score
elements.

Don't go crazy with the colors. Apply them sparingly (for example, to accent important instructions with red). But leave the notes and major elements in black. *Remember:* The colors may not come out the way you'd like them to when you print the score, because a printer's output doesn't always replicate what you see on the screen.

Inserting symbols and pictures

Pictures and symbols are also a great way to add some spice to your music, and emphasize important elements of the score. And certain musical symbols, such as keyboard pedal instructions or various percussion instruments, need symbols to get the point across.

To add symbols to your score, just press Z to bring up the Symbol dialog box (shown in Figure 14-21). Pick the symbol you want, and click on where you want it in the score.

Sibelius has lots of symbols for all kinds of musical instructions, from special repeat signs; to keyboard, guitar, and percussion instructions; to unusual symbols for contemporary music.

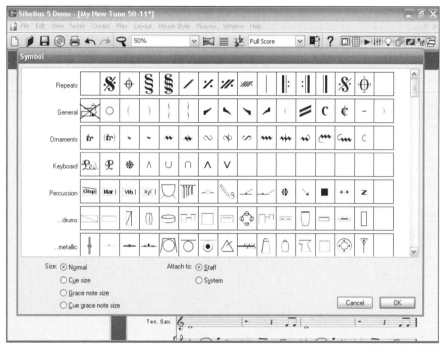

Figure 14-21:
Inserting
symbols in
your score.

You can also insert pictures of anything in your score, such as logos or band pictures, by importing your own TIFF files into Sibelius (Sibelius 5 only imports TIFF files). Choose Create⇨Graphic, select the TIFF file you want to insert, and click on the score to position it where you want it. After it's inserted, you can move the graphic around the score and resize it using the anchor in the lower right-hand corner of the graphic.

If you don't like any of your own pictures (hey, maybe you're no Richard Avedon), check out the Sibelius `Graphic Files` folder, which holds many images already created for you to use. This folder is usually in the `Example Scores` folder, which is created when you install Sibelius. The `Graphics Files` folder contains pictures of many different kinds of instruments and icons you can use freely.

Chapter 15

You're a Real Composer Now

- -

In This Chapter

▶ Composing a countermelody for your tune

▶ Adding intros and outros to your music

▶ Synchronizing a digital video with your musical score

A piece of music includes many elements beyond just the melody, harmony, and rhythm. The part of the tune before the main theme is called the *introduction*. The intro sets up the style and mood of the piece, and can be short or long. The tune has to end somehow, too. If you're playing live, you can't just use a recording studio's *board fade* (the gradual fade out of the music at the end) — you need to figure out an outro. Background music is also important to the overall concept of the music.

Let's look at these finishing elements of music, and also check out some ways to add and synchronize video files with your score.

Composing Background Melodies

A piece of music needs more than just the melody. A good tune often has other melodic phrases in addition to the main theme. A *countermelody* is a melodic note sequence, that is played at the same time as the main melody, and is often called the *background melody* in pop or jazz music.

This time, try adding a short background, or countermelody, to "My New Tune":

1. **Open the file My New Tune-15-01.sib.**

2. **Delete the first bar of both the trumpet and tenor parts, so it looks like Figure 15-1.**

3. **Create a countermelody and place it in the third and fourth bars of the trumpet part.**

If you don't know how to create notes using the Keypad, turn to Chapter 7. To make the new countermelody shown in Figure 15-2, I added a dotted quarter length D, a dotted quarter length F, and a quarter note G in the third bar. In the fourth bar, I added a quarter note A on the first beat of the bar.

If you want to see how it should look, open `My New Tune-15-02.sib`.

4. **Copy and paste the new third and fourth trumpets bars to the tenor sax part.**

   Be sure to lower the part and octave after you paste, to allow for the different range of the instruments. It should look like Figure 15-3, or you can open `My New Tune-15-03.sib` on the CD.

5. **To have the horns play this line twice, copy the third and fourth bars of both of the trumpet and tenor parts, and paste them to bars seven and eight.**

   I already did it for you in `My New Tune-15-04.sib`. Now you have your completed countermelody as played by the horn section (see Figure 15-4).

Listen to "My New Tune" on the CD at `Author/Chapter 15/Audio Examples/My New Tune-15-04.mp3`.

Figure 15-1: Changing the trumpet and tenor parts.

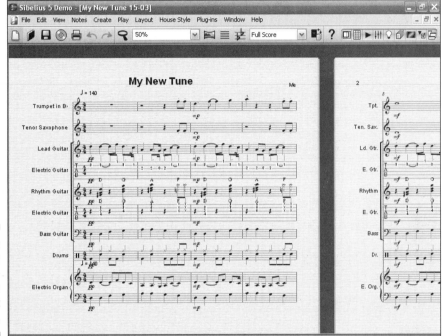

Figure 15-2:
Adding a counter-melody in the trumpet part.

Figure 15-3:
Adding the counter-melody to the tenor sax part.

Figure 15-4:
The completed horn section counter-melody.

Adding Intros and Outros

Most music doesn't just start immediately with the melody and end abruptly when the melody has been played. The melody is just a small part of an arrangement. Beginnings, endings, solo sections, time and key changes, and a host of other elements make an arrangement more interesting.

Tunes often have a beginning section called an *intro,* which can be short and sweet or complicated and lengthy. An ending section, sometimes called an *outro,* helps signal to the musicians and the listener that the tune is winding up, and going to end.

When you're composing your original song, consider adding an intro and outro to your piece. It'll make it sound more professional and make a better overall impression with your audience.

In the beginning . . . : Adding an intro

Try adding an intro section to *My New Tune*.

1. **Open My New Tune-15-04.sib.**

2. **Press Esc to make sure nothing is selected, and then choose Create⇨ Bar⇨Other (Alt+B/Option+B).**

    The Create Bars dialog box (shown in Figure 15-5) appears.

3. **In the Number of Bars box, enter 4, and click OK.**

    You get a big arrow to help you place the four new bars.

4. **Click on the very first bar line of the tune.**

    Sibelius places the four bars at the beginning of the tune, as shown in Figure 15-6.

I created an intro for you, shown in Figure 15-7. Open My New Tune-15-05. sib, and you see that I've added:

✔ A new rhythm guitar intro, playing an A chord on the fourth beat of each of the four measures

✔ A new drum intro, imported from Dom Moio's Basic Rock Figures Combinations #3.sib

✔ A new bass intro, based on the kick drum part

Figure 15-5: Creating intro measures in the Create Bars dialog box.

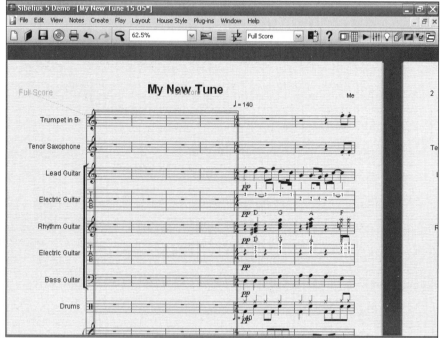

Figure 15-6:
Four
introductory
measures
inserted.

You can use the intro I created for you, or you can input something completely different. Either way, spend some time playing around with different intros to find one you like.

The big finish: Adding an outro

No tune is complete without a nice end to it. Although recorded music has the ability to *board fade* (fade out the song during the outro), live music needs to end cleanly.

Follow these steps to write an outro for "My New Tune":

1. **Choose Create⇨Bar⇨At End.**

   A blank measure is added to the end of the piece.

2. **Repeat Step 1 three more times.**

   You now have a total of four blank measures at the end of the piece.

I've created an outro for you in My New Tune-15-06.sib (see Figure 15-8). Here's what I did:

✔ Added a new lead guitar, trumpet, tenor, and organ outro part based on the bass line, which is a reprise of the intro bass line

✔ Repeated the rhythm guitar intro

✔ Reprised the drum intro part for the outro

✔ Inserted an End Repeat bar line at the start of the outro, to make the main section of the tune play twice

✔ Inserted rehearsal marks at the fifth bar of the tune and at the start of the outro

✔ Created an ending chord for the bass, drums, and organ

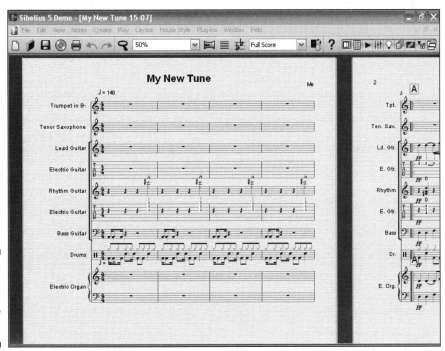

Figure 15-7:
An intro built into "My New Tune."

Rehearsal marks

Rehearsal marks are really a big help for the band. These big letters or numbers help the musicians think of your piece in sections and find their way in the music more easily. For example, the melody of the tune may be the A section, and a development or solo section may be labeled B. This makes it easy to start the band in the middle of the tune during rehearsal.

You can easily insert rehearsal marks in your score by highlighting the bar line where you want the rehearsal mark to be, and pressing Ctrl+R (⌘+R). This automatically inserts a big letter at the top of the bar in your score. When you print out the parts, the rehearsal marks will be duplicated on every part.

Figures 15-9 and 15-10 show the final opus in Sibelius's new Panorama mode. This new view fits the screen more easily, and shows more of the full score. You can hear the finished piece in `My New Tune-15-07.mp3`.

Listen to "My New Tune" on the CD at `Author/Chapter 15/Audio Examples/My New Tune-15-07.mp3`.

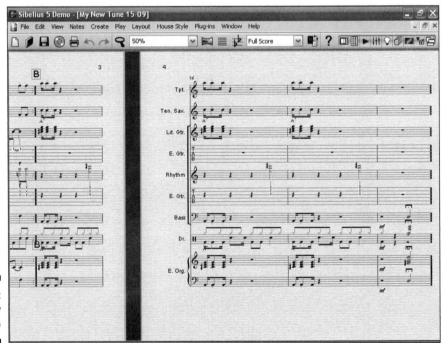

Figure 15-8:
The new outro

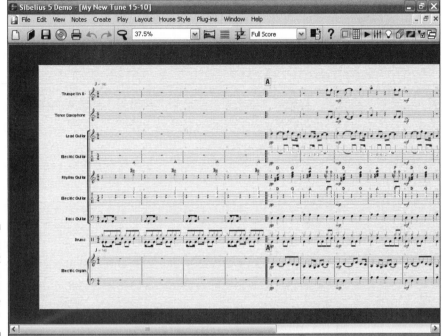

Figure 15-9:
The first half of the finished "My New Tune."

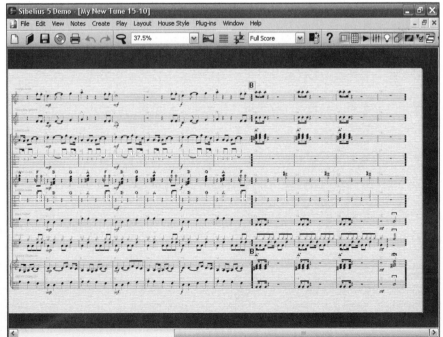

Figure 15-10:
The second half of the finished "My New Tune."

Adding Video to Your Score

Composing background music for a film or video is one of the most exciting challenges a composer can face. Most professional film and video production studios use very expensive and complicated equipment, and the options available to the home composer have always been very limited. But today, most digital audio workstations (DAWs) and notation software let you add a digital video file to your score and synchronize your music to what's happening on the screen.

Sibelius does video sync with music, and it's pretty easy. You can even do it with the demo software included on the CD.

Inserting a video

To insert video file into your score, even if it's a blank score, follow these steps:

1. **Open your score, or start a new score.**

2. **Choose Play⇨Video and Time⇨Add Video.**

   The Add Video dialog box (shown in Figure 15-11) appears. Sibelius will let you add most standard video file formats, such as AVI, MPG, WMV, and MOV video formats.

3. **Select the video file you want to use, and press OK.**

You can add external MP3 files by following these same steps.

Now if you play back your score, the video will start from the beginning and play along. The video starts and stops every time you start and stop the playback.

After you've inserted the video, you can press Ctrl+Alt+V (Option+⌘+V) to open or close the video window. Using the video window, you can resize the video so it takes up various sizes on the screen.

If the video has a soundtrack with it, you can control the volume of the video's playback using the horizontal volume slider at the bottom of the video window. You may want to mute the Sibelius playback, if you want to hear only the video soundtrack.

To remove a video that has already been inserted into your score, choose Play⇨Video and Time⇨Remove Video.

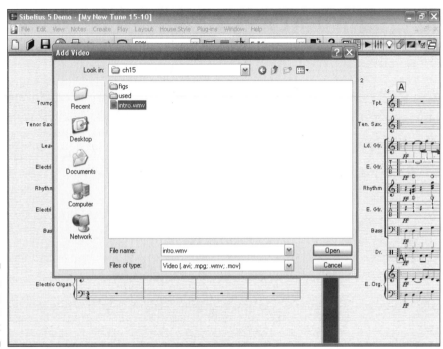

Figure 15-11:
Selecting
the video
file to insert

It's best if the video file is located in the same folder as the score. That way all videos that are associated with a particular project are kept and saved together. And Sibelius (and you) can more easily find the file when you open the project.

Because your score's playback is automatically synchronized with the video, you can adjust the tempo and playback position on the Playback window, and both score and video will update. In the same way that you play back the music to your score, you can use the playback position slider to jump to specific points in the score.

If you change the metronome marking at the start of your score and alter the tempo of the tune either faster or slower, the video will still run at the original speed. So you may need to adjust the tempo of your score to match the events onscreen.

Using hit points

When film or video music corresponds with something happening on the screen, it's known as a *hit point*. Composers use hit points to emphasize onscreen action, such as a cymbal crash when a dish drops and breaks, for example. Hit points also help composers locate areas in the film when the film's mood changes, such as from happy to suspenseful, and the music needs to change with it.

In most digital music software, you can create hit points to match events in the video to events in the music, or to allow you to aim for a hit point when composing a section of music.

In Sibelius, you can create hit points by clicking the button in the lower left-hand corner of the video window during playback. Hit points show up at the top of your score in a box (see Figure 15-12) and align themselves to the nearest beat in a bar. You can then choose Play➪Video and Time➪Hit Points to edit or label the hit point.

If you've already inserted hit points, you can ensure that Sibelius lines up a bar line at the exact time code position of your hit points. Choose Plug-ins➪ Composing Tools➪Fit Selection to Time, and experiment with this important feature.

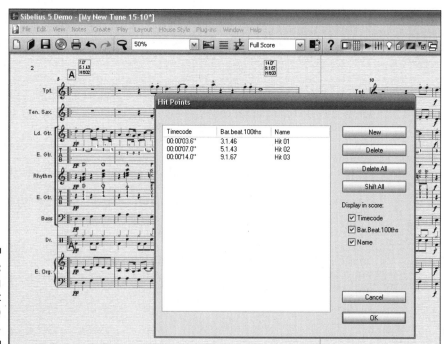

Figure 15-12: Inserting video hit points into your score.

Chapter 16

Fine-Tuning the Mix: Playback Options

*W*hen it comes down to it, a computer is a computer, it's not a band. The digital music software and hardware manufacturers expend tons of time and money in making the electrons moving through the cold transistors of your PC sound like flesh-and-blood musicians playing.

Originally, computers' attempts at making music were recognizable by their beeps and boops and weird swoops. And to suggest that the rhythms laid down by a electronic drummer were anything close to swingin' was humorous.

Today, advanced computer algorithms modify the output to add lifelike variations in the rhythm and pitch. Thousands of samples and sound sets have been created to let the digital music producer insert realistic instrument sounds into his piece. Modeling software and plug-ins were developed to replicate almost every type of analog or acoustic sound, from vintage analog synthesizers like the Moog, to famous guitarists' amplifiers (such as Jimi Hendrix), to every conceivable band and orchestra instrument.

If you're using a notation software program, like Sibelius or Finale, you probably really don't care that much about how lifelike your computer sounds when you're playing back the score on the screen. If you're like me, you want the ability to hear certain sections you wrote, to help proofread your notes and find mistakes in the harmony, for example. But you know that your computer is never going to sound like a roaring, full big band, no matter how much you tweak the sound card output.

Everyone wants his opus to sound great. You may be able to musically visualize the band cookin' on your hot tracks, but it's pretty deflating to play back your score to someone and have it sound tinny and nasal with no rhythmic feel. And if you're creating pop, dance, video, or other commercial music, such as background tracks for a vocalist or instrumentalist, the sound quality of the final product is very important. If you're going to use the playback to demo the song to a publisher, or show your musical group how the piece goes, the closer to reality the playback sounds, the better.

In this chapter, I show you how you can make a silk purse out of this sow's ear and make your computer sound like a pro.

Changing the Playback Device

The *playback device* is the hardware and software combination in your computer that converts the bits and bytes of the digital information stream into the sound you hear.

Because most computer owners want to watch video (either streaming from YouTube or on a DVD), listen to iTunes or CDs, and play video games with their expansive sound effects and musical scores, no computer is sold today without at least a minimal-quality sound card with speaker or headphone connections. The problem is that these bundled sound systems truly *are* minimal. The frequency range and bit depth (measurements that help determine how rich and true-to-life the music sounds) are not very high-quality. Also, the software sound set that comes with the average computer is very limited; you may only have the Microsoft GS Wavetable SW Synth, a MIDI sound set that comes with Windows PCs.

The Microsoft GS Wavetable SW Synth is the name of the MIDI sound set that comes with the Windows operating system. It translates MIDI code into specific instrument sounds, and provides a relatively minimal group of instrument sounds for MIDI playback. Apple's DLSMusicDevice driver is the Macintosh default MIDI sound set.

You probably want to improve the way your computer makes music, especially if you're going to invest big bucks in a digital audio workstation. You can do this in two main ways:

  ✔ Modify your Sibelius playback options and your audio engine properties.

  ✔ Get virtual instrument libraries that make your digital music sound more realistic.

KONTAKT Player 2

Sibelius 5 uses a virtual instrument rack called KONTAKT Player 2, to load, store, retrieve, and edit the sounds. KONTAKT Player plays the sounds from Sibelius Sounds Essentials and many other sample libraries, including those in the Sibelius Sounds range, and those produced by other vendors such as the Garritan Orchestra libraries (www.garritan.com) and the Tapspace virtual percussion libraries (www.tapspace.com).

KONTAKT Player 2 allows up to 16 sounds to be loaded simultaneously, and more than one instance of KONTAKT Player 2 can be used at once, allowing as many sounds as your computer can handle. KONTAKT Player 2 also includes a number of built-in effects, including reverb, compression, equalization (EQ), filters, and delays, which can be applied globally to all slots in the player to use less computer power.

Sibelius playback options

Sibelius supports a variety of hardware and software playback devices, including:

- External MIDI hardware, such as sound modules and keyboards with sounds built-in

- Internal MIDI hardware, such as built-in synthesizers for some soundcards

- Virtual instruments that use Virtual Studio Technology (VST) or Audio Unit technology, including Sibelius's supplied KONTAKT Player 2

When you first install Sibelius, it automatically sets up your playback devices for you. As you acquire additional virtual instruments or MIDI hardware, the list of playback devices Sibelius can use expands. In most cases, the initial sounds are fine — you can hear what the notes and rhythms sound like, and get a good idea of what you just wrote. But eventually you're going to want to make your opus sound better, and you need to know how to add sound sets and change the playback device. Sibelius offers lots of sound set add-ons for sale, and it's always adding new sound sets.

To change the playback devices Sibelius uses, choose Play➪Playback Devices. The Playback Devices dialog box (shown in Figure 16-1) appears. This dialog box gives you a bunch of options for setting up playback configurations. You see groups of playback device settings that determine which devices are available to Sibelius and how they should be used for playback.

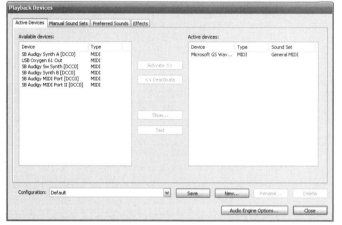

Figure 16-1:
Your
playback
devices
listed.

In the full version of Sibelius, you can set up as many playback configurations as you like, using different devices in each one, and switch between them at any time. In the demo version of Sibelius, you can only use one default playback configuration.

If you have any virtual instruments installed, you can activate multiple copies of the same virtual instrument. Sibelius can load an unlimited number of virtual instruments, limited only by your computer's specifications. (See the following section for more on virtual instruments.)

Sibelius can play back through any internal or external MIDI device you have connected to your computer, as well as VST (Windows and Mac) and Audio Units (Mac only) virtual instruments.

In the Available Devices list on the left-hand side of the dialog box, you see all the external and internal MIDI devices and virtual instruments installed on your computer. To activate a device, select it and click Activate; the device appears in the Active Devices list on the right. Each MIDI device disappears from the Available Devices list on the left after you activate it, because you can only activate a MIDI device once.

Activating your virtual instruments

A *virtual instrument* is Sibelius's name for a computer program that emulates the performance of a real instrument — whether it's an electronic instrument like an analog or digital synthesizer, an acoustic instrument, or an other-worldly sci-fi sound. By adding sound sets to your computer, you can build a seemingly infinite number of instrument sounds and sonic shapes.

Software plug-ins have an advantage over hardware devices because of their wide range of virtual instruments. With nearly every hardware device, your choice of sounds is limited to those that the original manufacturer included, although some manufacturers are offering ways to upgrade the number of built-in instrument sounds. But in the world of software, the number of virtual instruments at your disposal is limited only by your budget.

Sibelius comes with sampled sounds called Sibelius Sounds Essentials, a sound library consisting of a set of general MIDI sounds, as well as instruments from Sibelius Sounds Rock & Pop, Garritan Personal Orchestra, the Garritan Concert & Marching Band, Garritan Jazz and Big Band, and Tapspace Virtual Drumline.

If you purchased and installed the full version of any of the virtual instrument sound sets sold by Sibelius, such as the full versions of Garritan Personal Orchestra, Garritan Jazz and Big Band, or Garritan Concert & Marching Band, you'll see KONTAKT Player2 in the list of Available devices.

If you want to try out playback through these sample libraries, follow these steps:

1. **In the Playback Devices dialog box, select KONTAKT Player 2 and click Activate.**

   After a few moments, KONTAKT Player 2 appears in the list of Active devices.

2. **Click the KONTAKT Player's Sound Set column on the right of the Active Devices dialog box to choose the appropriate sound set from the list, according to which sample library you have installed.**

   Sibelius automatically uses the sounds from these sample libraries for playback.

If you activate a virtual instrument, it's a good idea to deactivate your computer's built-in sounds, so select Microsoft GS Wavetable Synth (Windows) or DLSMusicDevice (Mac) in the Active Devices list and click Deactivate.

In the demo version of Sibelius, you can add and remove devices from the default configuration, but you can't create your own or save your changes. So if you make any changes in the Playback Devices dialog box while using the demo, you need to make them again the next time you run the demo.

You can also purchase and install other sampled sound sets and use them with Sibelius. Some other manufacturers of virtual instruments include:

✔ Art Vista (www.artvista.net)

✔ Bardstown Audio (www.bardstownaudio.com)

✔ Dan Dean Productions (www.dandeanpro.com)

✔ Kirk Hunter Studios (www.kirkhunterstudios.com)

✔ Post Musical Instruments (www.postpiano.com)

✔ ProjectSAM (www.projectsam.com)

✔ Spectrasonics (www.spectrasonics.net)

✔ Miroslav Vitous (www.ilio.com/miraslov)

✔ Vienna Symphonic Library (www.ilio.com/vienna/instruments_
index.html)

Changing the audio engine properties

If you want to change the properties of your audio engine (that is, the buffer size or sample rate of your audio card as it plays your Sibelius score), choose Play⇨Playback Devices. Click the Audio Engine Options button at the bottom of the Active Devices tab of the Playback Devices dialog bog. The Audio Engine Options dialog box (shown in Figure 16-2) appears.

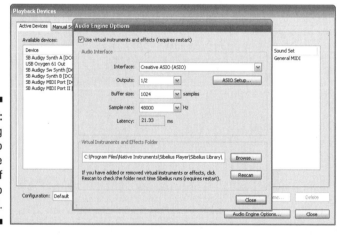

Figure 16-2:
Changing
the audio
engine
options of
your audio
card.

Here you can determine:

- ✔ Which audio card Sibelius will use for playback
- ✔ Which speaker outputs the audio will use, if it has more than one
- ✔ The size (in bytes) of the audio buffer it should use
- ✔ The default sample rate the audio card should use
- ✔ Where Sibelius should look in your computer for the virtual instruments

After you make changes in the Audio Engine Options dialog box and click Close, you get a prompt saying that you need to close Sibelius and restart it to have the changes take effect.

The Playback Devices dialog box (Play➪Playback Devices) has three other tabs:

- ✔ **Manual Sound Sets (see Figure 16-3):** This tab allows you to tell Sibelius what sounds are provided by a MIDI device or virtual instrument for which no sound set file is available, or for a virtual instrument that does not allow Sibelius to load sounds automatically. When Sibelius knows what sounds are available on a device, it can automatically use it during playback, without your having to tell it to do so.

- ✔ **Preferred Sounds (see Figure 16-4):** This tab is for telling Sibelius which device to use for particular sounds. For example, you may have a wonderful piano sound available on a specific device that you want to hear whenever your scores require a piano. This page allows you to set that kind of preference.

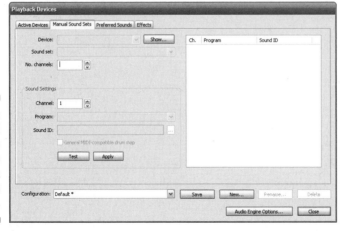

Figure 16-3:
The Manual Sound Sets tab of the Playback Devices dialog box.

✔ **Effects (see Figure 16-5):** This tab allows you to activate different effects that you have installed on your computer, such as reverbs, compressors, choruses, and so on.

You can use external effects with Sibelius, by choosing the Effects tab. New Macs come with their own effects such as AU Matrix Reverb. Windows users can download free effects to use with Sibelius from sites such as Kjaerhus Audio (www.kjaerhusaudio.com).

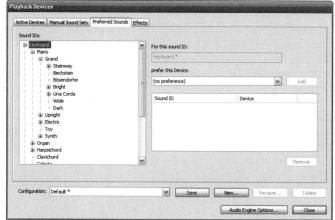

Figure 16-4:
The
Preferred
Sounds tab
of the
Playback
Devices
dialog box.

Figure 16-5:
The Effects
tab of the
Playback
Devices
dialog box.

Changing the Playback Feel

There is an alternative to the mechanical way your computer plays music. Besides changing the MIDI device that plays back your music, you can change the way Sibelius actually plays the notes, by changing the playback performance style or feel. If you composed a jazz tune, you can make the instruments in your score play the notes with a swing feeling. If your tune is Latin, rock, or funk, there's a performance style that goes with that, too.

To make Sibelius play a little more funky, choose Play⇨Performance. The Performance dialog box appears. Here you can change different aspects of how Sibelius plays the notes in your score. You can change how Sibelius plays the rhythmic feel — funky, straight, or swingy. You can add or subtract reverb to the mix, and decide if the horns will pay the full duration values of the notes, for example.

In the Rhythmic Feel drop-down list, you have many different rhythmic styles to choose from (see Figure 16-6).

For "My New Tune," you might choose Funk in the Rhythmic Feel drop-down list. Load My New Tune-16-01.sib and play around with the feeling of the music. Some of the changes are very subtle, and others you'll hear right away.

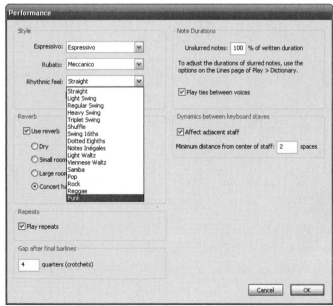

Figure 16-6:
Picking a new rhythmic style for your tune.

Mixing It Up

The Mixer in Sibelius allows you to adjust the volume and pan of individual instruments or whole families of instruments during playback. To show or hide the Mixer, simply press M or choose Window⇨Mixer.

Click on the first button, the Show/Hide Staves button, in the upper right of the Mixer box to list the instrument names that are being used in your score. You can expand the mixer by dragging on the lower right-hand corner of the mixer window, and make it as large or as small as you want.

Each staff in the score has a staff strip, allowing you to change the volume, pan, solo/mute, initial sound, and playback device of the staff. Click the little arrow at the left of each instrument name, and the mixer expands and displays the mixer's information for that instrument (see Figure 16-7).

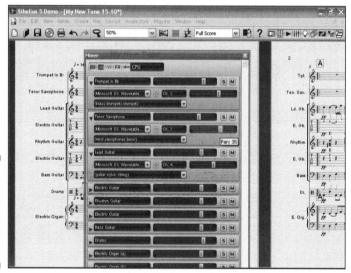

Figure 16-7:
Changing the instrument's mixer settings.

Here's what you can do to change the instrument's settings:

- ✔ You can raise or lower the volume of the instrument.
- ✔ You can change the playback device used by the instrument. You can also route its output to any effects you have in your current playback configuration.
- ✔ You can make the playback output of the instrument stereo pan from side to side or center it.

Sibelius 5 has four effects strips, allowing you to load one or more effects (including reverb, chorus, delay, flange, and so on). Each of the four buses has its own effects bus strip, allowing you to show and hide the effects' windows in order to change settings specific to each effect.

If you're using a virtual instrument sound set, Sibelius loads the sounds it needs each time you open or start a score, whether or not you're going to play back the score. Sometimes waiting for the sounds to load is a pain, especially if you're on a slow computer. If you're not going to play back the score right away, you can press Cancel when the sounds start to load. Sibelius asks you if you want to cancel the loading of the sounds (and sometimes it loads them whether you cancel or not).

If you want to see which sounds have been loaded, open the Mixer, select the icon at the top that says VI (short for *Virtual Instrument*), then click on the cog next to the word KONTAKT Player, and you see all the sounds that have been loaded.

Saving and Burning Your Opus

When your score sounds the way you'd like it to in terms of the overall mix, reverb, and effects, you can burn a CD to share your work of genius with others.

First, save your score the way you would normally, after tweaking the sound output. Then select the CD icon at the top of the main Sibelius screen to export the score as audio. This exports your audio as a WAV (Windows) or AIFF (Mac). (I describe all the details on how to export your audio in Chapter 8.)

After you've exported this score, and any others you've composed, to audio, you can use Roxio, iTunes, Toast, or other programs to assemble these files onto a CD.

Converting your WAV or AIFF files to MP3 files is a good idea. MP3 is the standard audio format for most music players nowadays, and MP3 files only take up about 10 percent or so of the size of the other two formats. Some high-fidelity quality is lost, but normally it's such a small amount that it's not noticeable.

I use Sony's Sound Forge to convert audio file formats, but iTunes and Audacity are a couple of free programs that can do this. Also, www. sibeliusmusic.com allows you to upload MP3 files of your music, so everyone can hear your genius!

Part VI
The Part of Tens

The 5th Wave   By Rich Tennant

"Guess who found a Kiss merchandise site on
the Web while you were gone?"

In this part . . .

No *For Dummies* book would be complete without a Part of Tens, and *Composing Digital Music For Dummies* is no exception.

In this part, you find lots of great information to continue on the path to digital music greatness. I fill you in on ten digital music terms you should know, ten composers whose music you should be familiar with, and ten handy Sibelius tips and tricks to make your life easier.

Chapter 17

Ten Digital Music Terms You Should Know

In This Chapter

▶ Getting hip to the lingo

▶ Throwing around digital music terms like a pro

▶ Understanding what you're saying — and what everyone else is saying

*O*kay, I admit: I introduce a lot more than ten digital musical terms in *Composing Digital Music For Dummies.* But in this chapter, I offer up the ten most important of them and provide a thorough definition of what each term means. Whether you want to impress your fellow musicians or you just want to understand what the pros are saying, this is the chapter for you.

Beats

Beats are the background tracks of a hip-hop tune. More than just the rhythm of the piece, like the drum or bass part, it can include any instruments or sounds that are not the singer's voice. Used to set the mood and style of the piece, beats can be made in low-budget studios with Mac or PC software, and common digital processing tools.

Although some hip-hop artists produce their own beats, some major producers, like Timbaland and Kanye West, are recognizable and highly prized beat composers, in great demand in the record industry.

Digital Audio

Up until the digital revolution, all sound reproduction was based on the same principles that the human ear uses to distinguish sounds. Analog recording systems captured audio waves and turned them into electrical signals. These signals could be used to cut shapes into vinyl or an arrangement of magnetic ions on a piece of recording tape. Then the process was reversed to play the recording back. An amplifier took the signals and turned them into audio that was recognizable as music to our ears.

After the development of the computer, analog-to-digital conversion programs were developed that would take the sound wavelengths and change them into digital bits (0 or 1), just like the programs that run on your computer.

The early digital audio converters were very limited by the low sampling resolution, resulting in a very unrealistic sound. Current digital audio recorders and digital audio workstations have a very high bit rate. An example of digital audio with a very low sampling resolution would be early video game machines, such as Nintendo.

Digital music is easy to share and distribute, because the fidelity of the performance doesn't degrade with replication, which is what happens when you duplicate a tape several times.

Latency

Latency is the time it takes in digital audio systems to convert the signal from analog to digital, process it, and then convert it back to analog. Latency can be a big headache when it throws off the precise timing required to make all the hardware and software parts work together correctly.

Sometimes the audio interface introduces latency when it converts the signal from analog to digital, before sending the signal to the computer. Even though the conversion appears to be instantaneous, it takes a few milliseconds, creating some latency.

Although latency may not be a very big issue for a small digital music system, it starts to affect the quality of the music in large studios, those with many MIDI devices connected together. Latency is also a big issue for musicians performing live with MIDI devices, because the music is being played in real time to an audience.

Latency can occur again after the data has moved from the interface into the computer. The audio processing software and the computer itself can create big delays as they move the data around. Often, installing more memory (RAM) can help latency immensely.

The term *latency* is also used to describe how long it takes MIDI devices to respond to MIDI messages, especially if several devices are daisy-chained together. Too many MIDI devices connected one after another can cause the MIDI messages to take too long to get to the last device, causing a

MIDI timing problem. For this reason, most MIDI setups don't connect more than three devices together in a chain. A better solution is to connect each MIDI device directly to a multi-port MIDI interface.

MIDI

The acronym *MIDI* stands for *Musical Instrument Digital Interface,* and it's the international standard for digital music instrument communication. Introduced in 1983, MIDI is a computer communications *protocol* (a set of standard rules computers use to talk to each other) that lets electronic musical instruments, computers, and other equipment communicate with each other, control each other, and synchronize with each other in real time.

MIDI does not transmit any audio signals or music per se — it's just a computer code that sends event messages (also known as MIDI messages) to a MIDI-aware device. The MIDI-aware device could be a keyboard synthesizer, a sound module, a drum machine, or even a theater's lights and curtains.

Each event message is a combination of numbers ranging from 0 to 127, telling the MIDI receiving device to do something. For example, there is one message for playing a note (known as Note On) and there is a separate message for terminating that note (known as Note Off). Other messages may contain instructions such as the pitch and intensity of the notes, volume, vibrato, panning, and tempo.

Multitimbral

A MIDI or digital music device that can produce more than one timbre at the same time is called *multitimbral.* A multitimbral instrument could be a sampler, a digital music workstation, or a synthesizer.

Multitimbral instruments let a musician play different instrument sounds at the same time, usually by assigning each instrument a specific range on the keyboard. For example, a very common way to split a multitimbral keyboard is to have the lower left-hand side of the keyboard assigned to a bass sound, while the upper right-hand side of the keyboard is assigned a piano-type sound. This way, the musician can play the bass part with his left hand and the melody and chords with his right. Or a sequencer may send MIDI data to a specific area of a keyboard, while the live musician plays on another part of the same keyboard.

Polyphony

Polyphony is a traditional musical term that's also used in electronic music. In electronic music, polyphony refers to how many notes a digital music device can sound at one time.

A polyphonic instrument is one in which multiple notes can be heard at once; it could be almost any type of MIDI device. Synthesizers, samplers, and tone modules can all be polyphonic.

The number of voices is limited, however, if the sound being played requires more than one voice. For example, a 16-voice polyphonic synthesizer can play 16 notes at once. But if the sound is a complex creation and is actually made up of four different timbres, called *patches,* then only four distinct voices can be heard at once.

Most modern synthesizers can play multiple timbres at the same time. They're called *multitimbral synthesizers.* (See the following section for more on the term *multitimbral.*)

Sampler

A *sampler* is a computer music device that can be either hardware or software. The sampler doesn't generate its own sounds, but it contains a library of sounds and combinations of sounds called *instruments.* These instruments can be any type of sound, from traditional acoustic instruments to weird digital noise. The samples can be edited with a DAW or sequencer in a studio, or played by a MIDI device like a sequencer or a keyboard controller on a live gig.

Hardware samplers are not as popular for digital music creation as they used to be. Software samplers have really taken over the music production market.

Most samplers are *polyphonic* (see the preceding section), and many are also *multitimbral* (see the "Multitimbral" section, earlier in this chapter). DropZone (shown in Figure 17-1) is a polyphonic, multitimbral sampler plug-in that comes with several SONAR products.

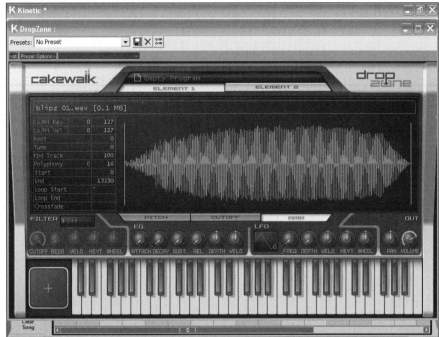

Figure 17-1:
The
DropZone
sampler
plug-in.

Sampling Rate and Bit Depth

Sampling rate is the number of samples per second used to convert an analog audio signal into a digital audio signal. It's usually measured in kilohertz (kHz).

Bit depth is the amount of data contained in each sample, using the unit bits. Common examples of bit depth include CD audio, which is recorded at 16 bits, and DVD audio, which can support up to 24 bits. The greater the sampling rate and bit depth, the more realistic your digital music will sound and the greater the audio fidelity of your output. Most digital audio software will record at least 96 kHz and 24-bit depth, and some digital recording software, like Sound Forge, will record up to 32-bit 192 kHz. By comparison, commercial CD audio playback uses 48 kHz resolution and 16-bit depth.

Sequencer

A *sequencer* can be either a piece of software or a hardware device that allows the user to record MIDI data, and then play it back and edit it. A sequencer does not record audio (either analog or digital); it just controls the digital data information going to and from other MIDI devices, such as synthesizers and tone modules. The MIDI devices are what actually produce the audible sound.

In the first days of computer music, and even up to the last decade, all sequencers were hardware devices. Today, they are primarily software products. As the personal computer has become more powerful, software sequencers have been able to replicate the functions of the hardware varieties and provide many more features, such as Internet updates and bug fixes.

The term *digital audio workstation* (DAW), which originally referred to a hardware device that only recorded and edited audio, is often used today as a synonym of *sequencer*. But today, a DAW usually has many more features than a sequencer has.

Chapter 6 provides more information about software sequencers, including some comparisons of the most popular software sequencing packages.

Software Synthesizer

Most digital music hardware is being replaced by software versions. This is also true of the keyboard synthesizer, which is evolving into a MIDI keyboard controller using a software synthesizer (softsynth) program.

A softsynth can run on a regular Mac or PC, and replicate synthesizer sounds through the audio card of the computer, or input synthesizer sounds into the digital audio recording program.

A softsynth has two main advantages over a hardware synthesizer:

- ✔ **Expense:** A softsynth is almost always cheaper than a hardware synthesizer.
- ✔ **Upgradeability:** The program can be easily upgraded and the sample library expanded quickly and simply over the Internet.

Stand-alone hardware synthesizers are still preferred for live performance, however, and can be more stable and reliable than software synthesizers.

Software synthesizers come in many varieties. A softsynth can be a VSTi or DXi plug-in to a DAW or sequencing program, emulating older, popular synthesizers, like the Yamaha DX7 or the Sequential Circuits Prophet-5.

VSTi (Virtual Studio Technology instrument) was developed by Steinberg as a universal platform for softsynths and samplers. Cakewalk, initially, did not go with VSTi — it created DXi, which is based on Microsoft Direct X code. But now Cakewalk's products support VSTi as well.

Some softsynths may have a large sample library. Because softsynths are computer-based, the software synthesizer's sample library is only limited by the amount of free space on the hard drive and by how much you're willing to pay for libraries.

Figure 17-2 shows the popular Native Instruments ABSYNTH 4 software synthesizer, which can be operated as a computer-based synthesizer using a MIDI controller, or as a plug-in for a DAW, sequencer, or other MIDI program.

Figure 17-2:
The
ABSYNTH 4
software
synthesizer.

Chapter 18

Ten (Or So) Composers You Should Know

In This Chapter

▶ Rediscovering the classical composers you learned about in school

▶ Getting acquainted with some of the best composers who've worked in your lifetime

Music composers come in all shapes and styles, from the traditional classical composers every music student learns about, through the contemporary avant garde and jazz arrangers, to the hip-hop beat producers of today. To study a composer's music is to understand what his world was like and feel what he felt.

Distilling the pool of all great composers to ten is impossible, and every musician, if asked, would come up with a different list. I tend to favor American composers, at least starting in the 20th century, covering the blues, jazz, film, and Broadway genres.

In writing this chapter, I picked ten (or so) — I couldn't limit it to just ten — that I feel represent the best of several genres. I list them in order chronologically. As you read this chapter, keep in mind that the best composers frequently cross genres, and the best music is often hard to categorize.

Wolfgang Amadeus Mozart (1756–1791)

Probably the world's best known child musical prodigy, Mozart composed over 600 works, which makes him the most prolific and influential composer of the Classical Era. His compositions are widely regarded as the peak of symphonic music, and Mozart is considered one of the greatest composers who ever lived.

Mozart's works are still played worldwide and are always popular with audiences. He could even be considered the first rock star, because he partied hard and died young.

Ludwig van Beethoven (1770–1827)

Regarded as one of the greatest composers in history (if not *the* greatest), Beethoven was a German composer who almost single-handedly moved music from the Classical Era to the Romantic Era.

Although his enduring fame is that of a composer, he was also an accomplished pianist and had a considerable reputation as a virtuoso. Somewhat of a misanthrope, Beethoven had a disdain for authority, especially for those who outranked him socially, and had few successful personal relationships. Even though Beethoven began to lose his hearing fairly early in life, he continued to compose, creating some of his most famous pieces after he was deaf.

George Gershwin (1898–1937)

Born in Brooklyn, New York, George Gershwin was the quintessential American popular composer; he composed Broadway show tunes, popular songs, and major concert-hall works with equal success. Gershwin's music has been a staple of the American songbook for decades — and will be for decades to come.

Much of Gershwin's music is seen as representative of the American ethos. He composed major concert-hall works such as *An American in Paris* and *Rhapsody in Blue,* Broadway hits like *Porgy and Bess,* and Jazz Era standards like "Embraceable You," "Fascinating Rhythm," "A Foggy Day," "I Got Rhythm," and "Summertime."

Although George Gershwin wrote most of his vocal and theatrical works in collaboration with his brother, lyricist Ira Gershwin, George is better known by the general public than Ira. Practically every singer who has ever graced a stage, from Ella Fitzgerald to Sting, has sung a Gershwin song at one time or another. In 2005, the British newspaper *The Guardian* determined that Gershwin had been the richest composer ever for his era.

Duke Ellington (1899–1974)

Probably no composer has done more for the uniquely American musical art called jazz, than Edward Kennedy "Duke" Ellington. A prolific composer, band leader, and pianist, at the time of his death Ellington was considered amongst the world's greatest composers and musicians.

The official Duke Ellington Web site (www.dukeellington.com) estimates that, by the end of his 50-year career, he had played over 20,000 performances worldwide. The French government honored him with its highest award, the Legion of Honor, while the United States bestowed upon him the highest civilian honor, the Presidential Medal of Freedom.

Ellington's band was a breeding ground for some of America's greatest jazz musicians, including Johnny Hodges, Ben Webster, Harry Carney, Cootie Williams, Clark Terry, Oscar Pettiford, and Louis Bellson.

Some of Ellington's best known hits, such as "Take the 'A' Train" were written by his long-time collaborator Billy Strayhorn. The two had a musical partnership lasting over 25 years. Strayhorn, a brilliant composer in his own right, often finished tunes sketched out by Ellington.

Duke wrote and recorded hundreds of pieces of music during his lifetime, and his suave demeanor impressed all who were fortunate enough to know him.

Aaron Copland (1900–1990)

Considered "the dean of American composers," Copland is credited with defining a unique American sound through orchestral works, choral works, ballets, and film scores.

Copland sought to blend 20th-century contemporary classical forms with American folk styles to evoke the vast American environment. Some of his best known works include *Appalachian Spring, Rodeo, Billy the Kid,* and his most recognizable piece, *Fanfare for the Common Man.*

He incorporated percussive orchestration, changing meter, *polyrhythms* (the simultaneous sounding of two or more independent rhythms), *polychords* (two or more chords, one on top of the other), and *tone rows* (a nonrepetitive ordering of the 12 notes of the chromatic scale, also referred to as a 12-tone scale). Outside of composing, Copland served as a conductor, most frequently for his own works.

A controversy over programming Copland's *Lincoln Portrait* at Dwight Eisenhower's 1953 inauguration led to Copland being summoned to testify in a secret session of the House Un-American Activities Committee. Refusing to implicate any of his colleagues and skillfully fielding questions about his own politics, he managed to survive the ordeal without betraying any of his friends or principles.

Copland was very skilled as a conductor, wrote many books and articles, often taught and lectured, and founded the Tanglewood Festival in Lenox, Massachusetts.

Alfred Newman (1900–1970)

The very successful and influential film music composer Alfred Newman received 45 Academy Award nominations, a record that is shared with John Williams (see later in this chapter). Newman won the Oscar nine times. Just in the year 1940 alone, he was nominated for an incredible four films. Between 1930 and 1970, Alfred Newman wrote music for over 200 films and acted as musical director of dozens of other movies.

Newman was the eldest of ten children and came from a musical family. His brother Lionel Newman scored three dozen films, several TV series, and conducted for hundreds of films. His brother Emil Newman scored over 50 films. Continuing the musical tradition of his family, Newman had five children, three of whom became prominent composers in their own right. His son David has scored over 70 films, his son Thomas has scored over 50 films, and his daughter Maria is an eminent musician and composer. The famous singer/songwriter and film composer Randy Newman is his nephew.

Willie Dixon (1915–1992)

Willie Dixon titled his autobiography *I Am the Blues.* Though some musicologists would probably find that statement a bit pompous, it would not be an exaggeration to place Dixon at the top of the list of those responsible for American blues rising out of its parochial beginnings and into an international force.

Born as William James Dixon and raised in Mississippi, Willie Dixon was a blues bassist, singer, songwriter, and record producer, who understood the commercial potential for American blues far beyond his contemporary musicians of the period.

Dixon rode the rails to Chicago during the Great Depression, eventually becoming the primary songwriter and producer for legendary Chess Records, where he was credited as being the man who changed the style of the blues by creating the "Chicago blues sound" that survives to this day. The Chicago blues is a blues style that uses electrically amplified guitar, drums, piano, bass guitar, and sometimes saxophone, in addition to the original Delta guitar and harmonica instrumentation.

Dixon was one of the greatest and most prolific artists ever to sing the blues, with more than 500 compositions to his credit. It is said that his quarterly BMI royalty report was so long it had to be delivered in multiple boxes.

Broadcast Music, Incorporated (BMI) is a performing right organization. Performing right organizations collect license fees on behalf of their song-writers, composers, and music publishers and distribute them as royalties to those members whose works have been performed.

Dixon's songs have been recorded by countless performers, including Muddy Waters, Howlin' Wolf, and Bo Diddley. One of his best-known compositions, "Back Door Man," was recorded by the Doors, and several of his songs reached an international audience in the 1960s when they were popularized by such British artists as the Rolling Stones, Cream, the Yardbirds, Jeff Beck, and Led Zeppelin.

Thelonious Monk (1917–1982)

An eccentric, prolific, and totally unique jazz pianist and composer, Thelonious Sphere Monk was credited, along with Dizzy Gillespie and Charlie Parker, with the creation of bebop, however Monk's musical progression soon evolved past bebop as he developed his own personal musical style.

His impression on the evolution of jazz — both through his angular and dissonant compositions, and his highly unusual approach to piano — cannot be overstated. Monk was famous for his use of space and silence in his playing, and for allowing the other members of his band to have room to develop their ideas onstage.

Monk approached composing unusually, trying to create a new architecture for jazz writing — combining melody, harmony, and rhythm in a new way. His compositions, such as "'Round Midnight," "Epistrophy," or "I Mean You," are still favorites of jazz musicians of every generation.

John Williams (1932–)

Over the course of over 60 years, John Towner Williams has composed some of the most famous film scores in history. He is currently the most in-demand Hollywood composer and has written some of the most memorable film scores ever, including the scores for *Jaws, Star Wars, Superman, E.T.: The Extra-Terrestrial, Raiders of the Lost Ark, Jurassic Park,* and *Schindler's List,* as well as the *Harry Potter* theme.

Williams is a five-time winner of the Academy Award, and his 45 nominations (as of this writing) make him joint second-most-nominated individual with fellow composer Alfred Newman (see earlier in this chapter).

From 1980 to 1993, Williams succeeded the legendary Arthur Fiedler as principal conductor of the Boston Pops Orchestra. Williams was a recipient of the Kennedy Center Honors Award in 2004.

John Lennon (1940–1980) and Paul McCartney (1942–)

The British pop writing duo of Lennon-McCartney may be the most famous songwriting pair in history. Both lead singers, John Lennon was a guitarist and Paul McCartney was the bassist of what's considered to be the most important pop/rock band in history, the Beatles.

Originally close friends, Lennon and McCartney wrote many hit songs together and helped change the way popular music was written, recorded, and distributed. There was occasional controversy over authorship of a few songs, but for the most part, in the early years at least, the partnership was quite amicable and generous.

The pair wrote songs together from 1958 until 1969. As time went on, the songs increasingly became the work of one writer or the other, often with the other partner offering up only a few words or an alternate chord.

By 1970 the Beatles had broken up, and both composers began successful solo writing careers. Among other projects, John Lennon penned the immensely influential album *Imagine.* McCartney created the band Wings, and has produced a large catalog of songs as a solo artist.

McCartney is listed in *Guinness World Records* as the most successful musician and composer in popular-music history, with 60 gold discs and sales of 100 million singles. His song "Yesterday" is listed as the most covered song in history and has been played more than 7 million times on TV and radio.

(More Than) A Few More

Here are more than a few additional composers to look up in your spare time:

- John Coolidge Adams
- Johann Sebastian Bach
- Samuel Barber
- Béla Bartók
- Irving Berlin
- Leonard Bernstein
- Carla Bley
- Benjamin Britten
- John Cage
- John Coltrane
- Claude Debussy
- Edward Elgar
- Philip Glass
- Joseph Haydn
- Jimi Hendrix
- Charles Ives
- Robert Leroy Johnson
- Stan Kenton
- Carole King
- Henry Mancini
- Curtis Mayfield
- Darius Milhaud
- Charles Mingus
- Harry Partch
- Henry Purcell
- Maurice Ravel
- Smokey Robinson
- Richard Rodgers
- Nino Rota
- George Russell
- Arnold Schoenberg
- Dmitri Shostakovich
- Stephen Sondheim
- Igor Stravinsky
- Morton Subotnick
- Peter Tchaikovsky
- Timbaland
- Dimitri Tiomkin

Chapter 19

Ten (Or So) Sibelius Tips and Tricks

In This Chapter

▶ Saving time with Sibelius shortcuts

▶ Exporting your score to MIDI and graphics formats

▶ Changing your score's tempo anytime you want

Sibelius is a great program and a lot of fun to use. And, like any great program, in Sibelius you can do stuff in more than one way. In this chapter, I've compiled what I think are the best shortcuts and tips to help you get the most out of the software.

Undoing Your Mistakes

Ctrl+Z (⌘+Z), the Undo function, is the most useful feature of Sibelius.

Everyone deletes the wrong thing sometimes, or puts a note in the wrong place. When you find yourself in this situation, you can easily back up a step by pressing Ctrl+Z (⌘+Z).

Ctrl+Z (⌘+Z) works great when you want to undo your last step or steps. But what if you want to *keep* the last couple things you did and *undo* something you did three or four steps ago? Choose Edit⇨Undo History to bring up the Undo History dialog box, which lists the last several keystrokes.

In the Undo History dialog box, you can skip over your last keystrokes and reverse something you did several steps before. You can set how far back you can undo, by choosing the Other page of File Preferences. You can even undo up to 20,000 past steps, so you can undo right back to the beginning of the score, if you set the level large enough. Of course, you lose all your undo history after you close your score or quit Sibelius.

Ctrl+Z (⌘+Z) is very useful not only for erasing your mistakes, but also as a composing tool. The ability to back up and start over at any time lets you try "what if" composing. You can use Ctrl+Z (⌘+Z) to try different harmonies, rhythms, melodies, and so on — and if you don't like what you've done, just back out with Ctrl+Z (⌘+Z) and try something else.

If you change your mind again, and decide you really liked it after all, you can press Ctrl+Y (⌘+Y) or choose Edit⇨Redo History to undo your Ctrl+Z (⌘+Z). Ctrl+Y (⌘+Y) is also really useful for repeating commands, like adding bars.

Changing the Way Your Score Looks

The Properties window is a small window that gives you a lot of power over how your score looks. You can bring it up on your screen either by pressing Ctrl+Alt+P (Option+⌘+P) or by choosing Window⇨Properties.

Figure 19-1 shows some of your Properties choices, in particular, the Notes submenu. You'll know you have the Properties window open because it says "Edit Passage" at the top. For example, using the Properties window you can change

✔ How many times a passage repeats, using the Playback Properties

✔ The note head from a black dot to an *X*, a slash, or another shape (This is very useful when writing chord changes or drum parts. You have 24 note heads to choose from.)

✔ Change the font and point size of text in your score

✔ Change the shape or properties of a slur or other line

You can change the size, shape, or other properties of almost everything that's on your score through the Properties window. But the Properties window is primarily for advanced users — most of the standard defaults for a score are fine for most composers.

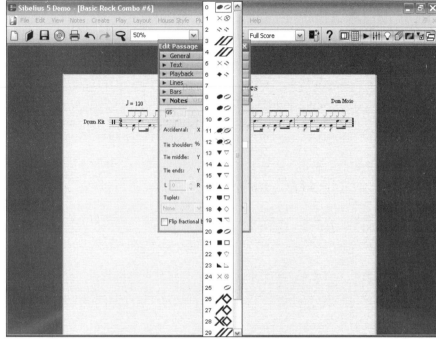

Figure 19-1:
Changing
the
notehead in
the
Properties
window.

Using Keyboard Shortcuts

You can scroll, drag, or click with your mouse to do everything you need to do in Sibelius. But when you learn the corresponding keyboard shortcut, you'll never go back.

Here are some of the tasks I use shortcuts for:

- ✔ **Rewinding playback:** Ctrl+[(⌘+[) starts the playback from the beginning of your score.

- ✔ **Adding instruments:** If you want to add, say, a trumpet to your score, you can just press I instead of choosing Create➪Instrument. Pressing I brings up the Add Instrument screen (see Figure 19-2).

- ✔ **Entering dynamics:** Select the note where you want the dynamic first, press Ctrl+E (⌘+E), and then right-click to get the dynamic you want (see Figure 19-3).

- ✔ **Repeating a note:** Select a note and press R to repeat that note. The pitch and duration will be repeated as long as you hold down the R key.

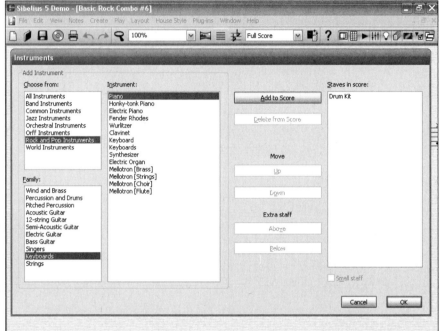

Figure 19-2:
Adding a
new
instrument
is easy —
just press I.

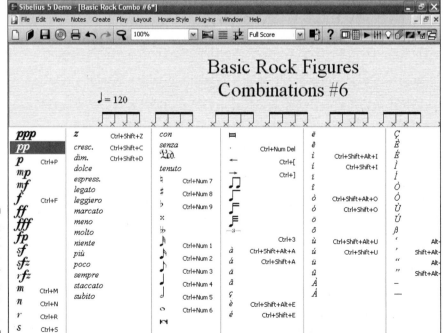

Figure 19-3:
Press Ctrl+E
(⌘+E) to
enter
dynamics
into the
score.

✔ **Copying and pasting passages:** Copy whole passages simply by selecting them and pressing R to paste them. Copying and pasting passages is a great way to fill out a part like a drum or guitar part that uses slash marks.

✔ **Jumping to another measure in a score:** You can quickly jump to any measure in your score by pressing Ctrl+Alt+G (Option+⌘+G), which brings up the Go to Bar dialog box (see Figure 19-4).

You can find a complete list of keyboard shortcuts by choosing File⇨ Preferences⇨Menus and Shortcuts. Plus, almost every menu choice shows you the shortcut when you choose it.

Getting to Know the Keypad

The shortcut Ctrl+Alt+K (Option+⌘+K) brings up the Keypad (see Figure 19-5). The Keypad has a wealth of functions that you'll often use. It lets you quickly edit notes, chords, and rests.

The Keypad menu box looks like your computer's numeric keypad, and that's not a coincidence. You can click on each part of the Keypad with your mouse, or you can use your computer's numeric keypad to accomplish the same tasks.

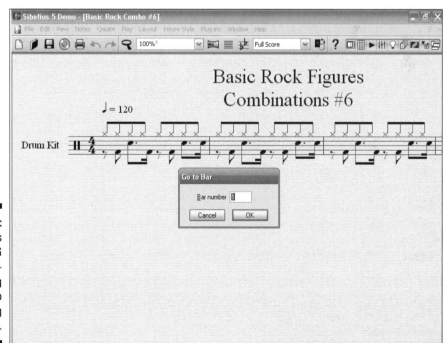

Figure 19-4:
Press Ctrl+Alt+G (Option+⌘+ G) to bring up the Go to Bar dialog box.

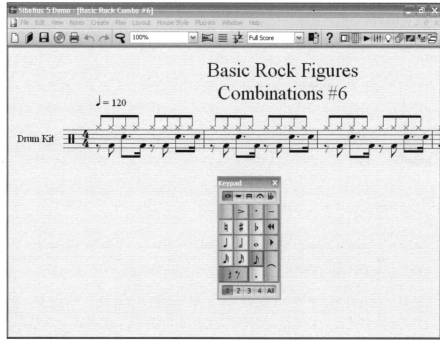

Figure 19-5:
The Keypad
lets you edit
notes,
chords, and
rests.

The Keypad has five layouts, which means that each button on your numeric keypad can do five different things.

Like everything in Sibelius, there's more than one way to get the menu you want. To select any one of the five Keypad layouts, you can:

- ✔ Click on one of the five icons at the top of the Keypad.

- ✔ Press the plus (+) key on the Keypad to cycle through each of the five layouts.

- ✔ Press the function keys F8 through F12 to cycle through the layouts (if you have a Windows PC).

By default, Mac OS X 10.3 (or later) assigns the keys F9, F10, and F11 to the Expose feature, and Mac OS X 10.4 also assigns F12 to the Dashboard feature. This means you may get unexpected results when using the function keys to change between different Keypad layouts in Sibelius, when using a Mac. You can change the way your Mac uses F9 through F12. If you use Mac OS X 10.3, use the Expose pane in System Preferences to reassign the Expose shortcuts to other function keys, such as F2, F3, and F4, for example. If you use Mac OS X 10.4, use the Dashboard and Expose pane in System Preferences to reassign both the Expose and Dashboard shortcuts to other function keys, such as F2, F3, and F4, and so on.

The five layouts are:

- ✔ Common Notes
- ✔ More Note Choices
- ✔ Beams and Tremolos
- ✔ Articulations
- ✔ Accidentals

The first layout, Common Notes, is the layout that's used most often. It contains the most used notes, rests, articulations, and accidentals. (See Chapter 3 for more information on articulations and accidentals.)

Deselecting to Start Off

Before starting any task at all in Sibelius, press Esc once or twice to deselect everything, and take Sibelius out of whatever mode it was in previously. If you get into the habit of hitting Esc as the first step of every task, you won't have to worry about messing up your last score change.

Exporting Your Score to Other Programs

Exporting your music to other formats is a great feature of Sibelius. Among other formats, you can easily export your score to a WAV (in Windows) or AIFF (on the Mac) audio file, export it to a musical instrument digital interface (MIDI) file to use with other software, or export it to a graphics file (like JPG, TIFF, or PDF).

Exporting your score to MIDI allows you to integrate your tune into some of the most powerful music composing programs on the market today, such as Logic Pro, SONAR, Cubase, or Digital Performer. MIDI is the common language that all music software and hardware speaks; having your tune in MIDI means you have an unlimited ability to use powerful tools to make your tune sound great.

Exporting your tune to a commonly shared graphics format (like JPG, TIFF, or PDF) means your score can be read by *anyone,* not just those who have a copy of Sibelius, or another notation program, but any computer program that can view graphics, such as Adobe Photoshop or Microsoft Word.

After you've exported your score to an image file, it's set. That is, you can't edit the score unless you reopen the score in Sibelius.

Working on Your Playback Devices

Experimenting with different playback devices (choose Play⇨Playback Devices) is a good idea, especially if you've purchased and installed extra sound collections.

Getting a decent, realistic sound during Sibelius's playback is often one of the biggest challenges with the software. In fact, some users prefer Finale's playback sound sets, and assert that Finale's sounds are more realistic. Often, the playback devices will do very odd things. I used the Sibelius Sounds Rock & Pop collection for much of this book, and the instrument sounds changed from one day to the next, for no apparent reason. For example, the fuzz guitar sound would become a nylon string guitar sound on its own. Often, I had to reinstall the Sibelius Sound collections, as they seemed to get corrupted easily, even on a PC with several gigabytes of RAM.

Whether playback accuracy is important to you may depend upon what you're using Sibelius for. Many composers don't care about playback, because they're using the software to create parts for other musicians to play. If you write a lot of improvisational music, as I do, it would be impossible for the computer to replicate a real performance.

If you want to burn your piece to a CD or convert it to MP3 file format for use by an MP3 player, I recommend exporting it to MIDI first, and then importing it into a good digital music composition program. Most MIDI software programs have a much better library of sampled sounds than Sibelius, and changing the sounds in a MIDI software program is much easier than changing the sounds in Sibelius. (I list lots of good MIDI programs in Chapter 6.)

Spend some time working to get the sound you want, and be sure to write down what you did to get it to sound good. You may need to refer to your notes later, when your computer decides to change it all without telling you first.

Creating Text to Help the Musicians

Notes alone don't tell the whole story of a piece of music. All music scores need text to communicate dynamics, style concepts, and other musical elements to the musicians. You can add text to almost every part of the score — choose Create⇨Text to see all the choices.

If you want to add general text (that is, text that's not a specific dynamic, for example), you can simply select a note or measure and press Ctrl+T (⌘+T). Sibelius will position the text above the note or measure selected.

Fiddling with the Tempo

Trying your tune at different tempos is fun. Sometimes music sounds better when it's played slower or faster than you originally intended. You can change the tempo of your piece either permanently (by changing the tempo indicated on the score) or temporarily (during playback, by changing the speed of the playback):

- ✔ **To change the tempo of the piece permanently** (that is, until you change it again), alter the metronome marking indicated at the start of your score. Press Esc a couple of times to be sure nothing is selected, press Ctrl+Alt+T (Option+⌘+T), right-click to get a quarter-note symbol, add the tempo you want (like 120), and hit Esc to finish. You can edit, copy, paste, and move the metronome marking just like any other text.

- ✔ **To change the speed of the tune during playback,** move the slider next to the metronome marking on the Playback window (see Figure 19-6). Bring up the Playback window by pressing Ctrl+Alt+Y (Option+⌘+Y). You can do this before pressing the space bar to begin playback, or anytime during the playback. Doing so doesn't change the written tempo of the piece — only the playback this one time.

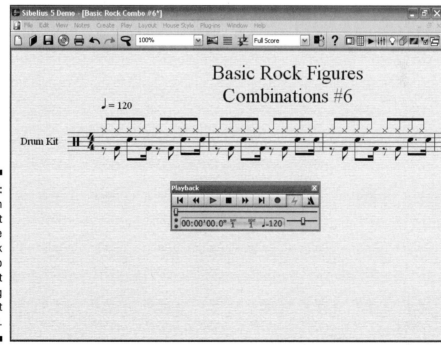

Figure 19-6:
You can experiment with the playback tempo without making permanent changes.

Part VII

Appendixes

The 5th Wave   By Rich Tennant

"Jake never knew how to end a song."

In this part . . .

Knowing which musical range most common instruments play in is helpful, especially when you use your notation software to print out parts for other musicians to play. Plus, it helps to create a more realistic sound in your MIDI files. So in Appendix A, I provide a chart of common instrument ranges and tell you which note range sounds best for each instrument.

In Appendix B, you can find information about all the nifty stuff that's on the accompanying CD, such as the demo copy of Sibelius 5, the Sibelius templates that you use to compose your tunes, and the sample MP3 audio files that let you listen to the examples I give.

Appendix A

Common Instrument Ranges

• •

*N*otation software lets you compose in either *concert key* or *transposed key.* This means that, when you write your notes into the score on your computer screen, you can write the notes as they actually sound (concert key) or as they would look to the transposing instrument (transposed key).

Some instruments are called *concert-pitched instruments,* because what you see is what you get. Piano, violin, flute, and some other instruments sound the note that's written. Guitar and bass are also concert-pitched, but they sound the written note down one octave.

Transposing instruments, however, read one note and play another. For example, when a trumpet reads a C on the part, the note that comes out will sound like a concert B♭, a full step lower. For this reason the trumpet is considered to be in the key of B♭. A written C for an alto saxophone will sound like a concert E♭, therefore the alto is called an E♭ alto saxophone.

So when a composer writes for the trumpet, he needs to compensate for this key change and write the trumpet part a full step higher than the pitch he actually wants to hear. If the composer really wants to play a C, he needs to notate a D. If he writes for the alto, he needs to write the pitch one-sixth of the scale higher, which makes the C he wants to hear an A.

Figures A-1 and A-2 show three measures of music for trumpet, alto saxophone, and piano. Each instrument is playing the same notes in each figure, but Figure A-1 shows the actual notes that the ear hears, and Figure A-2 shows how the part must be transposed in order for those notes to be heard. Fortunately, notation software automatically transposes the parts before you print them and hand them out to the musicians.

Although various instruments are pitched in numerous ways, you'll most often deal with three groups: the B♭ instruments, the E♭ instruments, and the F instruments.

The guitar and bass transpose down an octave, which means that if you want the guitar or bass to play a specific note, you need to write it an octave higher to get the sound right. (Obviously, this doesn't apply to chord symbols).

Transposing Instruments - Sound

Figure A-1:
A short
piece of
music as it
is heard by
the ears.

Transposing Instruments - Written

Figure A-2:
The same
short piece
of music as
written.

Often, professional composers (myself included) write directly into a trans-posed score rather than a concert score. The composers are so familiar with the instrument ranges and sound characteristics that they think in the trans-posed key of the various instruments. Writing a score in concert and then converting it to a transposed score is an unnecessary extra step. And in the days of pre-computer notation, paying a copyist to transpose the parts often incurred an additional cost.

Most composers have a hands-on familiarity with the instrument they write for, and most composers play several instruments. Writing in a transposed score rather than a concert score helps the composer visualize the tonal quality of the piece; it also helps the composer to see clearly what the part will look like to the musician.

Today, with the instant transposing ability of notation software, you really don't have to worry about all this transposing stuff. You can write your score in concert (true) pitch, and when you print out the part for the instrument you want, the software will automatically transpose it for you. Cool, huh?

Here's where it gets tricky, however: A problem rears its ugly head when it comes to the instrument's *range*. Acoustic instruments, in particular, sound quite different when the part is written in a very high range or a very low range than they do when playing in a range comfortable for them. And the part you want the trumpet or saxophone to play may not even be in a range that's physically possible for the instrument to play (although professionals and masters extend the common range of their instruments to great effect).

If you're importing samples from a plug-in or another software, ranges may not be an issue. You can experiment with the sample on several different pitches and octaves until you get the sound right. But knowing what the true range of, say, the trumpet is, will ensure that the trumpet part will sound the way it's supposed to.

Some software samplers limit the range of a sampled acoustic instrument in an effort to preserve the original sound of the instrument. For this reason, knowing the correct range of the instrument you're writing for is important. In this appendix, I give you a quick primer on the various ranges and tonal characteristics of the most common instruments.

In all the figures that follow, I show a fairly complete range of the instrument, one that a professional would be expected to be able to play. If you're writing for a student ensemble, or even a group of people whose level of proficiency you're not sure of, be sure to keep your parts in the middle half of the range. Unless you're *trying* to go for the effect of someone straining to hit a high note, you're better off knowing that your notes will be played without someone having to be sent to the hospital after trying to hit that high C!

The String Family

The string family is commonly divided into two groups:

- **Bowed:** The bowed group includes the instruments people think of when they think strings: violin, viola, cello, and double bass.

- **Non-bowed:** The non-bowed strings are the instruments that are technically strings, but that are played in a different context from the bowed strings: guitar, banjo, mandolin, electric bass, and harp.

Bowed strings

An instrumental family with a heritage almost as long as mankind itself, the bowed strings group consists of the instruments commonly called the violin family: violin, viola, cello, and double bass (also called a string bass).

Figure A-3 shows the usable range for the bowed strings. The range of the instruments are listed from high to low, with the violin on the top and descending down through the viola, cello, and double bass on the bottom. Orchestras use many bowed strings to project a full, rich sound.

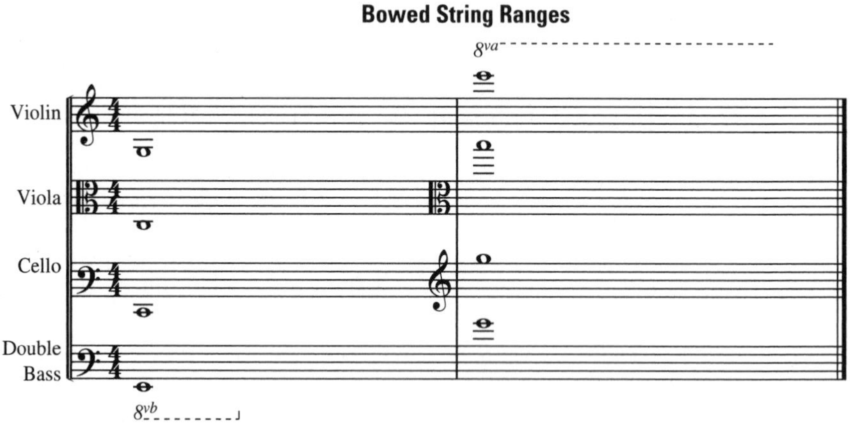

Bowed String Ranges

Figure A-3:
The musical range of bowed string instruments.

In most popular music the bowed strings usually play long, sustained, sweeping parts, and are sometimes added to a vocal track later in a process known as *sweetening*. In electronic music, the *pad* is a synthesizer sound used to replicate a string section's sweep, but often with a more modern edge.

In country music and bluegrass, the violin is often referred to as a fiddle. When the violin family plucks the strings with their fingers, instead of using a bow, it's called *pizzicato*.

When you see *8va* or *8vb* on a part, that means the note is actually an octave higher than the line it's written on (in the case of *8va*) or an octave lower than the line it's written on (in the case of *8vb*). The *8va* and *8vb* notations lessen the number of ledger lines the composer has to write for a note that's way out of the staff. It also helps the musician read the note more easily, without having to count a bunch of ledger lines.

Non-bowed strings

The non-bowed strings are usually plucked with a pick or the fingers, although they're sometimes bowed to create a special sound effect.

Although the non-bowed strings — harp, guitar, banjo, mandolin, and electric bass — are technically all in the same family, they're very different from each other in the way they're played and in how they're used in music.

The guitar and bass are the most similar, with the bass strings the same as the bottom four strings of the guitar, but sounding an octave lower. The electric bass is in the same range as the double bass (see the "Bowed strings" section). Guitars come in many different varieties — acoustic, electric, 6-string, 12-string, pedal steel, and so on — and, through electronics, the range and type of sound that guitars create can greatly expand.

The harp is in its own special category. It's amazingly old, dating from the Greek age. The modern harp has a very complicated pedal system that is usually notated in the score.

Mandolin and banjo are very popular instruments in folk, bluegrass, and country music styles. The mandolin normally has eight metal strings in four pairs that are plucked with a *plectrum,* a type of pick. Banjos most often are found in four-string or five-string versions, and banjo players usually use a *thumb pick* to pluck the notes or strum a chord.

Figure A-4 shows the common ranges of the non-bowed strings.

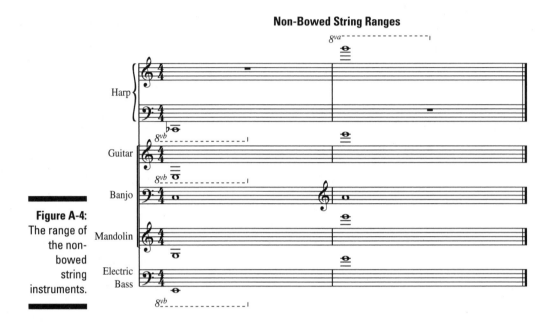

Non-Bowed String Ranges

Figure A-4:
The range of the non-bowed string instruments.

The Woodwinds

The woodwind family is probably the largest and the most varied family of instruments. It consists of the flute family (flute, recorder, piccolo), the oboe family (oboe, English horn, bassoon, and contrabassoon), the clarinet family (Bb clarinet, Eb clarinet, bass clarinet), and the saxophone family (soprano, alto, tenor, baritone, and bass). Sometimes, the woodwinds are divided up between the non-reeds (the flute family), the single-reeds (the clarinet and saxophone families), and the double-reeds (the oboe family).

The ranges of some of the more common woodwind instruments you'll come into contact with are shown in Figure A-5.

Woodwind Ranges

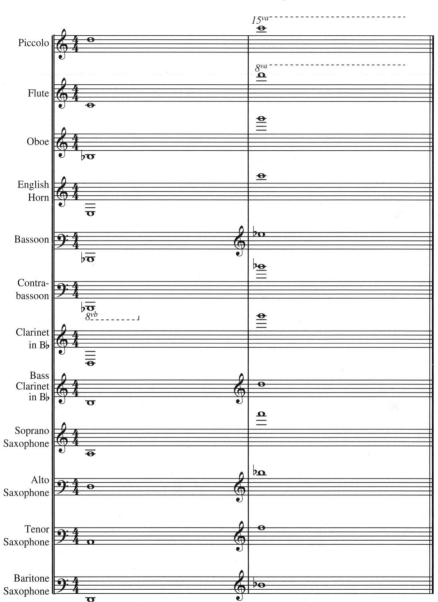

Figure A-5:
The range of the woodwind family.

The Brass Family

When you compose for the brass family, you're going to most likely use one or more of these instruments: French horn, trumpet, trombone, bass trombone, and tuba. The brass are the loudest of the wind instruments and are very versatile, appearing in almost every type of music, from jazz to rock, in orchestras and films.

Their range is somewhat more limited than other instruments, and the outer limits of the range is more dependent upon the skill of the musician. Brass instruments can change their tone dramatically with mutes. Figure A-6 shows you the range of instruments in the brass family.

Brass Ranges

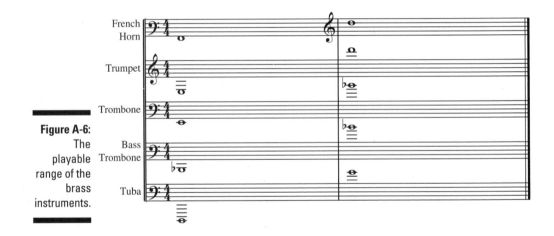

Figure A-6: The playable range of the brass instruments.

Keyboards

When I refer to keyboards here — the piano, harpsichord, and organ — I'm referring to the standard historical keyboards found in bands, orchestras, chamber ensembles, and churches. MIDI keyboard controllers are another animal altogether; through electronics, MIDI keyboards can extend their range to way beyond the written ranges I list here.

The venerable piano is traditionally the instrument used by most composers to write music, especially because its range is larger than that of the guitar and MIDI keys.

Technically, the piano is a percussion instrument, because the strings are struck by a hammer when the note key is pressed. But except for some special instances, the piano is used as a melody and chordal instrument and is not usually thought of as a percussion instrument.

Figure A-7 lists the range of the standard three keyboards.

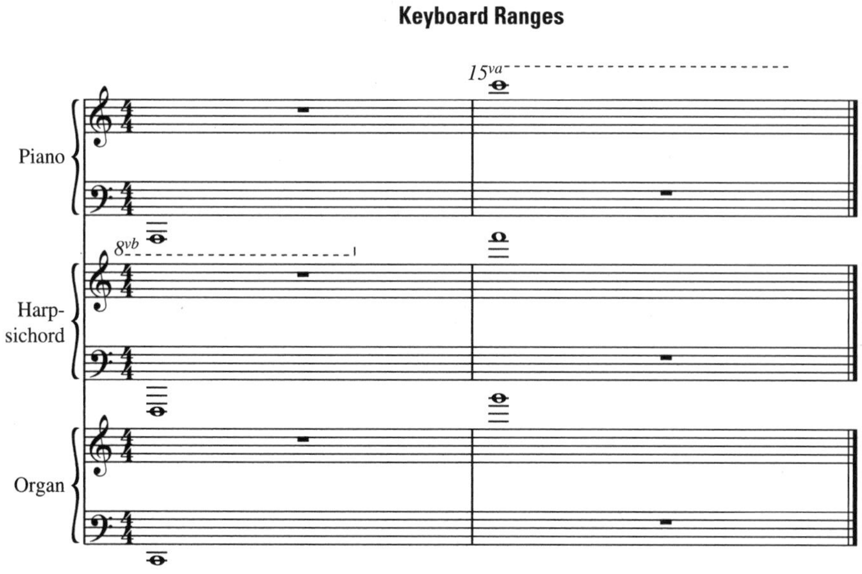

Keyboard Ranges

Figure A-7: The effective musical range of the standard keyboard instruments.

Percussion Instruments

All percussion instruments are played by striking or hitting the instrument with hands, mallets, sticks, or beaters. Percussion instruments come in two major flavors:

✔ **Pitched:** Pitched percussion instruments are called that because they have a definable pitch and range that can be written and played. Pitched percussion instruments include

- Chimes (tubular bells)
- Glockenspiel
- Xylophone

- Marimba

- Tympani

- Vibraphone

✔ **Non-pitched (or indeterminate pitch):** So-called non-pitched percussion instruments — like a snare drum, claves, wood block, or conga drum — actually *do* have a pitch. For example, tom-tom drums in a trap set are "tuned" by the drummer to sound high or low, depending upon what sound he wants to project. But the tom-toms don't play a pitched part that changes along with the key signature of the music.

Figure A-8 illustrates some common pitched percussion instrument ranges.

Pitched Percussion Ranges

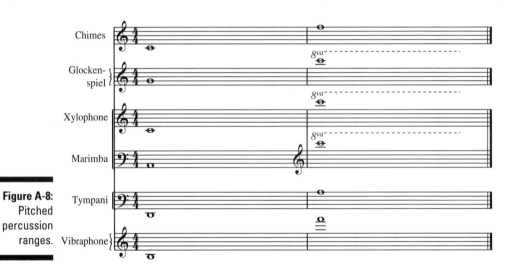

Figure A-8: Pitched percussion ranges.

Voices and Choirs

The majority of choral music is written in soprano, alto, tenor, and bass (S/A/T/B) voices. Choirs are very effective in singing the melody to a song in *unison* (everyone singing the same note); singing long, sustained background parts; or singing a punchy countermelody to the main melody.

Experienced, trained, professional singers are in great demand in the music industry, especially singing backgrounds in pop music, jingles, record and film sessions, and country and jazz performances. Figure A-9 shows the range of a good professional choir.

The ranges of the five voice parts shown in Figure A-9 — soprano, alto, tenor, baritone, and bass — vary wildly from group to group, and from singer to singer. Although the figure shows the approximate ranges of an accomplished vocal group, most often you'll have a much more limited range available for your tune. As always, you should write for the more limited vocal range, unless you know for sure the singers can hit the notes you write.

Vocal Ranges

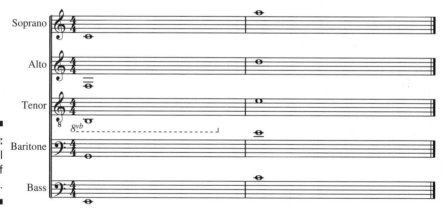

Figure A-9: The musical range of voices.

Appendix B

About the CD

● ●

*I*f it's information about the CD that you're after, you've come to the right place. In this appendix, you find out everything you need to know about the CD — including system requirements, what's on the CD, and what to do if you run into trouble (with the CD, at least — I won't come bail you out of jail or anything).

System Requirements

Make sure that your computer meets the minimum system requirements shown in the following list. If your computer doesn't match up to most of these requirements, you may have problems using the software and files on the CD. For the latest and greatest information, please refer to the ReadMe file located at the root of the CD-ROM.

The recommended minimum computer requirements for a Windows computer are:

- Windows XP Service Pack 2 or Windows Vista
- At least 512MB of RAM
- 350MB free hard drive space
- CD-ROM drive

You must be running at least Windows XP Service Pack 2 to install and run Sibelius 5. If you have Windows 95, Windows 98, Windows Me, Windows 2000 or Windows NT 4.*x,* you may want to purchase a more recent version of the Windows operating system.

If you want to load a lot of sampled sound sets, such as Sibelius Sounds Essentials and KONTAKT Player 2, and intend to use scores with numerous instruments, you should have at least:

✔ Windows XP Service Pack 2 or Windows Vista

✔ 1GB total RAM

✔ 3.5GB total hard drive space

✔ DVD-ROM drive

✔ ASIO-compatible soundcard

You can use Sibelius Sounds Essentials if your computer doesn't meet the recommended requirements, but you may find that you cannot use as many sounds simultaneously.

The minimum computer requirements for Macintosh are:

✔ Mac OS X 10.4 or later

✔ At least 512MB RAM

✔ 350MB free hard drive space

✔ DVD-ROM drive

Sibelius 5 is a universal binary application, which means that it runs on both older Macs with PowerPC processors and new Macs with Intel processors.

If you're running a version of Mac OS X earlier than Mac OS X 10.4, you cannot install and run Sibelius. You may want to upgrade.

To get the most out of the book, an Internet connection is helpful, but it's not mandatory.

You'll probably want to hear the MP3 examples on the CD through a set of external speakers or headphones. Most computers have an audio output to plug your speakers or headphones into. (In Chapter 4, I describe hardware choices in more detail.)

If you need more information on the basics, check out these books published by Wiley Publishing, Inc.: *PCs For Dummies,* 11th Edition, by Dan Gookin; *Macs For Dummies,* 9th Edition, by Edward C. Baig; *iMac For Dummies,* 5th Edition, by Mark L. Chambers; *Windows 98 For Dummies,* by Andy Rathbone; *Windows 2000 Professional For Dummies,* by Andy Rathbone and Sharon Crawford; *Microsoft Windows Me For Dummies, Millennium Edition,* by Andy Rathbone; *Windows XP For Dummies,* 2nd Edition, by Andy Rathbone; *Windows Vista For Dummies,* by Andy Rathbone; *Mac OS X Tiger For Dummies,* by Bob LeVitus; or *Mac OS X Leopard For Dummies,* by Bob LeVitus.

Using the CD

To install the items from the CD to your hard drive, follow these steps:

1. **Insert the CD into your computer's CD-ROM drive.**

   The license agreement appears.

   Note to Windows users: The interface won't launch if you have autorun disabled. In that case, choose Start⇨Run (for Windows Vista, choose Start⇨All Programs⇨Accessories⇨Run). In the dialog box that appears, type **D:\Start.exe**. (Replace **D** with the letter of your CD drive, if your CD drive uses a different letter. If you don't know the letter of your CD drive, go to My Computer, where you'll find the drive listed.) Click OK.

   Note for Mac users: The CD icon will appear on your desktop. Double-click the icon to open the CD, and double-click the Start icon.

2. **Read through the license agreement, and then click the Accept button if you want to use the CD.**

   The CD interface appears. The interface allows you to install the programs and run the demos with just a click of a button (or two).

What You'll Find on the CD

The following sections are arranged by category and provide a summary of the software and other goodies you'll find on the CD. If you need help with installing the items provided on the CD, refer back to the installation instructions in the preceding section.

Shareware programs are fully functional, free, trial versions of copyrighted programs. If you like particular programs, register with their authors for a nominal fee and receive licenses, enhanced versions, and technical support. *Freeware programs* are free, copyrighted games, applications, and utilities. You can copy them to as many PCs as you like — for free — but they offer no technical support. *GNU software* is governed by its own license, which is included inside the folder of the GNU software. There are no restrictions on distribution of GNU software. See the GNU license at the root of the CD for more details. *Trial, demo,* or *evaluation* versions of software are usually limited either by time or functionality (such as not letting you save a project after you create it).

Author-created material

All the templates and audio examples provided in this book are located in the
`Author` directory on the CD and work with Macintosh and Windows XP and
later computers. The structure of the `Author` directory is:

```
Author/Chapter 02/Audio Examples/James Bernard
Author/Chapter 02/Audio Examples/Tom Salta
Author/Chapter 06/Audio Examples
Author/Chapter 07/Audio Examples
Author/Chapter 07/Templates
Author/Chapter 10/Audio Examples
Author/Chapter 10/Templates
Author/Chapter 11/Audio Examples
Author/Chapter 11/Templates
Author/Chapter 12/Audio Examples
Author/Chapter 13/Audio Examples
Author/Chapter 13/Templates
Author/Chapter 14/Audio Examples
Author/Chapter 14/Templates
Author/Chapter 15/Audio Examples
Author/Chapter 15/Templates
Author/Chapter 16/Templates
Author/Software/Sibelius 5 Demo
Author/Extras/Audio/Hip Hop Beatz
Author/Extras/Audio/Synclavier II
```

Sibelius 5

Demo version.

Sibelius 5 is software for writing, playing, printing, and publishing music
notation. Sibelius is the primary tool for opening and editing the included
templates.

With Sibelius, you can create audio files (which can be converted to MP3s or
burned to CDs), produce instrumental parts, compose for video, and sell
your music online. For information on purchasing Sibelius 5 or other Sibelius
products, go to `www.sibelius.com/products/index.html`.

Troubleshooting

I tried my best to compile programs that work on most computers with the minimum system requirements. Alas, your computer may differ, and some programs may not work properly for some reason.

The two likeliest problems are that you don't have enough memory (RAM) for the programs you want to use, or you have other programs running that are affecting installation or running of a program. If you get an error message such as `Not enough memory` or `Setup cannot continue`, try one or more of the following suggestions and then try using the software again:

- **Turn off any antivirus software running on your computer.** Installation programs sometimes mimic virus activity and may make your computer incorrectly believe that it's being infected by a virus.

- **Close all running programs.** The more programs you have running, the less memory is available to other programs. Installation programs typically update files and programs; so if you keep other programs running, installation may not work properly.

- **Have your local computer store add more RAM to your computer.** This is, admittedly, a drastic and somewhat expensive step. However, adding more memory can really help the speed of your computer and allow more programs to run at the same time.

Customer Care

If you have trouble with the CD-ROM, please call the Wiley Product Technical Support phone number at 800-762-2974. Outside the United States, call +1 (317) 572-3994. You can also contact Wiley Product Technical Support at `http://support.wiley.com`. John Wiley & Sons will provide technical support only for installation and other general quality-control items. For technical support on the applications themselves, consult the program's vendor or author.

To place additional orders or to request information about other Wiley products, please call 877-762-2974.

Index

• N •

Notes

Wiley Publishing, Inc., End-User License Agreement

5. **Limited Warranty.**

    (a) WPI warrants that the Software and Software Media are free from defects in materials and workmanship under normal use for a period of sixty (60) days from the date of purchase of this Book. If WPI receives notification within the warranty period of defects in materials or workmanship, WPI will replace the defective Software Media.

    (b) WPI AND THE AUTHOR(S) OF THE BOOK DISCLAIM ALL OTHER WARRANTIES, EXPRESS OR IMPLIED, INCLUDING WITHOUT LIMITATION IMPLIED WARRANTIES OF MER-CHANTABILITY AND FITNESS FOR A PARTICULAR PURPOSE, WITH RESPECT TO THE SOFTWARE, THE PROGRAMS, THE SOURCE CODE CONTAINED THEREIN, AND/OR THE TECHNIQUES DESCRIBED IN THIS BOOK. WPI DOES NOT WARRANT THAT THE FUNC-TIONS CONTAINED IN THE SOFTWARE WILL MEET YOUR REQUIREMENTS OR THAT THE OPERATION OF THE SOFTWARE WILL BE ERROR FREE.

    (c) This limited warranty gives you specific legal rights, and you may have other rights that vary from jurisdiction to jurisdiction.

6. **Remedies.**

    (a) WPI's entire liability and your exclusive remedy for defects in materials and workman-ship shall be limited to replacement of the Software Media, which may be returned to WPI with a copy of your receipt at the following address: Software Media Fulfillment Department, Attn.: *Composing Digital Music For Dummies,* Wiley Publishing, Inc., 10475 Crosspoint Blvd., Indianapolis, IN 46256, or call 1-800-762-2974. Please allow four to six weeks for delivery. This Limited Warranty is void if failure of the Software Media has resulted from accident, abuse, or misapplication. Any replacement Software Media will be warranted for the remainder of the original warranty period or thirty (30) days, whichever is longer.

    (b) In no event shall WPI or the author be liable for any damages whatsoever (including without limitation damages for loss of business profits, business interruption, loss of business information, or any other pecuniary loss) arising from the use of or inability to use the Book or the Software, even if WPI has been advised of the possibility of such damages.

    (c) Because some jurisdictions do not allow the exclusion or limitation of liability for conse-quential or incidental damages, the above limitation or exclusion may not apply to you.

7. **U.S. Government Restricted Rights.** Use, duplication, or disclosure of the Software for or on behalf of the United States of America, its agencies and/or instrumentalities "U.S. Government" is subject to restrictions as stated in paragraph (c)(1)(ii) of the Rights in Technical Data and Computer Software clause of DFARS 252.227-7013, or subparagraphs (c) (1) and (2) of the Commercial Computer Software - Restricted Rights clause at FAR 52.227-19, and in similar clauses in the NASA FAR supplement, as applicable.

8. **General.** This Agreement constitutes the entire understanding of the parties and revokes and supersedes all prior agreements, oral or written, between them and may not be modified or amended except in a writing signed by both parties hereto that specifically refers to this Agreement. This Agreement shall take precedence over any other documents that may be in conflict herewith. If any one or more provisions contained in this Agreement are held by any court or tribunal to be invalid, illegal, or otherwise unenforceable, each and every other provision shall remain in full force and effect.

BUSINESS, CAREERS & PERSONAL FINANCE

0-7645-9847-3   0-7645-2431-3

Also available:
- Business Plans Kit For Dummies
  0-7645-9794-9
- Economics For Dummies
  0-7645-5726-2
- Grant Writing For Dummies
  0-7645-8416-2
- Home Buying For Dummies
  0-7645-5331-3
- Managing For Dummies
  0-7645-1771-6
- Marketing For Dummies
  0-7645-5600-2

- Personal Finance For Dummies
  0-7645-2590-5*
- Resumes For Dummies
  0-7645-5471-9
- Selling For Dummies
  0-7645-5363-1
- Six Sigma For Dummies
  0-7645-6798-5
- Small Business Kit For Dummies
  0-7645-5984-2
- Starting an eBay Business For Dummies
  0-7645-6924-4
- Your Dream Career For Dummies
  0-7645-9795-7

HOME & BUSINESS COMPUTER BASICS

0-470-05432-8   0-471-75421-8

Also available:
- Cleaning Windows Vista For Dummies
  0-471-78293-9
- Excel 2007 For Dummies
  0-470-03737-7
- Mac OS X Tiger For Dummies
  0-7645-7675-5
- MacBook For Dummies
  0-470-04859-X
- Macs For Dummies
  0-470-04849-2
- Office 2007 For Dummies
  0-470-00923-3

- Outlook 2007 For Dummies
  0-470-03830-6
- PCs For Dummies
  0-7645-8958-X
- Salesforce.com For Dummies
  0-470-04893-X
- Upgrading & Fixing Laptops For Dummies
  0-7645-8959-8
- Word 2007 For Dummies
  0-470-03658-3
- Quicken 2007 For Dummies
  0-470-04600-7

FOOD, HOME, GARDEN, HOBBIES, MUSIC & PETS

0-7645-8404-9   0-7645-9904-6

Also available:
- Candy Making For Dummies
  0-7645-9734-5
- Card Games For Dummies
  0-7645-9910-0
- Crocheting For Dummies
  0-7645-4151-X
- Dog Training For Dummies
  0-7645-8418-9
- Healthy Carb Cookbook For Dummies
  0-7645-8476-6
- Home Maintenance For Dummies
  0-7645-5215-5

- Horses For Dummies
  0-7645-9797-3
- Jewelry Making & Beading For Dummies
  0-7645-2571-9
- Orchids For Dummies
  0-7645-6759-4
- Puppies For Dummies
  0-7645-5255-4
- Rock Guitar For Dummies
  0-7645-5356-9
- Sewing For Dummies
  0-7645-6847-7
- Singing For Dummies
  0-7645-2475-5

INTERNET & DIGITAL MEDIA

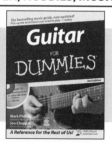

0-470-04529-9   0-470-04894-8

Also available:
- Blogging For Dummies
  0-471-77084-1
- Digital Photography For Dummies
  0-7645-9802-3
- Digital Photography All-in-One Desk Reference For Dummies
  0-470-03743-1
- Digital SLR Cameras and Photography For Dummies
  0-7645-9803-1
- eBay Business All-in-One Desk Reference For Dummies
  0-7645-8438-3
- HDTV For Dummies
  0-470-09673-X

- Home Entertainment PCs For Dummies
  0-470-05523-5
- MySpace For Dummies
  0-470-09529-6
- Search Engine Optimization For Dummies
  0-471-97998-8
- Skype For Dummies
  0-470-04891-3
- The Internet For Dummies
  0-7645-8996-2
- Wiring Your Digital Home For Dummies
  0-471-91830-X

*Separate Canadian edition also available
Separate U.K. edition also available

SPORTS, FITNESS, PARENTING, RELIGION & SPIRITUALITY

0-471-76871-5

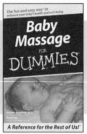
0-7645-7841-3

Also available:

✔Catholicism For Dummies
0-7645-5391-7

✔Exercise Balls For Dummies
0-7645-5623-1

✔Fitness For Dummies
0-7645-7851-0

✔Football For Dummies
0-7645-3936-1

✔Judaism For Dummies
0-7645-5299-6

✔Potty Training For Dummies
0-7645-5417-4

✔Buddhism For Dummies
0-7645-5359-3

✔Pregnancy For Dummies
0-7645-4483-7 †

✔Ten Minute Tone-Ups For Dummies
0-7645-7207-5

✔NASCAR For Dummies
0-7645-7681-X

✔Religion For Dummies
0-7645-5264-3

✔Soccer For Dummies
0-7645-5229-5

✔Women in the Bible For Dummies
0-7645-8475-8

TRAVEL

0-7645-7749-2

0-7645-6945-7

Also available:

✔Alaska For Dummies
0-7645-7746-8

✔Cruise Vacations For Dummies
0-7645-6941-4

✔England For Dummies
0-7645-4276-1

✔Europe For Dummies
0-7645-7529-5

✔Germany For Dummies
0-7645-7823-5

✔Hawaii For Dummies
0-7645-7402-7

✔Italy For Dummies
0-7645-7386-1

✔Las Vegas For Dummies
0-7645-7382-9

✔London For Dummies
0-7645-4277-X

✔Paris For Dummies
0-7645-7630-5

✔RV Vacations For Dummies
0-7645-4442-X

✔Walt Disney World & Orlando
For Dummies
0-7645-9660-8

GRAPHICS, DESIGN & WEB DEVELOPMENT

0-7645-8815-X

0-7645-9571-7

Also available:

✔3D Game Animation For Dummies
0-7645-8789-7

✔AutoCAD 2006 For Dummies
0-7645-8925-3

✔Building a Web Site For Dummies
0-7645-7144-3

✔Creating Web Pages For Dummies
0-470-08030-2

✔Creating Web Pages All-in-One Desk
Reference For Dummies
0-7645-4345-8

✔Dreamweaver 8 For Dummies
0-7645-9649-7

✔InDesign CS2 For Dummies
0-7645-9572-5

✔Macromedia Flash 8 For Dummies
0-7645-9691-8

✔Photoshop CS2 and Digital
Photography For Dummies
0-7645-9580-6

✔Photoshop Elements 4 For Dummies
0-471-77483-9

✔Syndicating Web Sites with RSS Feed
For Dummies
0-7645-8848-6

✔Yahoo! SiteBuilder For Dummies
0-7645-9800-7

NETWORKING, SECURITY, PROGRAMMING & DATABASES

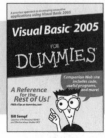
0-7645-7728-X

0-471-74940-0

Also available:

✔Access 2007 For Dummies
0-470-04612-0

✔ASP.NET 2 For Dummies
0-7645-7907-X

✔C# 2005 For Dummies
0-7645-9704-3

✔Hacking For Dummies
0-470-05235-X

✔Hacking Wireless Networks
For Dummies
0-7645-9730-2

✔Java For Dummies
0-470-08716-1

✔Microsoft SQL Server 2005 For Dummi
0-7645-7755-7

✔Networking All-in-One Desk Referen
For Dummies
0-7645-9939-9

✔Preventing Identity Theft For Dummie
0-7645-7336-5

✔Telecom For Dummies
0-471-77085-X

✔Visual Studio 2005 All-in-One Desk
Reference For Dummies
0-7645-9775-2

✔XML For Dummies
0-7645-8845-1

ALTH & SELF-HELP

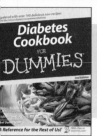

0-7645-8450-2

0-7645-4149-8

Also available:

- Bipolar Disorder For Dummies
  0-7645-8451-0
- Chemotherapy and Radiation
  For Dummies
  0-7645-7832-4
- Controlling Cholesterol For Dummies
  0-7645-5440-9
- Diabetes For Dummies
  0-7645-6820-5* †
- Divorce For Dummies
  0-7645-8417-0 †

- Fibromyalgia For Dummies
  0-7645-5441-7
- Low-Calorie Dieting For Dummies
  0-7645-9905-4
- Meditation For Dummies
  0-471-77774-9
- Osteoporosis For Dummies
  0-7645-7621-6
- Overcoming Anxiety For Dummies
  0-7645-5447-6
- Reiki For Dummies
  0-7645-9907-0
- Stress Management For Dummies
  0-7645-5144-2

UCATION, HISTORY, REFERENCE & TEST PREPARATION

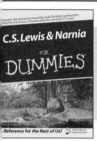

0-7645-8381-6

0-7645-9554-7

Also available:

- The ACT For Dummies
  0-7645-9652-7
- Algebra For Dummies
  0-7645-5325-9
- Algebra Workbook For Dummies
  0-7645-8467-7
- Astronomy For Dummies
  0-7645-8465-0
- Calculus For Dummies
  0-7645-2498-4
- Chemistry For Dummies
  0-7645-5430-1
- Forensics For Dummies
  0-7645-5580-4

- Freemasons For Dummies
  0-7645-9796-5
- French For Dummies
  0-7645-5193-0
- Geometry For Dummies
  0-7645-5324-0
- Organic Chemistry I For Dummies
  0-7645-6902-3
- The SAT I For Dummies
  0-7645-7193-1
- Spanish For Dummies
  0-7645-5194-9
- Statistics For Dummies
  0-7645-5423-9

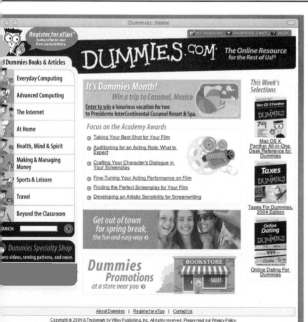

Get smart @ dummies.com®

- **Find a full list of Dummies titles**
- **Look into loads of FREE on-site articles**
- **Sign up for FREE eTips e-mailed to you weekly**
- **See what other products carry the Dummies name**
- **Shop directly from the Dummies bookstore**
- **Enter to win new prizes every month!**

* Separate Canadian edition also available
† Separate U.K. edition also available

Available wherever books are sold. For more information or to order direct: U.S. customers visit www.dummies.com or call 1-877-762-2974.
U.K. customers visit www.wileyeurope.com or call 0800 243407. Canadian customers visit www.wiley.ca or call 1-800-567-4797.

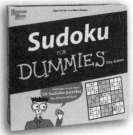